I WILL WALK WITH YOU
An Alzheimer's Love Story

Julie Thomas Tullos

I WILL WALK WITH YOU
An Alzheimer's Love Story
© 2025 Julie Thomas Tullos

www.JulieTullos.com

Adriel Publishing

Cover photograph by Julie Thomas Tullos

ISBN: 979-8-9931690-1-9

www.JulieTullos.com

For Skylar

I believe that Imagination is stronger that knowledge,

That myth is more potent than history,

That dreams are more powerful than facts,

That hope always triumphs over experience,

That laughter is the only cure for grief,

And I believe that love is stronger than death.

"The Storyteller's Creed"

TABLE OF CONTENTS

PROLOGUE

She holds an unlit cigarette in her hand. Just as if she were going to smoke it. But she doesn't pick up the lighter. There are a dozen unlit cigarettes spread out over the table. A few have ketchup on the ends, from dipping into an opened packet of ketchup. Fruit gummy snack packages are everywhere, mostly empty, with the grape ones scattered about, unwanted. A lip liner, a Southern Living magazine, and Junior Mints boxes are strewn about as well. Her empty purse, save a clean pair of panties, lies on the floor at her feet. A pair of pants are draped over a chair. I couldn't assume they were clean.

We still laugh sometimes. Her sense of humor hasn't left. If it's a good day she'll laugh at her ineptitude, if it's a bad day she'll get teary. She tries to use the cigarette in her hand to color with my four-year-old. She laughs when I say "Mom. You can't color with that." So she picks up the lip liner instead. I gently take it from her and hand her a marker.

I know the lid will be left off the marker and the coloring page will just have scribble on it.

I know how hard she tries to stay with us.

I know she can't.

CHAPTER ONE

Growing Up Susan

Mabel. Thomas Howell. Maudie. John William. These are the names of her grandparents. Somewhere back there, is a Cherokee Indian, a Scot, and someone buried in Canada. Intriguing tales and mysteries never solved. A habit of secret keeping that started who knows how far back and would last through the generations until her own children grew up, when that habit would be laid aside, with care and reverence but with an aching desire to finally tell the truth.

In 1915 T.H. Wade was born to Mabel and Thomas Howell Wade, who was to become Susan's father in 1946. T.H. was *not* Thomas Howell, it was simply T.H. Wade, with nothing intended behind the initials although we can presume it was meant as an homage to Thomas Howell. He was described in his high school yearbook as "quiet and brainy." His life is full of mysteries, such as: Why didn't he serve in the Second World War? He was served a draft notice, classified as fit for service. Yet he didn't go. His elder brother David served as a doctor in the Army, so why was T.H. presumably exempted? Why did it take him thirteen years to complete a bachelor's degree? Where was he and what was he doing? All that is known is that on May 8, 1943, he married Jewel Margaret Willsie in San Antonio. He finally finished his college degree in August of 1946.

Jewel Willsie, on her mother's side, originated with the Bevell family from Paris, Texas, a place, in the dawn of the 20th century, known for racial violence and mob lynchings. The family, in those days, were very against drink - "the devil's beverage" - and even signed a temperance pledge. Jewel was born during the Spanish Flu epidemic and was placed into an oven to keep her warm. Jewel's mother, Maudie, and father, John William Willsie, married in June of 1911. Maudie grew up to be a formidable woman, and Susan remembers her grandmother as "crazy" and "odd" which may indicate that she suffered from the effects of dementia. Not much else is known about the family history here, except for a rare story of a sister or cousin that died young from eating too many green apples. John William's story is a complete mystery.

Jewel's name was a scourge to her, although it signified what a precious gift she was to her parents in a time of darkness and depression. There's not a lot of family lore regarding Jewel (who renamed herself Judy) as a child - in fact there is none. Judy was aiming to be a nurse and applied for acceptance to the State Tuberculosis Sanatorium Training School for Nurses in San Angelo, Texas. But before she could attend, she contracted tuberculosis herself and was treated at the Sanatorium for seven months before accepting her position as a student there in early 1940. Susan's mother Judy - our Granny - was graded harshly in "acceptance of criticism" and "even temper" during her studies (family traits to be handed down) but otherwise managed to get mostly A's and a few B's. During one two-week period of time Granny Judy disappeared from school to "have an operation" but we are left in the dark as to what for, as it was never mentioned again.

Granny Judy did have a beau. A Mr. Hugh Davis, in the spring of 1943. It seemed quite serious, but all of a sudden we find that she married T.H. Wade in May of 1943. What happened to Hugh? Who knows. Did Granny Judy see more ambition and a better future with T.H., or was it simply love at first sight?

Was it Granny Judy that encouraged T.H. to finish his degree work? Possibly. He finally graduated with a Bachelor of Business Administration degree from The University of Texas in August 1946. Susan had been born a month earlier. T.H. and Granny Judy prospered and soon moved into a large house in the Hyde Park area of Austin. This is where she and her younger brother, David Howell (Datch – pronounced Day-tch), would grow up, and ultimately the house my Granny Judy lived in for most of her adult life. T.H. became the business manager for Oak Ridge Sanatorium, where his elder brother was psychiatrist-in-chief.

Mysteriously, a receipt dated January 1, 1954, signed by David Wade, T.H.'s elder brother, gave T.H. all his interest in Oak Ridge Sanatorium for $1.00 and "other valuable consideration." Nobody in the family knows or knew the reasons behind this generous gift, except for possibly Granny Judy - but she was absolutely not sharing that information. T.H. went on to partially own several nursing homes in the Austin area.

By the 1960's T.H.'s personal life took a rapid downturn. He ended his own life prematurely in

January 1966. Granny Judy went on to live until age eighty-eight, dying from Lewy-body dementia in January of 2006, forty years after her husband.

Susan, born July 22, 1946, was a happy and carefree child. Surrounded by animals, her first word was "Fella," the name of the family dog and she received a kitten on her fourth birthday following a week-long stay in the hospital for appendicitis. The kitten was called Lucifer.

In a baby photo of Susan you can see a shock of hair swept forward, just as she passed down to her own daughter and then granddaughter. Thick and heavy, Susan opted to keep her hair short (or her mother did as per the style at the time). She was a busy little girl, joining the Girl Scouts and the Texas Reading Club while maintaining an A average in school.

In junior high she was popular, earning a best actress award in drama at school, and elected the cheerleader mascot. She had many friends and was content and confident. In her own words "I had a secure foundation, and I was secure within myself." High school rocked her boat somewhat, as she did not go to the same school as most of her friends and did not find it easy to make new ones. She changed along with the decade and discovered that the father she adored was also an alcoholic and a progressively violent one. Escapism into books was the choice she had, and the choice she eagerly made.

Susan met her lifelong best friend, Panchita Jones, at Camp Mahaba in Belton, Texas. They were fast friends from the beginning, sharing a love of books and swimming. Panchita recalls a time at camp that summer when Susan won first place in the final horse show, and

Panchita came second. And they were both bitter about not receiving either the Junior Counselor title or the Junior Lifeguard certification because "someone got an ear infection, so they closed the pool."

Panchita recalls Susan as "the cool one" because of all the pets the family had (including a monkey and a raccoon!), the family's pink Thunderbird, and having a television in her bedroom.

Despite a seemingly ideal childhood, Susan grew up with a family history of mental illness that wasn't talked about. Wasn't discussed or acknowledged, even as Susan discovered her father's weaknesses.

A seemingly ideal life, hiding dark secrets.

CHAPTER TWO

Family Secrets

It's January 1966. She pulls out of the driveway in her yellow mustang convertible that her Daddy bought for her. She is headed to another college semester at Centenary College in Shreveport, Louisiana. This will be the spring semester of her junior year, and she is looking forward to seeing old friends after Christmas break. Her major is Zoology, though she has no idea what she will do with such a degree. The medical field calls to her, as she has a notion that that's what intelligent people do. Although, in saying this, she couldn't actually imagine herself studying or performing anything to do with medicine!

As she leaves, she takes a glance back at the house she grew up in. Something feels different. Something feels off. She had said goodbye to her parents and younger brother but suddenly she has an intense feeling of grief. As if it's the last time. She draws a deep breath and shakes loose the uninvited feelings. She drives on, hits the highway and is coasting towards Shreveport.

A few days later she is home again. Lost and feeling alone, like life has just turned into grey clouds there is no escaping from. Her beloved daddy has died, having committed suicide probably due to an undiagnosised bipolar disorder. Her younger brother is just 14, but she can't think of his needs now. She can barely breathe on her own, much less make sure her brother is okay. She won't be going back to Centenary, she knows this. The fighting with her mother is untenable, so she eventually takes an apartment with her best friend, Panchita, and enrolls in the University of Texas. She has no idea what she's going to do next.

She rolls along South Congress Street aimlessly in her car, smoking cigarettes (because her mother hates the habit) and doesn't make it to many classes. She struggles to stay connected to a world without her daddy in it. She feels adrift and unmotivated.

On a fall day in 1967 she's convinced to go on a double date with her friend and classmate Margaret. Margaret's boyfriend is a young man from Texas A&M University named Ron. Susan's blind date was the young, incredibly handsome and dark-haired David Lee Thomas, who was in the same Corps unit.

In David Lee's words: "We went to a football game and I was hooked! Have to also mention that I was an extremely good-looking stud at the time! Yes, I remember those times like yesterday!"

The couple went through some exceedingly tough times as Susan was young and confused, due to her father's death. According to David Lee, Susan's mother Judy was angry, bitter and put blame and fault onto everything. "Also, she did not like me at all. A very difficult woman," he recalled.

Susan broke up with David Lee but soon wrote him a letter asking him to come to Austin. "I was picking cotton in the valley, but I hightailed it back to Austin when I got that letter."

Dad recalled this story about the proposal: "Once I was back at school I decided to surprise Susan, so I went to Austin to ask her to marry me. Discovered she was out with a guy named Peter Lee! I sat down on the steps and waited until Susan got home. Very awkward — but the guy dropped Susan and took off. Next day we went to College Station. We stopped under a big tree on the side of the road and I proposed. I had the ring in my pocket the whole time! Some years later I gave her an A&M ring which she replaced the diamond ring for. She wore that A&M ring for over forty years."

Due to her love of books and reading, Susan became a librarian. She served in many different communities, including her favorite - the library in Copperas Cove, Texas, where she met lifelong friends Kathryn and Mariam, among others.

Mom was a children's storyteller at heart, and I remember many car rides listening to other storytellers telling wonderful stories that Mom was interested in. If she had had her way she would have continued to improve her storytelling skills into something amazing. But sadly, life would get in the way.

Family secrets didn't dissolve after a happy marriage, a young family and a move back to Texas though.

Susan's younger brother suffered from mental illness as well, which was kept hidden through all her growing up years. Datch was unsurprisingly on a path of destruction ever since their father committed suicide on the back patio with a gun. Datch shot at a random car when he was twenty-eight and killed the woman in the passenger seat. Granny Judy did everything she could to get him off. She spent much of the money left to her from her husband's death, a fact which did not sit well with Mom. With help from high powered lawyers funded by inheritance, Datch was convicted of manslaughter and spent just five years in prison and mental institutions. I could swear Mom told me he was once diagnosed as having schizophrenia, but this is a fuzzy memory.

When I was a kid, Uncle Datch seemed nice enough to me, although there was always a frosty air when he was around. Mom laid down a hard no, when he offered to take us out in his car to his 'ranch' - the place where he worked, saving and rehabilitating animals. She drove us there herself. The ranch house where Uncle Datch slept was full of reptiles, including a python and some cobras, among other things. I remember being horrified enough by these poisonous snakes that I didn't venture far from my mother. My brother also remembered the 'reptile house' quite clearly. Another time, Uncle Datch came bearing gifts at Christmas and received a stony reception from Mom and a "prodigal son" greeting from my Granny Judy. Mom was always uncomfortable having us kids around her brother, but we never knew why until years later, as adults, we finally learned probably half the truth.

Years after Granny Judy's death, Mom found a letter that Judy had written to her husband T.H. after his passing. A letter that was kept and handed down to me. It is unbearably sad and says a lot about a mother's undying love for her children, even when they disappoint.

A letter to T.H. after death:

Dear One:

In leaving could you not foresee the countless responsibilities you bequeathed to me - but these are nil compared to the loneliness, the heartbreak of trying to do what I believe is the best for our son. A son we failed to instill with unselfishness or responsibility. As he grew up we gave him the pleasure of having everything. He now believes he can continue to have whatever he wants no matter what the hurt or cost to me. In his selfish interest there is no thought of what he can do for me or how lonely I may be - no responsibility daddy dear - to your dead memory, me, or even himself. I love him so and he treats me as dirt - he can't realize the ache in my very depth for him - and he doesn't care.

Daddy dear since you are so near our Heavenly Father would you intercede to Him for help for our boy - to grow in love to God - to family and to accept and expect responsibilities equal to his mental capacity. I hope you are very happy there. I miss and love you.

Love as always - Judy

CHAPTER THREE

Growing Up David Lee

David Lee was born March 5, 1946 to Marjorie Isabel Havel and James Dalton Thomas, and grew up in the small farming community of Wharton, Texas. He learned to raise livestock, farm cotton, and fix broken machinery on the side of the road when necessary. He told us a story about having strep throat, a fever and a terrible headache when he was just a kid, maybe twelve, but just kept popping aspirin and working alongside his old man. He was one of four children, and the only boy. Three sisters kept him on his toes. His older sister by eighteen months, Patty, loved to play tricks on him, somehow convincing him to climb a tree (more than once) high enough that he then couldn't get down. The baby sisters were Gail and Diane, seven and nine years younger than him.

Dad became a talented mechanic and welder, and President of the Future Farmers of America (FFA), while in high school. He was a hell raiser, riding motorcycles and water skiing in rice canals, pulled behind a pickup.

In another story, he told us one day he was working with his old man in the barn behind the house - the old man was cutting metal with a welding torch. Dad went to pick up a recently cut piece of metal, and the old man told him, "Don't touch that son, it's hot." Dad picks it up anyway and drops it just as quickly, burning his fingers. "You needed to feel it for yourself, Son?" Quick as a flash Dad replied, "No sir, I was just done looking at it." Quick witted and smart mouthed David Lee couldn't wait to see the world outside of that small hometown.

David Lee was on a path to join the Army. He graduated from Texas A&M in December 1968 and he and Susan were married on January 25, 1969. They began to settle into military life. Right after David Lee and Susan were married, they were assigned to West Point, Kentucky and then Fort Benning, Georgia for basic training. They were keen to see the world and gladly took off for Germany in 1970, after Dad's officer pinning ceremony. Mom met a great friend in Germany, Brenda, who was married to Richard Knox, and they made good use of their youth and time by exploring Europe together when the men were busy at the base. In Dad's military service he was a tank and automotive material management officer for twenty-five years - thanks to his agriculture degree he received from Texas A&M University!

After that they were assigned first to Fulda, then to Mannheim/Heidelberg in Germany where my brother David Dalton Thomas was born in July 1971. I followed in June 1975 after they were stationed in Ft. Hood, Texas.

The young couple were separated during the Vietnam War in the early seventies, then later in their marriage in 1988 Beirut and Desert Storm in the early 1990's. Many, many letters criss-crossed the ocean during these times. Most were heavy letters filled with detail and chit chat, but a few were simple love notes. In one card to Susan, David Lee wrote *"you are the strength that I live for,"* and in one from Susan to David Lee, she simply said *"you are my everything."*

In his time of service David Lee earned many awards and medals including a Bronze Star medal 3rd award, a Ranger tab, and a parachutist badge. He went to airborne school to become a helicopter pilot but for reasons unknown to me (maybe due to injuries from a youthful motorcycle accident) he ended up working on tanks for almost his entire career. At one point he was a Battalion Commander during Desert Storm and also a Director of Maintenance. He earned the nickname "Bullworker," an homage to his tireless work ethic. Dad's military career ended with retirement in June of 1994.

After leaving the service, he used his considerable wood working skills to open "Solid Oak Wood Products" - a business which he and Mom worked on together for many years.

Admittedly handsome as a movie star (he admitted it himself) and full of courage and brevity you got the feeling he was a ladies' man from a young age. With dark brown hair and what Mom called "brown bedroom eyes," he had a fine physique from working hard all his life and hands that knew what work was. Dad sure wasn't a slouch, he believed in working hard, then working harder. You don't have to do it fast, but you do gotta get it done, was the moral of a story he liked to tell us kids. He didn't suffer fools gladly and once committed to something (like Susan) he wasn't going to back out. He once told me - you don't cut the neighbor's lawn because you want them to pay you back. You cut the neighbor's lawn because it needs cutting. He was a man full of integrity and the belief that you do what's right because it's right and nothing more.

Another of his favorite things to tell me as an adult was "blame doesn't matter" - what is done is done and there's no sense casting blame about. Just hunker down and fix the issue, whatever it is. Blame is for cowards.

Speaking of hunkering, you could often find Dad sitting on his haunches, one knee down and one knee up, smoking a cigarette. His favorite way of viewing the world was from this position. He started smoking at the age of ten with friends behind the barn, stealing his old man's smokes, and was soon hooked. Never to be free from the demands of nicotine again, Dad smoked for sixty-five years, a fact he was almost proud of. In the Army he got serious about drinking and whiskey became a fast favorite. He would drink to dull the pain of a motorcycle accident in his teens, and to drown out the bullshit of the Army world. Dad couldn't abide ass-kissing and refused to do it himself. A fact which more than likely cost him being promoted to a full colonel in his late Army years, something he would be bitter about for the rest of his life. I used to tell him it didn't matter to me that he wasn't a full colonel - I for one appreciated his integrity in refusing to be dishonest with anyone.

Dad didn't really believe in secrets. But he believed in Mom more, and his love for her superseded everything else.

This is a story about Alzheimer's and Love.

CHAPTER FOUR

Dementia

February 2017 - July 2018

Alzheimer's changes can start up to ten years before symptoms are seen. However, if you are not looking for it, you are not going to see it.

During their time in central Texas in the 1980's, Mom was bitten by a tick and developed Lyme Disease. Her notion that the medical profession was an intelligent and caring one collapsed. Her belief in the ability of her own mind was shaken. This two-year time period between being bitten and being diagnosed was a steady downhill spiral into severe physical illness and mental deterioration. She eventually had three positive diagnostic tests for Lyme and was still not treated or taken seriously. She finally took control of her own fate long enough to call the National Lyme Foundation and get the name of a specialist in Dallas, Texas. That action probably saved her life. She did not share details of her diagnosis with many people outside the family. Her motto was to suffer in silence and let people think what they will.

It's possible that this Lyme Disease changed the course of her future and at least partly caused her early death from Alzheimer's.

Mystery still surrounds the family history - there was always a *"don't ask, don't tell"* unspoken quality to Mom. And Dad would not, and did not, share stories about any of it, ever. Secrets were a way of life.

"

Suffer in silence, and let people think

what they will.

"

After her Alzheimer's diagnosis, she was not about to tell friends or even family why she disappeared from their lives. She tucked herself away in East Texas with Dad and focused on creating an environment she could control. Dad knew better than to tell anyone what was happening. Even his older sister, Aunt Patty, whom he was close to, was not privy to what was going on. My Aunt Patty did disclose eventually that Mom had confided in her that she had Alzheimer's, while on a trip to Monday Trade Days in Canton, Texas. I am still not sure that I believe it.

While dementia slowly seeped into Mom's brain, she hid it. She compensated. She didn't want to know. She fell back on a lifetime of secrets – this is all she knew. So when it started, she carried it around without telling anyone for who knows how long. When did she first realize something wasn't right? Did she confide in Dad? Instinct tells me she didn't. I think Dad figured it out faster than the rest of us but being forever her knight-in-shining-armor, he kept her secret as his own.

Why didn't I see it? All the crying jags I put down to depression, which were probably sourced from fear and frustration. Frustration wasn't hers alone. I couldn't figure out what she could possibly be depressed about. I used to get upset, because *she* was upset. I wanted her to be happy, so that I could be happy. So that I didn't have to feel bad. Don't assume I was un-empathetic. I wasn't, I hated that she was upset. I hated that my heart broke every time she cried. I hated that I couldn't fix whatever was wrong. I watched as she struggled and I tried to help, but of course, I didn't know what the real issue was.

She used to come visit me. She'd stay a couple of nights. Then all that changed. She'd be anxious when she arrived, and after a few hours, maybe that night, she'd tell me that she had to go home tomorrow. She couldn't stay two nights. She would get angry at me when I questioned why? I took it personally. It wasn't personal. Not to me, at least. But it was to her. In the summer of 2017, she drove to my house in Pilot Point (about three hours away) for the last time. It was the last time because she got confused on the way here and had a panic attack. She could not remember the way. By the time she got here she was frazzled and extremely upset. She was crying and angry at everyone, especially herself. We had to call Dad immediately. Dad was supposed to be on his way to my cousin David's funeral but had to change plans and come to my house instead to pick Mom up and take her home. There was no way she was going to be able to drive home by herself. Dad asked my brother to represent us at the funeral, but

Aunt Patty was still extremely unhappy with him. He could not tell her why - just that "something has come up with Muff (Mom) and he couldn't make it." The secret was still safe, for the time being. It was a heartbreaking ordeal. She never drove to my house again; I'm not sure she ever drove again, period. Dad started taking her everywhere. We couldn't risk her getting in an accident or truly lost.

I noticed she no longer put softener in the washing machine. When I asked her about it, she said that she never used laundry softener on the towels. And I let it go. I thought it odd when I asked her to wash the sheets on my bed at her house because I was coming to stay and she responded with "I'll try." The fact that I even had to ask should have keyed me in. Normally she did it without me saying a word.

I would take my daughter Skylar, who we call Baby Girl, to visit her grandparents and stay at their house. In the mornings once Mom got up I liked to go back to bed but Mom would not be happy about having to watch toddler Skylar while I slept. I couldn't understand why she didn't want that special time with her granddaughter. I get it now. It was just too much. It screwed up her routines that she relied on to keep herself and all of us in the dark.

I noticed that she stopped playing the online game "Words with Friends" with me – we used to play every evening before we'd each go to bed. She stopped reading People magazine. I don't know any of those people anymore, she told me. I didn't question it. I noticed that she couldn't handle Skylar's meltdowns. Hell, I couldn't handle her meltdowns so I definitely did not take note that it was a strange development. I noticed that she couldn't tell me what I was like at that age (two), that she couldn't tell me what she would do in certain situations because she "didn't remember when I was that young."

I remember when she told me that she was having trouble with numbers and could I please do the card thing when we were out shopping, and could I please fill out the checks for her and she would just sign them. This troubled me. When I did say something about her memory, she would just blow it off. She refused to visit any doctors. When I look back and I think "oh she was fine just a few years ago" I know I am lying to myself. She wasn't fine. She was scared and lonely and very worried. She didn't want to know the truth. Nobody wants to be told they have Alzheimer's. Nobody wants to realize that what's coming is like a fire consuming your brain while your body is still very much alive.

She stopped talking to friends. She would think that they hated her. That she had done something to make them mad. She would tell me things that they said to her – which I knew couldn't possibly be true. But she absolutely believed it had happened. Even when she hadn't even talked to her old friends, it was very real in her mind. She stopped leaving the house. She blamed her stomach – said she just couldn't go out. I worried more but chalked it up to anxiety.

One morning my husband, Tony and I were at her house, and she was sitting at her table. Normally she would have been up and fussing around, busily cooking bacon and french toast or biscuits. Nothing was happening so I asked Mom "should I cook breakfast?" And she said "well I was wondering when someone was going to do it." My husband looked at me, a long look full of words, and stood up to come help me at the stove. We didn't say a word to each other. We didn't need to. I didn't know that Dad had been preparing her breakfast each morning for a few months now.

And then. She was at my house one day, looking through a recipe book, filled with family recipes and pictures. She looked up at me and said, "this is neat!" I paused. Hesitated. Looked at her and said "Mom. You made that." "Well I did a great job!" she laughed. I didn't laugh. It hit me then. All at once, like a mack truck. She spent a year creating that recipe book for me. And she didn't remember any of it.

Mom. Mom. Please remember.

I should've known. But I didn't.

Trouble with numbers is an early sign. Isolating from friends is an early sign. Not wanting to leave your home is an early sign. I missed them. I missed them all.

Mom is starting to fixate on things. Once Mom asked Dad about her granddaughter. Where is Skylar? I think something has happened to her, I think she is upset. Is Skylar ok? She is wringing her hands and almost in tears. Dad texts me, "Mom has become very fixated on Skylar, any way you can have her FaceTime Mom to let her know she is ok?" I reply, "Yes, as soon as we're home from the park."

Dad says "she has also decided that the Prevagen (a supplement made from jellyfish that is supposed to slow down memory loss) capsules are too big to swallow. Been taking them fine for months!"

Dad is in a great deal of pain. His heart is absolutely crushed over what is happening. He desperately wants to fix it, he has always 'fixed it.' He is the caretaker, he tells me "Been married fifty years and I can't help her."

I can't imagine. He rarely talks about what is happening. He tries his best. He is not a patient caretaker though, and this is breaking him.

Mom was diagnosed with dementia in February 2017 at age seventy. The doctor never followed up with us after that initial diagnosis. Her cognitive function had declined at a rate that had us all very concerned. And because we had zero idea from the beginning what to expect, or what to think, we did not follow up on things we probably should have. We were given no instructions or suggestions or anything at all after that diagnosis. I remember very clearly that she could not draw the clock. She did not do well on any of the tests, she couldn't really understand why we were even there.

"

We were basically flung into empty space with no life support, or even a good luck pat on the back.

"

For eighteen months we struggle through, cognition declining with every new day. Sometimes she is very, very angry. Other days she is just sad and teary. Still on some days she is somewhat upbeat, as if nothing is wrong. She becomes fixated on her stomach. Spends a lot of time in the bathroom. Refuses to leave the house, refuses to see any doctors about anything. However, getting extremely angry when told you can't go to the doctor *that day* just because you want to. Dad and I know she wouldn't get in the car anyway. The effort to get appointments becomes futile. She won't take her pills. She insists that she already has, but you know damn well that she hasn't. She fully believes that what she did yesterday, a week ago, a month ago, still applies to this day. All sense of time is lost. There is constant frustration on everyone's part.

Dad and I have become texting buddies. We commiserate, we bitch about things, we simply tell how our day is going (it's never going well for Dad), I entertain with Skylar stories, we say goodnight, we say "love you" every day. We do not take each other for granted but lean on each other as we used to lean on Mom.

I look for books to read on the subject of frontal lobe dementia. I research the difference between frontal lobe dementia and Lewy-Body Syndrome, which is what my Granny died from. I realize Mom is awfully young for this diagnosis. Seventy when she was diagnosed, and who knows how many years before that she was compensating and hiding what she must have *known* and wouldn't tell.

I look for books and find nothing helpful. A book about communicating with Mom doesn't address the issues we specifically need. I look at the book *Still Alice* - something both Mom and I read years ago and realize I am afraid to read it again. I look at it on the shelf, and I turn away. I just can't do it.

By April 2018, Easter, you can really see that Mom is struggling. She absolutely insists on putting a huge bag of kit-kats in the grocery cart even though Dad has already put a smaller bag in there. When we visit for

Easter, Mom and Dad both have a great time helping Skylar look for the Easter Bunny eggs. But by the next day Mom is tired. She is exhausted from trying to hold it all together. At this point, I still don't really understand, and I just feel upset and disappointed. I'm sure when we all leave to go home, she will be really relieved. She won't have to pretend so hard anymore. I have a picture of Mom from that day. Her hair is wild, and she has bags under her eyes. She's looking at me with daggers, just because I wanted to take her picture.

When we visit a few weeks later, Mom needs help to help Skylar bake a cake. She can't understand the directions. Her hair is still wild - she needs a haircut badly. She does, however, get a great deal of pleasure from interacting with Skylar in this way. I just want Mom to go back to being the way she used to be. I don't understand at all just how bad it will get.

Skylar turned four that year. Mom and Dad and my brother and his kids came for the party, and a bunch of littles from Skylar's preschool. It is utter chaos and when David William, my autistic nephew, blows out the candles on her birthday cake she gives him daggers. I know that look well. Somehow, she knows not to cry. Mom is overwhelmed and later she complains to Dad that "it should have been just family." Which of course is not what a four-year-old's birthday party is going to be when she has a bunch of friends from school who want to eat cake and create mayhem! Skylar had a blast, and Mom's comment irritates me. Shouldn't it be what Skylar wants?! Not what Mom wants, I say to Dad. I should probably be more understanding, but I don't really know why she would say that. Later when everyone has left, I get the sweetest picture of Dad helping Skylar open her toys that she received. Grandpa is in his element with this sort of thing.

We go visit them in East Texas several times over the summer, just to hang out and relax. Grandpa has a small pool for his Fu-Fu (a nickname he created for Skylar when she was born) and we spend a lot of time watching her splash around. These are lazy, easy days and we are all happy for a while. We spend the summer ignoring what is happening in front of our eyes. None of us want to make any waves.

Late in the summer I go to Oklahoma City for surgery on my lower back. It is the first time I've ever been in a hospital without Mom being there or even knowing what is going on. Dad and I decided not to tell her because she would only worry and get confused about it. When I wake up from the anesthesia my husband is there. He stays with me and then drives me the four-hour long drive home. The recovery is terrible; I am in a lot of pain and can barely move. They tell me that the amount of inflammation I had and the years which I ignored the pain will make the recovery slow. Damn straight, as Dad would say.

Skylar had stayed with my best friend Val, we call her Miss Pooh, for the few days we were gone. I miss Mom. I have lots of help during this time from my stepdaughter Ali (Skylar's older Sissy), and my friend, Kathy, who makes dinner and helps me change the sheets on the bed. She feeds my four-year-old and braids her hair. Skylar is about to start preschool in September at the only Mother's Day Out in our area. She goes Tuesdays, Wednesdays and Thursdays and those five hours are a lifesaver for me.

CHAPTER FIVE

Diagnosis

August - September 2018

Dad calls, frustrated because he can't get through to the neurologist and Mom needs to go. He also doesn't think he can get her there, that she'll refuse to go.

I'll take her, I say. I'll make the appointment. I call the office and track down the right person and make the appointment for six weeks later. Of course they can't get her in before that.

I make the arrangements to go to their house in Tyler, Texas and pick Mom up and take her to the doctor, then drive home again. Tyler is a three-hour drive, but I am undeterred. I can do this. I figure out what to do with Skylar and rearrange my schedule in order to make it all happen.

The appointment is on a Monday. The Friday before, the office calls and tells me we will have to reschedule because the doctor has jury duty. Are you shitting me? Wouldn't they have known this weeks ahead of time? I am annoyed but I take the earliest spot they have - 11:40 on the following Thursday.

A week and a half later, after having rearranged everything all over again, I get up at the crack of dawn to drive to my parents' house, to pick Mom up and drive her to the appointment. Dad has told her about the appointment, and she swears she isn't going.

When I arrived at the house to get Mom she was absolutely insistent that she was **not** going. I had arrived early enough to spend an hour at the house before we had to leave. Mom does not understand why she needs to see this doctor again. I try to tell her it's because you have a condition and we need to follow up on that. A check up, Mom, that's all. No, she says, my stomach hurts and I can't go. You want me to poop everywhere?

I am trying to be calm but am quickly becoming unraveled by her anger. Mom, I drove all this way to take you! Please just come on and go to the doctor! She is in tears, throwing things and crying that her stomach hurts. I am dying inside but I insist that we go. "**Fine**" she yells at me. I said I know you are mad at me Mom but even if you are mad, we still have to go. "You're being a **jerk,**" she mutters under her breath. I turn away to hide the pain.

She stomps out to the car and I follow. We are leaving way too early but there is no way I am not leaving **right now** while I have the chance. In the car she can't figure out the seatbelt, so I lean over to help her and she cries "Leave me alone!" I back off. We are both terribly upset but I try not to let her see the tears hiding behind my eyes. This isn't really Mom, I tell myself. This isn't really her.

We drive in silence for a while, and I am aware of her muttering under her breath. After some time, I can tell that she has calmed down. I honestly don't remember if we talked about anything else on the way. And then she was fine. She didn't remember how upset she had gotten.

At the doctor's office we were of course pretty early so I knew we would have to wait a long time. Mom didn't bring her purse inside with her - she had left it in the car. When I was done checking her in, I offered to go get her purse if she wanted it. No, she said. I am afraid I won't remember where you've gone. Just stay with me. A moment of clarity of her own condition, which she very rarely acknowledges.

I help her find the bathroom and walk with her. All earlier anxiety over her stomach is gone. I go up to the receptionist and tell her quietly that I would like to talk with the nurse or doctor on my own without Mom hearing - could they arrange that? She said certainly, I will let them know.

When we are finally led back, I see the receptionist hand the note about a private discussion to the nurse. She reads it and I am reassured that I will get to talk to someone. The nurse takes Mom's weight and blood pressure and asks how things have been. I decline to go into too much detail since I will have to repeat it all to the doctor anyway.

Once the doctor himself finally appears (trying to keep a woman with dementia patient while waiting is akin to keeping a two-year-old occupied) - he is brash. I instantly don't appreciate him. He does not have much concern or sympathy. He is on a time crunch, you can tell. He asks Mom how she is and he can clearly see that she cannot answer his questions without looking to me. She mentions that her stomach gets upset and she has diarrhea a lot. At this point he gets completely sidetracked by the diarrhea and what is causing it. That's not why we're here, I scream inside my head. We don't even know if the stomach is actually a problem, or if it's just anxiety. Do you feel anxious, he asks Mom. No, not really, Mom answers. I close my eyes. This is such bullshit. I can't even tell the doctor that yes, of course she's anxious. I look imploringly at the nurse who is taking notes. She looks away.

The doctor suggests a new MRI, based on her inability to have a conversation. He can see she has seriously deteriorated *from the last time he saw her. He says, yes, I think we've progressed to Alzheimer's, not just basic dementia. I stare at him. He's almost jubilant. Unfortunately there's really nothing we can do - are you taking the Neumenda? Christ, I think - you should **know** that by reading her chart! Ok, he says, stop taking that for a week and see if the diarrhea gets better. I am almost apoplectic at this point. Let me get this straight - you want to stop the only medication that may actually be helping her cognitive function? To see if it's causing the diarrhea. I can assure you it's not. Mom has had stomach problems for twenty years.*

I'll put in for the MRI, he says. They'll call you to schedule it. I'll see you again in six months.

***Six Months.** Where the heck will we be in six months? I look at the nurse as she shepherds us out the door, never once trying to get me on my own so I can relay my own concerns and questions. She won't catch my eye. I mentally give up on this office.*

Do you want to go to lunch Mom? No, I just want to go home. So we do.

Did you know that Alzheimer's can't even be officially diagnosed? It's just a matter of guessing really. Watching the patient deteriorate in her logical capabilities until the doctor says Yep. She's progressed to Alzheimer's. An MRI can show blockages, shrinkage or other abnormalities but even that can mean different things.

Mom has Alzheimer's. It's only official because the doctor's office called today, after the MRI results were in (going to get the MRI was also traumatic, but we made it).

I talk to the nurse on the phone. The doctor himself hasn't bothered to call me. I am at the park with Skylar when I get the call. The nurse tells me that the MRI showed significant decline in cognitive function. Well shit, I say, of course it does. We didn't need an MRI to know that. It also showed brain shrinkage and a lot of blocked blood vessels. I wonder how this happens. Does she have any amyloid plaques on her brain? I ask. Well, we can't actually tell that by an MRI or anything. Only after the patient has died and we do an autopsy can we know for sure. Here's where you can find the pamphlet that shows the decline of patients that have been diagnosed. Mild… moderate… severe. The average lifespan after diagnosis is four to ten years.

I am more than angry. The nurse is so unconcerned. I scream, I cry, I ask her how *she* would feel if it were *her* mom. Why do we have to wait six months to see the doctor again? Is there *nothing* more he can do for her? The nurse falters but swears nothing else can be done.

I have always been a strong woman, Dad says, when I tell him about the phone call (after he has heard the devastating news). But it doesn't matter, I say. Strong or not, I can't change what is happening. Mom was always strong, too. Dad doesn't believe in blame or fault. What caused this? It doesn't matter, he says. It's here, it's with us and we have no choice but to cope.

I want to fall into the abyss. I want to scream THIS IS BULLSHIT! I want to wring that doctor's neck.

This is only the beginning of the end. What more is there to come? I am afraid. Terrified. We are all so aware that we are actively walking forward into the fire. We *will* actively walk towards it. Anything, anything for Mom.

CHAPTER SIX

Moving Forward

October - December 2018

In late October Tony, Skylar and I meet Mom and Dad at a place called Yesterland Farm in Canton, which is only about forty-five minutes from their house in East Texas. Tony and Dad go on to the house, leaving Mom with me. It soon becomes apparent that doing this with Mom at this stage was a bad idea. She is overwhelmed quickly and can't understand Skylar's behavior - she is four years old after all. Skylar is a demanding, high energy little kid and I try to regulate her, but Mom is upset every time Skylar is upset. The whole day is a minefield that I'm trying to navigate through with both of them. Skylar is (mostly) having a great time, but being just four, she is amazed and overwhelmed by all the activity. There are little train rides, a small roller coaster, fun houses, pumpkins everywhere, swing sets and round-a-bouts and a million other things designed to make kids go crazy. Mom doesn't even know what to think - she is way out of her comfort zone. I remember thinking that I couldn't wait to get them both home so I could relax! I'm sure Mom felt the same way.

I tell Dad I'm going to work on getting home health to come out. He says "I don't know how that's going to work, Mom doesn't like strangers coming into the house and trying to make her do stuff." I tell him to try and think positive. We need the help. He responds with "I'm probably the most positive person you know, but I'm way the hell into reality." He's defeated before we even start. It frustrates me but I also understand his point. He's been dealing with Mom's issues for almost fifty years. I know he's tired and discouraged.

They are getting ready to move closer to me in Pilot Point, Texas. They are looking at houses, and the main concern is that Dad needs to be able to see Mom at all times, unless she's asleep. We finally find a home that is pretty wide open. Dad can be watching TV in his recliner and see Mom sitting in her chair at the table. Mom has sat at a table reading or watching TV for her entire adult life. It is where she is comfortable, where I can always find her. She shakes parmesan cheese onto her palm to eat or organizes M&M's and pops them into her mouth while reading. Microwave popcorn is another favorite. I wonder later how, exactly, this unhealthy diet might have contributed to her dementia. She used to smoke at the table, too, but now they smoke on the back porch, or in the garage.

Anytime I text Dad to ask how he's doing his reply is always "about the same, very discouraging." I tell him to try and keep his spirits up, that maybe the new house will help make things better. He answers, "the whole thing has turned out very difficult and upsetting." He is as honest with me as he has ever been with anyone. I am his outlet; my brother is his distraction. I guess it works, but I try not to offload too much on him with my own feelings. I save that for my husband. My brother calls Dad every day at 4 pm. Dad really looks forward to those calls. I think they are what keep him going right now. They talk about football, and about the garage "man cave" my brother is building. I don't know what else they talk about but they're good at "shooting the shit" as Dad would say.

When I complain that my house is a wreck Dad says that while he was mowing the grass, Mom pulled out every single thing in the kitchen and put it all on top of the countertops then started crying when she thought that Dad was criticizing her. He absolutely wasn't but was probably extremely dismayed to realize that he couldn't even put it all back or she would get even more upset.

Having been an Army wife, Mom knows that packing is involved with moving, and she is very aware that they are going to move. She doesn't know what else to do. She wants to be busy, she wants to help, but she is very confused. I think that she doesn't always understand what she is doing when she is doing it. That's got to be very hard for her.

Dad tells me he is worried about getting the trash out. His back is hurting him a lot. I tell him when he moves here I'll be able to help him, and he can help me by watching Skylar while I get things done. He says "yeah we can watch a lot of dog show. Paw Patrol." I laugh and tell him Skylar will love that. It's currently her absolute favorite thing. She is completely obsessed with Paw Patrol.

I tell Dad to make Mom plenty of ginger tea. She loves hot tea and she forgets to drink water. So it will help with her stomach issues and also help to keep her hydrated. I've heard of a new thing called "Jelly Drops" which are like gummies filled with water, to keep older people hydrated. Mom loves gummies, and I love this idea. Unfortunately, they are not yet ready to be sold to the public. I don't think they'll be ready in time to help Mom at all, but it is a brilliant idea.

Dad still leaves Mom alone sometimes, when he has to go run errands. I'm anxious every time he does and even more anxious for them to get moved into the house we chose five minutes from mine in Pilot Point. When he leaves Mom alone, and quite frankly, he has to in order to get groceries and stuff, Mom will forget where he's gone and will get scared and angry.

One day in October I asked how everything was, as I usually did every day and this was his response: "Not good. Bad mood shift while I was gone! Very angry – thinks I had a good time! It was horrible, flooding, twenty mph and pouring! Mom would not eat - drank three hot beers – terrible – went to bed 6:40 pm! Will not let me help her!"

Mom spends a lot of time being angry. There are good days and bad days. Bad days of mood swings and anger and frustration and no conversation and tears. Good days where she tries so hard to be grateful. They're all bad days in my opinion, better bad days and worse bad days. Each day is just one more towards the last. There will be no improving, no recovery, no moving on from this. It is an impossible pill to swallow for all of us.

I tell Dad I hope things will get more bearable once they move here. He responds: "I hope! It's a path to destruction! I think she has lots of flashbacks to childhood! Her mother was a very nasty person! Lots of blame and fault!" I'm sure my Granny Judy had plenty of her own bitterness to swallow, with such a history of mental illness in her husband and son. And then her daughter so desperate to leave, and with a man she did not approve of!

I tell him I am worried that I will also get Alzheimer's, and he tells me that out of all the people in his very large family he never knew anyone who had it. I am praying there's enough of his side of the family's genes in me to outweigh the mental illness genes on Mom's side. As I watch Mom decline, I am hyper aware that all this could someday happen to me.

We talk about the new house. We are both hopeful that spending time with me and Skylar will help Mom stay happier and more relaxed. We are hoping it will slow down the progression but are aware that it probably won't. Dad is worried about Mom not being familiar with the new house. She has compensated for so long here that moving will make things harder for her, I know. I am worried that Mom will end up needing to be in a home and Dad will be all alone in the expansive new house he just bought. We come to visit for Veteran's Day and make Dad an American flag cake. We are helping to clean out and pack up the house, but it's hard because Mom really doesn't understand what is happening. She is all about throwing things out, though.

One day Mom throws away all the cookies I had made for Dad. He is so disappointed. It's the little things like that that help him get through the days. I am so sorry for him, but now he's learned he has to hide things so that Mom won't get rid of them. She has been going through the house lately, forcing Dad to get rid of things. "We don't need that!" she'll say, even though it's something like the gorgeous jewelry box that Dad gave her many years ago. It breaks Dad's heart, so he takes it out of the house and hides it in his truck where she can't see it. Otherwise she'll fixate on it and hound him every chance she gets. She made Dad get rid of the bouncy chair that Skylar slept in as a baby - something I wanted to keep for her to play with her baby dolls with - and Dad was afraid to tell me when I asked about it and searched the house high and low for it.

The sewing machine disappeared. We think that Mom took it to a repair shop a long time ago and forgot about it. Now we don't have a clue where it could be. She takes to hiding things in bizarre places, or else throwing away old pictures and memorabilia. My brother rescues the big box of family photos when he's there one day so that it doesn't get trashed.

She can no longer text me. Sometimes when I call her she is doing well and we have a good conversation. But she lets her phone run down and doesn't remember how to text. My emotions are all over the place. We used to talk daily - sometimes multiple times a day. It's a hard new reality for me. Dad says he has to get up early when Mom gets up, so he can plug in the coffee pot and turn on the TV. "Otherwise she just sits there."

Mom refuses or cannot understand that they've hired movers to come pack up all their stuff. She continually takes things out of closets and drives Dad mad with the mess. If he says anything at all she gets pissed off and upset. I try to tell him it's just her way of coping. She doesn't know what to do but thinks she is supposed to be doing *something*... so she pulls stuff out and stacks it everywhere. God knows how we'll find anything once it's all moved.

She refuses to take her pills. She will swear up and down she already did it. Or she gets very suspicious and thinks we are giving her things she doesn't need. We have resorted to trying to sneak the pills into her hot tea in the mornings. Especially the anxiety one, that is the most important one right now. Also, after over ten years of not smoking in the house, Mom has forgotten that they don't do that anymore. She gets incensed when Dad tells her to smoke outside or in the garage. She will sneak them when she thinks he's not looking and light up in the house. It's all the old habits and behaviors she remembers. None of the relatively recent things.

Dad and I commiserate over how fast she's deteriorating.

Mom is back to thinking her old friend, Panchita, is mad at her. I talk to her and get her to calm down. I will have to call Panchita tomorrow so Mom can hear her voice and be reassured that she's not mad. Mom comes up with stuff in her mind and absolutely believes it is real. I know it is real to her, she doesn't know she's making stuff up.

It's finally December, moving time is here. I am supposed to pick up Mom and the cat and take them to my house for a few days while Dad and Tony stay behind to supervise the packing and moving. Dad has successfully snuck the anxiety pill into Mom's coffee. When I get there, I am barely out of the car before Mom jumps in and says let's go. I am astounded. I figured we'd have tears and sadness over leaving the place she's lived in for almost twenty-five years. To this day I still don't know what to think of that!

So we drive. We sing songs and get McDonald's. She is as happy as I've seen her in a long while. When we get to Pilot Point I take her by the new house. I am very worried that she won't remember it, but she does. I ask her if it will feel like home and she says yes, but I think she is just saying what I want to hear. We head to my house where Mom will stay for a few days, until things are sorted at the new house. She does great with everything until about 3:30 pm in the afternoon when she starts complaining about her stomach and mumbling to herself. Dad reminds me to help with the CPAP machine that night. I tell Mom we need to put water in it but she insists it doesn't need water. She's pretty defensive right now so I drop it. I have never used a CPAP, so I am unsure if it does or not. I figure it doesn't matter that much at this stage anyway. Mom stands by the bed in her clothes. I can't get her to put pajamas on or brush her teeth, so I help her into bed. She sleeps right on the edge of the mattress, like she doesn't know how to scooch herself over to the middle.

The next day she helps me decorate my house for Christmas. I had already decorated their house before they even moved in so that it would be done before they got there. At one point Skylar accidentally drops a very special piece and it breaks. I am already on edge so I start to cry. I know my four-year-old didn't mean to drop it, I know she is upset too, but I can't help myself. Mom looks at me crying and comes over and puts her arms around me. I lean into her shoulder and am comforted by the familiarity of her. I am not entirely sure, but I think this is the last time she spontaneously puts her arms around me and lets me lean into her. Of course I don't realize this at the time, if I had known, I would have cried harder. There are many times in the coming years where she reaches out to me when she is scared or upset, but that is for me to comfort her, not the other way around.

Later that day, after 3 pm, Mom is very tired and things get difficult. She is obsessed with all the CPAP supplies and pills that were in the back of the car. She keeps messing with all of it and gets mad at me when I tell her she doesn't need any of that right now. I am wondering if 3 pm is the new "witching hour" or the start of sundowning. Mom always has had a time in the evening when she just shut down. Didn't want any more interaction or communication - sat in her chair at the table and watched TV or read her magazines and books.

By December 5th, Mom has been at my house for three days. Wearing the same clothes, she refuses to change or shower. On the 6th she finally spends the night in the new house. She still won't shower. Dad says that she's in a good mood and he doesn't want to screw that up. I say, yeah but she kinda stinks. It's a very short fuse we're working with here, Mom will get angry faster than I can say the word 'shower'.

That first night I am very anxious. I drink two glasses of wine to try and relax. I keep texting Dad to see if Mom is doing ok. He finally says that she's in bed and I should get some sleep. I tell him I am worried about her waking up disoriented. He is worried too, but we can't do anything about it.

For the next few days we are all busy unpacking and getting them settled. Mom desperately wants to help.

Dad says let her even if she puts stuff in the wrong places. She puts a bottle of shampoo in the bedroom designated as mine (when I sleep there). Puts stuff basically everywhere. I try to sneak around and move things when she's not looking. One night she has a drastic mood swing after I've left - we've had a pretty good day - and comes out to the porch to yell at Dad and tell him he hasn't helped her all day. She won't relax - she constantly wants to be up and moving around. Nowadays I look back and realize it's because she wasn't comfortable. She was anxious and disoriented, and as always, took it out on Dad. He finds it bewildering and very upsetting. He's only ever trying to help her. I know how hard this is for him.

A few days later Mom is waiting at the window for over an hour because Skylar and I are coming over. She no longer has any sense of time. Once we leave she has another massive mood change and goes to bed angry at 5:45 pm. At 7:30 pm she comes back in the living room and angrily tells Dad that he's "been sitting in here for hours!" She grabs her cigarettes and heads back into her room. Thankfully she does not have a lighter. Dad knows she needs to take her meds, especially her anxiety pill, but he is loath to bring it up with her. He, somewhat jokingly, tells me he will try some gentle approach first thing in the morning so that she can get mad and stay mad all day. I say, you could try the meds at night? He tells me she's been mad every night lately (which I am aware of). Then Mom hides the pill tray and we can't find it. Dad simply buys another one. Then her bottle of anxiety pills goes missing. Thankfully Dad has an extra bottle in his bag. So he sneaks one in her coffee.

They've been there nine days and no one has showered. Not Mom. Not Dad. Dad does ask me where the soap is. So I find it for him and he agrees to shower. Dad's issue is that he can't stand being cold. He simply doesn't eat enough to make a bird fat. He doesn't want to be cold when he gets out of the shower while he's drying off so he simply avoids showering as long as possible. At least he has a reason. Mom will swear up and down that she bathed when you know damn well that she didn't. In the morning she will come out of her room with three or four shirts on. She sleeps in her clothes usually, but she still knows that she's supposed to get *'dressed'* in the mornings. So she puts more clothes on. Sometimes it's extremely hard to get her to take any of them off. Sometimes I don't even bother. I wish like hell I could get her to bathe.

We are racking our brains trying to come up with Christmas presents for Mom. Finally, I settle on body lotion (even though she won't shower) and hand cream and a cup that says MOM. I am hoping that will help her know which cup is hers because she can never remember. She'll set it down somewhere and then that's the end of that.

My brother and his kids come for Christmas. The kids have a great time, and I hope that makes Dad feel better. We worked really hard on making this Christmas happen the best it could. But the day doesn't turn out well at all. My brother, Dad and I are all worried sick about Mom, and if we're honest, a little upset that Mom has made it unbearable. Mom is angry, resentful and confused. This is a very difficult reality we're facing and we just wanted one day of happiness. It didn't happen.

The next day we talk about home health care again. Dad is adamant that it won't work - that Mom won't let anyone help her. I am adamant that we try. I insist that Dad needs help, too, and it's worth a shot to have someone come. He finally gives in.

Mom still hasn't bathed.

CHAPTER SEVEN

A New Year

January - February 2019

Mom is crying. Telling Dad how much she hates this place and wants to go home. He is telling me it rips his guts out - "in twenty days it'll be fifty years of marriage - now in her time of greatest need I'm not able to help! Heartbreaking!" He tries to change the subject by telling her I'm coming to help take the tree down. Mom immediately goes to the tree and starts taking all the ornaments off and lays them on the table. Dad says Mom really wants to be involved and help so he'll help her finish taking the tree down and the other decorations instead of me. I tell him I think that's a great idea.

I try to encourage Dad to show Mom how to do things. Even if she doesn't remember five minutes later. I think if he would spend more time with her and reassure her that he loves her in that way it might go a long way. Take a walk across the street to see the ponies! Sitting there all day isn't helping anyone. But Dad is stubborn and negative about the situation and tells me there's no way - Mom won't listen to him. She will get upset. She will get angry. I think he's just tired and discouraged. He doesn't want to do anything that might set Mom off. Doesn't want to risk any moment of peace. I understand.

Dad also says he doesn't want to get too involved with the neighbors. He doesn't want them to know she has Alzheimer's. I raise my eyes at this one - aren't we beyond that? "Dad," I say, "you **must** stop listening to the limiting factors and using them as excuses! And just *do* what needs to be done. If they recognize that she has dementia chances are they will A) not mention it and B) be supportive and kind. She needs interactions! The time for people not knowing has passed." Maybe I am being pushy by saying these things. I get frustrated, too. Looking back, maybe I needed to listen to Dad more and say what I thought less often. I am trying to support him as well, but I am also hardheaded and probably should keep more of my thoughts to myself.

Dad thinks he is not a good caretaker. We both know that we both get depressed over Mom and then don't want to do everyday things like pay the bills. I tell him I am still working on getting home health care. He is completely resistant to the idea. Swears it won't work. That Mom will get upset because she will think that we think she is stupid. I tell him I don't believe that - I think these people know what they are doing and will take it easy on Mom. Dad and I have a bit of a spat over text about it but we both back off quickly. I tell him I am just talking to them, setting wheels in motion. He tells me he appreciates everything I do.

If I text Mom now she'll bring the phone to Dad and tell him she doesn't know what to do. She's been pretty nasty to Dad lately. He'll ask a simple question like "do you want coffee?" and she'll reply with a sneer and say "no, I have coffee. I've had it all day." Today he asked her if she wanted Skylar and me to come over later and she looked at him like he was speaking Russian. We're guessing that's a no. But fifteen minutes later she won't even remember that he asked.

He still has to leave her alone sometimes. He needs to go grocery shopping or just out by himself. I always try to come over when he needs to do that but occasionally I can't. Dad tells me that "you can only take so much of her moaning, groaning, talking to herself saying no one does anything for her, no one gets her anything." I fully understand. It's very difficult to be around Mom when she's like that, which is currently a lot of the time.

I want to take Mom to the movies. I tell Dad I'll pick her up at noon. A bit later he texts me to say she is throwing up and says she can't go! Even though it's hours away, it is clearly too much for her to think about. We decide to wait until the next day to go. Mom says yes, she wants to go!

But the next day Dad waits until about 11 am to tell her he's bringing her to my house, and she gets angry because nobody told her! She hasn't remembered any of the day before. Dad manages to convince her to go, and Skylar is very excited. She wants to spend time with her Granny Susan that she adores. It's been super hard on Skylar too. It is very difficult for a four-year-old to understand what is happening to her Granny Susan. But she is always patient and kind and just tries to get Mom to play or color with her like she used to. Skylar has been loving that she can go over to Granny Susan and Grandpa's anytime she wants. She loves their house (although she says she loved the one in East Texas more) and she loves that Grandpa has a playhouse and a trampoline. He moved these things to the new house just for her.

I can't recall now which movie we saw. Mom enjoys herself but I wonder if she can even follow along. It will turn out to be the last movie Mom ever goes to. I've taken to sneaking Mom's dirty clothes out of her bathroom and sticking them in the washing machine. Then Dad puts them in the dryer at night. I notice there is no toilet paper in her bathroom - and she never asks for any, which is very concerning. I put about four rolls in there, hoping it will motivate her to use it. She tells me about the lady who is coming that wants her to take a bath. She is calm about it. She has agreed to try it once.

Dad has been having trouble eating. He'll get Mom a Whataburger and she will take a few bites. He'll ask how it is and she'll say "it's ok, you don't care about me anyway." When Mom says something mean, it makes Dad so upset. He knows he shouldn't let it get to him, but he can't help it. It hurts. All he wants is to make her life better. To make her happy. My Aunt Patty told me that Dad has spent his entire life trying to make Mom happy. I believe it.

Another day I ask Dad how things are that day. He replies "well we started off with Mom telling me to go fuck myself cuz I couldn't understand what she was telling me. Another great day." I am just gutted for him. What a horrible thing to say. I understand that this isn't the Mom we grew up with, this isn't the Mom that we've known all our lives. But still, it's a very bitter pill, especially for Dad. No wonder he can't eat.

Physical therapy, speech therapy, lady wanting to give her a bath... Dad says this is getting out of hand - we just wanted one person a week. Nobody has actually come yet but they keep calling to set up appointments. I call them and tell them we've got to keep it to once a week - one person at a time - right now. We have to see how it goes before we commit to more than that!

Mom has been wild lately, muttering to herself and tapping on the table constantly. Dad keeps trying to slip her anxiety pill in her drink. Dad is desperate to leave the house. One morning he tells her "I would do anything for you; I love you and I'll always be here." She responds with "I don't think so." I tell Dad, just keep telling her. Her brain is sick, she doesn't know what she is saying.

It is a very bad month.

Dad tells me that Mom is "not wearing any pants today! Says she can't find um!" I reply "I hung them all in her closet. After I washed them. This is why I have an ulcer." He finds some pants in the bathroom and remarks that this is all probably a lot harder than I thought it would be. I have to agree. He jokingly says not to worry, it'll get a lot harder. I am not laughing. I am not prepared.

I decide to try notes all over the house, telling Mom where the cups are, the refrigerator, the trash, etc. She angrily rips them all down after I leave. Mom is also not eating. Won't touch her food. She eats an apple turnover every morning and then packs of fruit snacks all day. She was eating Whataburger but has stopped touching that as well. Same with Chick-fil-A, Sonic, and Dairy Queen. Dad doesn't cook so he simply goes to get food for her. Of course when I am there I cook but it's a crap shoot whether she'll eat it or not. She tells him she wants ribs. He gets them. She won't touch them. It's a never-ending story. Tony was there helping Dad do a few things and told me later that she was "tapping, banging on table, cussing, very angry." We have absolutely no idea why.

She sits in her chair and I sit in a blue wing chair across from her, that Dad wanted to move to the bedroom. It's in the way, he says, see if you can convince Mom to move it. But I like it, it's cozy and big and Skylar and I can sit in it together. So I let Mom win this battle and the chair stays where it is. We are watching some poor soul on TV, struggling in her 600-pound life. How depressing I tell Mom. Let's watch something else. HGTV. Fixer Upper is on, Chip and Joanna are funny.

After a while I get up to fix dinner. I get the chicken out of the fridge. Mom asks if she can help. Sure I say. But what can she do? I hand her the bag of salad, which she can't open. I open it with scissors and tell her to put the salad in three separate bowls. But she doesn't do it. Following instructions is now beyond her, for the most part. After a few bewildering moments, she goes to sit back down in her chair.

The speech or 'cognitive' therapist finally came a few days ago. She spent an hour showing us these apps on an Ipad that Mom and I could work on together, she mentioned crossword puzzles and Soduku. I am staring at the therapist like she has lost her mind. Where was all this two years ago when it might have helped? When it might have made a difference? It's way too late for all this shit now. Too damn late. Mom can't even name the apple when it pops up on the screen. She can no

58

longer text. She hasn't played Words with Friends with me for over a year. I tried to show her how to play Solitaire the other day - something she used to play all the time - and she looked at it like she had never seen it before. I can't, she said. I can't figure it out.

I'll show her something we used to do all the time, or watch or read or whatever and she'll say "No, I've never seen this before, I've never done this." She'll look at something she had owned for fifty years and say we never had this before.

She does remember some things. It is very selective and random. Or she'll see something, and she'll remember that she likes it, without remembering where it came from. Like my Granny Judy's dishes with the yellow roses. She loves those. Yesterday she remembered Dakota, my uncle Datch's dog even though she has forgotten her estranged brother that she never saw or spoke to again after Granny Judy died. She remembered Dakota, a great Dane, and said she missed him. He's been dead for thirty years.

Will I grieve when she's gone? When will the end actually come? I spend so much time grieving now while at the same time trying to embrace the remaining moments that I feel like I will be so exhausted when the end comes that I might just freeze up and not feel anything at all.

"

I don't even feel the heat of the fire, I just keep walking through it.

"

How will Dad handle it? Will he be ok? Will I be ok? Will Skylar be ok?

The end is coming much faster than any of us anticipated. The end is staring at us like a barrel of a gun. We were hoping for so much more time. I fear that years are going to end up as months. Is that a blessing or a curse? Neither or both? I know nothing anymore.

Mom thinks she can still do the laundry. She puts dryer sheets in the washer and washes the clothes I already washed. Eventually Dad figures it out and makes sure to take the dryer sheets out, add some detergent and wash them for real. Then he's got to be quick to get them in the dryer before the whole cycle starts again.

She has forgotten about smoking but has taken to carrying strange things around. Yesterday it was a cigarette and a razor. Today I took her to the doctor and suggested that she leave the cigarette, two $10 bills and a pair of underwear that she was carrying in the car. She snapped at me "don't tell me what I need!" When we went to get her hair done, she had a lighter in her hand the whole time. I think she's so used to taking her purse that she knows she needs 'something' but has forgotten what it is.

At Walmart she'll tell you she needs something but can't tell you what. Even if you walk in a big circle around the store, she still won't know. Dad and I do this a lot. One day I hit the jackpot and figured out she wanted candy! At home, she'll go to the garage to get a beer and come back with an ashtray. She hasn't taken to wandering or wanting to go outside and we are grateful for that. It would be awful if she got lost somewhere.

She will tell the home health nurse about all sorts of strange things. Once she told her she had eight kids, then she just had one. She also told her that her longtime friends, Brenda and Dick, were here in our house.

At the end of January Mom thinks that Skylar is coming to stay while Tony and I go to Maryland. When Dad finally got her to understand that it was Skylar and Tony going to Maryland and not me, she was devastated. Then she wanted to know what happened to me. (Nothing had happened except that I just didn't go on the trip).

Around this time, we decide that we need a puppy for Skylar. We pay the deposit on an English Springer Spaniel, and she will be ready to be picked up just after Valentine's Day. This turns out to be one of the biggest mistakes I've ever made. My best friend Val, and I think Kathy as well, asked what the hell was I thinking! Because I don't have enough to deal with right now! We go to visit the puppy that we've named Tess Cupcake (Tess for short), and she is the cutest thing I've ever seen. Brown and white with long floppy ears. I have no idea what having a puppy will entail, as I've never been a dog person, but I believe that I can handle one more thing. Time will show that I cannot.

There are rare days when Mom's in a good mood. More often than not she is angry, tired, sad and/or being nasty to Dad. Will or will not eat any food he gives her. There's no way of knowing what kind of day it will be. Dad and I take it in turns to be with her, though he bears the brunt of the work as I have a child, a husband and a business to also take care of. Still, I feel bad every day that I can't make it over there. Guilt and worry consume my days. Dad sends me a picture of some notes she tore up and says she burned one the other day. I am horrified by the implications. I ask if he's keeping my brother in the know and he says that my brother has more than enough problems of his own. I know this is true, but I still feel like he would want to be aware of how bad things have gotten.

I wish I could spend more time with Dad, to make him feel better. But Mom gets jealous and thinks we are talking about her. He has taken to texting me only at night, after she's asleep, or real short texts during the day. Dad talks about going to spend a night at my brother's or going to Canton for Monday Trade Days with Tony. We say we will make it happen, but for one reason or another it never does.

Dad prefers to go out to get Mom food at night. Panera, Whataburger and McAlister's have all been tried. The problem is that while he's gone, Mom forgets where he went and gets scared and angry, then refuses to eat when he gets home. I have to teach lessons (riding lessons) in the evenings after school so that is not a time when I can come over. I'm getting super worried about him leaving her alone. Especially after the burned note thing.

Dad tries to take Mom out to Dillards or anywhere, really, just to get her out of the house. It is nerve wracking for him, because he also has limited mobility, and can't walk a lot. He knows every minute they are out they can be one second away from total disaster with Mom. She doesn't know what she wants when they go out, and it is very difficult to keep her happy. She hardly ever leaves the house these days. Occasionally I get Dad to drop her off at my house, to watch me ride or keep me company while I clean. This usually goes ok, until Mom gets tired. We have to do a lot of guesswork to figure out the fine line before she basically has a meltdown and needs to go home. We try to get her home before that moment but sometimes we are not successful.

The mood swings are intense. I can leave her perfectly happy and fifteen minutes later she is angry and unhappy. Another day I take Mom out, but it ends with a tear fest in the car. She gets upset with me and I have been so stressed that I just start crying. Mom did not like me crying. Then when I get her home, Dad texts me later and tells me Mom is very confused and said I was upset and crying and that they should get me something and "put it up there." Dad and I couldn't puzzle that one out, but Mom finally went to bed so all is well.

Skylar and I head over to my parents' house early one morning. Dad needs a break. He'd like to go out without worrying about leaving Mom home alone. I ask Mom if she'd like to go out with Skylar and me, to breakfast? Hobby Lobby? We could go to Cracker Barrel and get her some black licorice. She gives me a look that says, "not really but I want to make you happy so okay."

But of course, her stomach hurts. Can't go anywhere. It's debilitating and sudden. Dad gives her some medicine and we wait. I do some laundry and I try to clean up a little. I attempt to get Mom to write Tony's birthday on her calendar. But she says "I'm tired of doing this stuff." After an hour she agrees to go out. We head out and Dad leaves right after us.

Immediately I can tell it's not going to go well. Mom is totally silent, except for little noises about her stomach hurting, and small gasps whenever I turn or go over a bump. Skylar is talking a mile a minute in the backseat. Unfortunately, everything is thirty minutes away. All the good stores and places to eat. We persevere but I am on high alert and tense. Skylar is tired from waking up at 5 am. She finally drops off with five minutes to go before we get to Cracker Barrel. Mom is extremely anxious and I ask her if we need to just turn around and go home. I already know the answer. We stop in at a Whataburger and I ask her if she can find the bathroom. I don't want to leave my baby girl alone, asleep, in the car. I park as close to the door as I can. Mom gets out of the car; I can see her muttering. This worries me so I get out as well and make my way to the front door so I can keep an eye on Skylar and also make sure Mom finds the bathroom.

She isn't in there long. I know it's just anxiety about leaving the house, it seems to paralyze her sometimes. Nothing is as it used to be. Gone are the days when we can just go shopping together, go to lunch, have a good time. These days every moment is extremely stressful.

Skylar is still asleep as we make our way back home again. I glance over at Mom, and it seems she is sleeping too. She is much more relaxed now that we are on the way home. She's not actually asleep but she's calm. Skylar wakes up ten minutes before we get back to the house and immediately launches into a meltdown because we are headed home and not out to eat. She is frustrated and I understand – but there's nothing I can do about it.

We finally make it to Mom's house and Skylar asks me if I will get her a pretzel from Sonic. Mom sits down on the couch in the living room. She seems vacant. Mom, do you want anything from Sonic? No, she says. Nothing.

I call Dad as I go to Sonic. I feel bad that I can't give him his worry-free day out. But at the moment I can't seem to make anyone happy. And I certainly haven't accomplished any of the things I had intended to do.

I will try again tomorrow of course. I will keep trying, and so will Dad. But how long will this go on? She does not want to do any of the stuff the therapist tells her to do. She does not want to bathe, or do laundry, or vacuum. But she doesn't want me to do any of it either. She certainly doesn't want to leave the house. I miss her. I miss Mom and the way she used to be. I miss going shopping, trying new places to eat. I miss her communicating with me. I miss talking to her on the phone. I miss playing Words with Friends, talking about books we're both reading, and texting.

Mom was wonderful. This situation is not.

"

There is only going to be a finish line, and we don't know where it is.

"

How can I talk about what is going on with my friends? It feels so disloyal. It feels like I am betraying her with every word I say, and every bit of this experience that I write about. But to keep it all in will destroy me. I don't even know how many of my family know what is truly going on. I think possibly none of them know, outside the immediate four of us. Keeping her secret is hard. It's killing Dad too. I know it would help him to talk about it as well. We can hardly even talk to each other about it – it's too depressing. And heartbreaking.

Before they moved here I told Mom how wonderful it would be to be able to just pick her up and take her out – get our nails done, shop and eat and enjoy each other. She agreed that it would be really wonderful. She would love it.

That is not how it has turned out. Not at all. And no one is more distraught about that than me and Dad. We know that we cannot fix this. It will never go away; it will never get any better.

How do you wish for something to be over? How do you wish for peace in this situation? Oh the guilt for even thinking it. The guilt. The fear. The agonizing decisions that are headed our way. We can't win – none of us. There is no winning here. There is only going to be a finish line, and we don't know where it is.

God please bring us peace.

We bring the puppy Tess home mid-February. She is the sweetest thing but proves to be more than we can handle almost from the get-go. I take about a thousand pictures of this little love bug. At first, we are completely in love but as time goes on we realize we bit off more than we can chew. I didn't realize how hard potty training would be! Tess is very loving, and she loves Skylar (as was the point) but she is getting bigger as each day goes on and Skylar is not. She has claws and she pushes Skylar over a lot, and even though I know it's not on purpose, it unnerves Skylar. Her dresses and shirts soon have holes in them from puppy teeth, which are sharp! We struggle along while Tess grows, getting bigger and stronger each day, and more rambunctious. What will I do with her when we are at horse shows? I wanted a horse show dog, but I don't have any idea how to train her to be one.

I introduce the puppy to Mom and Mom is not very amused when it pees on the carpet. To be honest, neither am I. This puppy is a little much for Mom to handle, too. One night Skylar is taking a bath. She has a "baby bathtub" that she plays with and she gets very upset when Tess drinks the water out of it! Mommy, make her stop! She whines at me. Of course, I think it's hilarious, but I drag the puppy away and shut the bathroom door. We have an older cat, Moby, who is not amused by the puppy either. He likes to thump Tess on the nose but Tess is undeterred and keeps coming back for more! These little interactions do give me a smile and a laugh most days, but on the whole I'm quickly figuring out that the addition of a puppy wasn't a great idea. About nine months later we give Tess to an adult riding client of mine where she will get a lot of love, time and attention.

CHAPTER EIGHT

Feelings

March-April 2019

We've got to get Mom to sign a Power of Attorney while she still can. Dad has the form; we just need her signature. I tell Dad to bring the form and Mom to my house, and I'll get her to do it. When they're there, I tell Mom I need her to sign this form in case anything were to happen to her then I need to be able to take care of Dad and everyone. I know it doesn't make sense to her, but this is what I think will work. She looks at it suspiciously and looks at me but takes the pen and signs "Susan C Thoms" with a sigh. She forgets the "a" in Thomas but beggars can't be choosers and I know it'll hold up so I let that go. You can tell she's forgetting how to write. She has to think to hold the pen and then the words are slanting upwards and the letters are further apart than they used to be. But we've got a signature and that's all that matters.

One day I ask her if she remembers my old horse, Jaxon, that we bought when I was fourteen and whom I owned for twenty-five years. She has absolutely no memory of him. This puts another crack in my heart.

We make plans for Dad to go visit my brother in Austin for two nights. Skylar and I will stay with Mom. Dad can't decide if he'll really go… he's very worried about leaving Mom, even knowing that I'll be here with her the whole time. I tell him he really needs to go, have some fun with my brother. He doesn't think he can relax enough to enjoy it.

Dad makes Mom a turnover every morning. Sometimes she eats it, sometimes she just stares at it or pushes it around her plate. She eats junk all day though - like Cheez-its and fruit snacks. I ask if he thinks Mom wants to go out anywhere. He reports "she says she can just hang out here - she doesn't have anything to give you." Dad gets her a salad from Clark's BBQ and Mom says it's horrible (it's not). A few days ago she thought it was delicious. Mom starts feeling bad and stays in bed. Dad and I are worried. Mom can't tell us what is wrong.

She stays in bed all day. She is wearing her clothes, not pajamas. She's been wearing the same outfit for a week. I imagine that she doesn't brush her teeth anymore. Dad says he goes into her bathroom all the time and there's no toilet paper. But she won't let us help her. Or anyone.

Next day Mom is up - Dad is trying to get her to take pills and drink stuff. Dad says she is moaning and groaning to hell and back - took pills but won't eat anything. Not much liquid either. There a nurse coming to check on Mom. Dad tries Mom's favorite - Whataburger - but she won't eat that either. She drank some tea, a little beer and went back to bed. Nurse Renee said Alzheimer's affects her taste and appetite. Mom is not showering at all. I couldn't tell you the last time she bathed.

I am getting a lot of headaches. Probably stress related. Tension. Migraines. Who knows.

They moved to my town in December 2018. By February I was getting pretty desperate, but I could not convince her to take a shower. She would get very upset with me if I mentioned it and Dad sure as shit wasn't going to mention it, so it just went on and on. Dad's birthday is March 5th. That's the first time she was admitted to the hospital. Complaining of severe stomach pain, cramps, diarrhea, etc. for weeks before she finally let us do anything to help her.

*Now, Mom in the hospital is no picnic. At that time she was still angry, still refusing help, still refusing to believe anything was wrong. It is a very fine path to tread, let me assure you, when you are trying to help someone who does not want to be helped and at the same time is very angry about the situation she finds herself in. It's a Friday night when we go in. We wait **four hours** before we are even admitted to the back – to the ER itself. We get to listen to a man (woman?) with pink nail polish agonizing over his (her?) asthma attacks that he can't get under control, apparently. He seems fine to me but is clearly enjoying his audience. Having Mom wait for hours somewhere is intense. It's hell, basically. We had to shuffle to the bathroom fourteen times. I had to endure endless questions of what are we doing here and when are we leaving? Also, the grunts and moans and cussing of the clueless staff and tongue clicking and complete and utter bewilderment.*

Mom is admitted to the hospital. Dad and I take turns sitting with Mom in the room. She sleeps a lot. Probably best. Mom keeps asking where Dad is. I keep telling her he went home for the night. It's so weird, it's like one minute she knows and is fine and the next she doesn't.

The next day Mom is crying when Dad arrives - probably confused and didn't know where Dad was - but she is a lot better once he gets there. She is extremely dependent on him, and he knows it. She gets released that day. I don't remember what was wrong, possibly she was dehydrated.

In a further twist, I come down with bronchitis and have to be on steroids.

Who do you tell that you're feeling bad when you used to tell Mom everything? People think you should be fine, you should be ok, that everything is normal. But nothing is normal. Nothing is right. The emotions that eat you up stay inside because to let them out ... well how can you? Where would they go? Who would hear them? Feel them? Understand them?

You are the strong one, the one that just keeps going. You figure shit out and you keep working at it when things are bad because you have no other choice. What else are you supposed to do? Somebody has to be responsible, and that somebody is you.

*Yet you still feel that you are not doing enough, that you are **not enough**. That there's not enough of you to give anything to anyone. You try to hide your misery from your loved ones but at the same time you wish they could understand. You let it out a little at a time, testing the water, testing the reaction. They cannot give you what you need though, and it's not their fault. You don't even know what you need.*

Everything is spinning and yet standing perfectly still. You can't stop what's happening, but you can damn well try to ignore it. You want to help the one person who needs you the most right now, but you can't reach her. Anything you say is met with resentment and anger, but sometimes those confused blue eyes well up with tears and you would give anything to say just the right thing then. If you only knew what that was. If you only knew what to do.

I know nothing. I have known nothing for years. Ever since my baby girl was born, I am standing still in swirling water. I am the same, but you can't find me anymore. How long have I known that Mom was changing? That she was slipping away? Were we all in denial or did we really not see it? And it's not just Mom – it's my very self. I remember back when Tony and I first met and all I knew and did was horses. And I was mostly happy. Or am I fooling myself? I remember crying after horse shows because my students didn't do as well as I'd wanted, and I was so afraid of disappointing everyone. Of not being enough.

But I also remember precious moments when it was just Tony and I. Precious, precious moments where we could just be. Be together, just us. And that's when I was happiest. Hot and sweaty from working hard all day, drinking wine on the front porch. Listening to music and being happy to be together. Not owing anything to anyone but our two selves. No responsibilities other than the horses. Which can still be a lot, but they have a way of showing they're grateful. Those velvety noses and soft nickers, when they let you pat their foreheads and lean on their large shoulders. These creatures know you, and they love you. Their dark eyes and twitching ears are full of understanding and care. And Tony doesn't talk a lot. He's a man of few words and emotions. My rock and protector, his calm to my chaos works for us.

And looking back, it's easy to say life was easier before my baby girl came along. Of course it was. I was three weeks shy of thirty-nine when she was born and I was 100% thrown for a loop. I planned everything out up until the exact moment she entered this world. Then all my plans fell to pieces. But *she is my light and my joy. She is everything I didn't know I needed in my life. But I did not imagine Mom not being really present for the experience. I never thought I'd be doing it so alone. Mom can't handle her for more than two hours even with me there and while I know it's not her fault it is still terribly upsetting. I had visions of Skylar spending days and nights at Granny and Grandpa's. Baking cookies and going to the zoo and doing all sorts of fun things together. None of that is going to happen.*

Mom is still with us but NOT. She is not here. She is not here. With me. I am alone.

Mom takes a fall in her bedroom one evening and the next day she is moaning and groaning - Dad and I wonder how much of this is normal and how much is new? She is holding her side and saying it hurts. Dad heats up a pad to put on her side where it hurts but she puts it on her neck instead. Following directions or making connections (pain = heating pad) is a thing of the past. He gave her some Ben Gay to rub on the area that hurts but she rubbed it on her hands instead. He finally just does it for her. Dad says they're going through hell and if it's not better in the morning we might have to call an ambulance. I say that maybe she broke a rib when she fell. She gets up at 4 am with terrible pain. Dad gives her three ibuprofen and a heating pad so she'll go back to sleep. Skylar also is sick with a bad ear infection. Dad says the night before he had hell getting her to take pills - she kept spitting them out, she wouldn't drink any water and swallow.

The next day Dad notices that Mom sneezed about seven times and never said a word about any pain in her side. Got up and went to bed and never made a sound! It's all very strange.

Despite my bronchitis I manage to go to their house while they are out getting an ultrasound to clean since I can't clean while Mom is there. It upsets her or she wants to "help". She'll get mad if I try to clean while she's there.

On March 16th Dad says Mom is terrible. Raising hell about her stomach - side - brain - he went to Sam's because he had to get the hell outta there. She is very confused. Later that day she settles down and starts doing better. Ultrasound is negative so we still don't know what is causing Mom's side pain, which she is still intermittently complaining about. Dad says he wishes he could fix his own stomach - had tests up the wazoo - found nothing! He says, "I still think mine is attributed to Mom's condition - just don't think you can be married for fifty years and watch this go down with no stress or emotional hell." I tell Dad I really sympathize with him and I hope that Tony is never in his shoes.

Mom has a lot of stomach pain, I surmise maybe it's the red dye in the fruit snacks she eats nonstop. Somehow, I manage to get Mom in the bathtub. I can't believe I'm in this situation, of giving my own (extremely modest) Mom a bath. Seeing her naked is something that has never happened in my lifetime. She doesn't even notice.

In a moment of clarity after the bath while we are getting her dressed, she looks up and says "I'm never going to get better, am I?" My heart clenches. I just answered I don't know because I didn't know what else to say. Should I have lied? Told her of course this was just temporary, and she'd be fine in a few days? I remember this moment very clearly. Then she is worn out and lays down to rest.

Dad and I talk about if he can be happy again after Mom is gone. At least, I mention it and he lets me. I'm really worried about it. He says he'll try to be. He asks if I have found a place for Mom, which is something I've been researching in my 'spare' time. I say that I have been working on it but can't fathom it. I'll have to go visit the places. Dad says, "yes we're all trying to believe it ain't gonna happen."

Mom gets up and Dad asks her if she feels better and she says no and goes back to bed. He gives her some ibuprofen. Still complaining about her stomach. Dad says if we can give her something like Celebrex which Dad takes it may ease her mind that she is taking something. He says we are really grasping at straws out of desperation. I say we *are* desperate.

Dad has an appointment with the hip doctor to help with his mobility, but obviously he can't leave Mom alone that long, I promise to be there with her so he can go to that. A lot of my time is spent juggling what I need to do for each parent, plus my daughter and my husband - who is remarkable about the whole situation by the way. He is calm and patient and does whatever he can to help. Without him I would have lost my mind months ago.

I try to get Mom to go to Walmart with me, but she won't go. She won't eat for me, either. I call the neurologist Dr. Garza's office after convincing Mom to take an anxiety pill - though I don't tell her that's what it's for. She thinks it will help her stomach feel better (which it actually might). Dr. Garza says to stop the Donepezil immediately and see if symptoms resolve (doctor speak for see if she stops complaining). I try subway sandwiches but that doesn't work - she won't eat it.

That evening she wakes up crying at 8 pm after having gone to bed at 5:30 pm. Dad tries to reassure her and says he is there for her, but Mom insists he is not doing anything to help her. I can't imagine how this makes Dad feel. I have a constant ache in my gut over the whole situation. Dad swears a day caretaker won't work - Mom won't put up with it. He says we are not there yet, but we are rapidly approaching it. Mom finally goes back to bed. We know it's just going to get worse from here. Dad says he moved here hoping Mom would have six months to a year with Skylar. I said I was hoping for two years, and this is all moving much faster than they say is normal.

The next morning Mom woke up about 7:30 am raising hell and calling everybody six bags of MFers! She eats one bite of toast. I tell Dad you better give her an anxiety pill and antidepressant pronto!! Now Mom has always been one to use the F word, she flung it around quite freely in her day. So that is nothing new, but of course now there's no reason for it, just a by-product of her mood and whatever is happening in her brain.

She's going out to have a cigarette she tells him. No need for you to come with me. He watches and says nothing as she goes out with neither a cigarette nor lighter in hand. His

stomach clenches into further knots. What can he do? She's probably out there getting angry because he's not helping her, yet she clearly told him not to. She'll come inside in a minute, either pissed as hell or having completely forgotten why she went out there.

Dad doesn't eat. How can he when his stomach is tied into knots? He manages a couple of sweets and a boost-like drink each day, which is really all the nutrition he gets, bar a few beers at night. Those beers are probably what's keeping him alive. The anger and resentment he faces each day is enough to drive any man out on the street. But he doesn't go. He wouldn't. This is his wife of fifty years.

"

This is the disease that's killing them both.

"

For many, I'm sure that Alzheimer's is a different experience. For my parents it means silence, walking on eggshells, resentment, anger, helplessness, and heartbreak. Every day is heartbreak. He lives in fear and so does she. But they can't talk about it. She refuses to acknowledge that anything is wrong with her, she refuses to let anyone help. She can no longer wash her own clothes or get her own food or make her own tea. She'll say "I can do that" whenever you try to get her a drink or wash the dishes or sweep the floor. She'll say it, but she never does it. There's a hint of resentment behind her words, a hint of longing as well. She wishes she could still do it. That much is obvious.

If she had told us years ago that things were going south, getting harder, we could've done so much more to delay the process. But she is a strong and stubborn woman, and I don't think she believed it herself until it was too late. We are all independent to a fault. Anything you can do, I can do also. It's only in my later years I have come to realize how much I can and should depend on Dad for more than just fix-its – it's his job as a parent and he wants to be my parent. He also needs my help; I am co-parenting Mom with him.

*This is a nightmare from which we cannot wake. Ever. It will haunt us for the rest of our lives, especially Dad's. How do you come face to face with your own mortality in the eyes of the woman you have loved for fifty plus years? How do you come to terms with the anger that is lashing out at you, **you** because you are the closest thing to her. The one she has always been able to count on. I remember when she first heard Shania Twain's song "You're Still The One" and how it really resonated with her. Must have been twenty years ago. Back when I took my parents' relationship for granted. When I didn't know what marriage is really all about.*

I understand why she is angry. I would choose a million things for her over this. We are not a 'que sera sera' family. We are a 'we're going to fix this dammit' family. So she is angry. Because she can't. Because we can't. A disease that has progressed more rapidly than any one of us would have imagined. So fast we were caught unaware and unprepared. She doesn't want the world to know what she is going through. If only she would understand that there would be support and love, not recriminations and advice, as she fears. You cannot give advice if you have not lived this. I beg you, all of you, if you are not on the inside looking out please don't try to understand Alzheimer's and what it does to the victim and to the caretakers. It is a 100% impossible situation.

Mom, please let us help you. Mom, please let us reach you. We still need you too.

CHAPTER NINE

Hospital Woes

I tell Dad I can barely concentrate on all the other stuff going on in my life from all the worry about Mom. Dad says if we can't get her to eat something the next day then we will be in deep shit. She seemed to be doing better but then he got a call from James (next door neighbor in Tyler) and she went back to bed. He figured she got angry because he wasn't giving her his full attention. She got upset yesterday when he was talking to Ann (the realtor for the house in Tyler). She doesn't like it when he is doing something else. At 6:44 pm he says he got her up because she was hollering that nobody would do anything! Tried some tea - started crying and saying when are we going - wanted to go somewhere - nobody would help her, why aren't we going, etc. then finally went back to bed. I tell him we are going to have to take her to the hospital in the morning. There's nothing left for us to do. Dad says they're just going to give her fluids. I say no, we will tell them she's in pain and they need to figure out why. Dad repeats that she just wants to go back to house in Tyler. He says it just rips his guts out that he took her away from her home but what else was he gonna do!! Just a killer. I tell him I understand, but we all thought it was best. He says it was for the best for everyone except Mom. He couldn't take care of her by himself, and I couldn't run up to Tyler three hours away every other day. Things are just really screwed. It was 100% an impossible situation.

Dehydration can cause all these symptoms, which is something we didn't know at the time. Confusion and talking crazy - I witnessed it later with Dad occasionally and I knew then what was happening. This is something you only learn if you have to take your mom to the ER because you can't figure out what is wrong. Which is what we did. Of course, they admit her and give her fluids, as Dad knew they would. But when you can't get her to eat or drink anything, this outcome is inevitable.

As soon as I can, I relieve Dad so he can go home. Sometimes it's hard to remember he needs a lot of rest, too. He's not getting any younger and he's under a tremendous amount of stress. I try not to lose sight of his needs. I get a video of Mom on the "happy pills" which I send to my brother. I tell him she's doing fine but talking nonsense. She was fixated on the table, which we had to move away from the window. She also can't figure out why it says "call me Susan" on the bulletin board. At 9:15 pm they give her morphine and a sleeping pill so I leave and go home to sleep.

My brother decides to come to see Mom and Dad. Dad is at the hospital complaining that he hasn't had a smoke in four hours because he didn't want to miss the doctor. The kidney doctor shows up and says Mom had very low kidney function yesterday, but it is better now after all the fluids. Mom finally starts doing better and I ask Dad if he thinks he will be able to handle her at home and he is not sure. He says we probably need a portable potty, walker, depends, wipes and stuff. I say it sounds like a super-duper good time. We are all just trying to keep a sense of humor here. It ends up, though, that right now Mom needs a rehab center. She is very weak. I think that's for the best and it will take some of the pressure off Dad, although he'll feel like he has to sit with her every day, all day. At least maybe he can relax and get some rest at night, at home alone.

Poor Skylar starts crying when I say I have to leave again. I have been gone too much. Dad and I start looking into rehab places. My friend Kathy is going to go with me to help me look at places. It's easier with a friend who will remember all the questions you need the answers to when you are overwhelmed with emotions and exhausted.

Mom has been diagnosed with emphysema - COPD - in the past. She used to do breathing treatments every day and each evening before bed. I tell Dad the wheezing is making her agitated and they're going to do a breathing treatment. Dad says she hasn't done a breathing treatment in months. This is something she used to do daily, on her own. She has forgotten of course.

In the hospital Mom is sleeping, they have started her on oxygen. One thing is that her blood pressure is too high. A C-Dif bacterial infection has been ruled out so the staff don't have to wear gowns and masks when they enter her room anymore. The hospital tells us Mom will stay there until she is discharged to a rehab facility. Dad and I choose a rehab in Denton for Mom, it has a private room available, and she could be moved the same day.

The next day Dad tells me Mom is doing much better, practically going to the bathroom by herself with the walker. But she still won't eat anything. But then she goes downhill a little. Dad says Mom seems pretty weak but at least there was no agitation or Haldol last night. They are still working on which rehab she will go to because of some problem with her being on Haldol - the rehab place says they can't administer that medicine. I say we can change the medicine, no problem. The doctor affirms we can change the medicine, too.

Later I ask Dad what is happening, and he says Nope - zero - nada - zilch - nothing - not shit. Ha ha.

I arrive later in the evening. Mom won't eat her dinner. Apparently, she only ate half the cheese stuff and cookies at lunch. She is drinking, though, so that's good. She's very tired. Skylar is with me and driving me crazy. It is impossible to entertain a four-year-old in a hospital room for very long.

In the morning Dad is there with Mom but he's very aggravated. He's mad at the "piss poor staff" - the nurse gave her pills and didn't give her any water - of course she choked and threw them up. Then the nurse left and never gave her the rest of the pills or replaced the ones she threw up! Dad says the dimwit aid helps her to the bathroom and then leaves with her still in there! He tells the nurse if they're not outta here in an hour he's gonna hit her. Dad is clearly very tired.

Finally, she is admitted to the rehab center. The next morning Mom eats all of her eggs but again choked on her pills because they didn't crush them up for her. The nurse said she had a good night. She is calm. Dad is planning to stay with her most of the day. I say I will be there after school with Skylar and can stay for an hour before I have to leave again because I have lessons that evening as per usual. Dad asks if I can come back again after lessons, but I know I can't - Skylar needs an early night.

At the rehab she's finally getting better. She's in good spirits and walking pretty good. Later that afternoon Dad texts me that Mom is fixated that there's something obscene going on outside the window and will not let it go. I tell him to close the blinds. I tell Dad we have to hire a day caregiver for Mom. He finally relents and says we can give it a try. I find someone through the home health agency - a referral - and arrange to meet the first person I call. She'll come to the rehab center to have a brief interview. Her name is Angie and when I meet her she seems perfect. She has been doing this job for years and knows how to take care of the elderly. I explain about the Alzheimer's and how Dad just can't cope. She is understanding and seems to be patient and kind. I tell her she's hired and can she start when Mom gets out of the rehab place? She says of course. I tell Dad all about her and he seems interested and hopeful.

When I try to take Mom to the dining room to eat dinner we end up sitting for thirty minutes with no food. Mom is annoyed and I realize it was a mistake to try this. She gets very agitated and we have to go back to her room. On Saturday I plan to be there about 4 pm to relieve Dad so he can go home. When I get there I tell Dad her legs look swollen again. Skylar starts bouncing off the walls about an hour later so I have to leave. Mom was getting aggravated or flustered or whatever. I told her three times to eat her dinner but she could not comprehend what I was saying. She didn't touch it.

Sunday I have a horse show but Dad asks if I'm going to be able to make it today. I feel terribly guilty that I have to go to the show and leave Dad there all day. He tells me that Mom keeps talking about me coming. She is very antsy about leaving - she will not sit down; all her clothes are out of the drawers (she is not getting released yet but she is definitely ready to go!) I am done with the horse show about 4:30 pm and I am incredibly tired - I don't want to have to go see Mom. We always have to get up for the horse shows around 5 am and it's an incredibly long day every time. Dad says he thinks she'll be ok until tomorrow.

I am worried that Dad is mad at me because I haven't been able to be there at night to make sure Mom eats. He sits with her from 8 am to 4:30 pm so I know he's stressed and exhausted. Dad says, "you have an awful lot of responsibility and are very busy, you're doing the best you can and I'm glad for it." I tell him I am really trying hard to do everything for everyone. Skylar makes it hard when she is hanging on me every second and I am trying to work.

Mom is hyper and talking crazy. Her legs are really swollen again. Dad grills Gina, the nurse, who swears Mom's not taking anything to cause the leg swelling but she noticed it this morning. He made it very clear that it had occurred since they got there. I agree, I first saw it Saturday night.

Mom wants Dad to tell me that "we were there - we knew it was there". Of course it's just gibberish.

It's finally April. It feels like March lasted about a thousand weeks. I go to be with Mom early so Dad can sleep in. Mom is perfectly fine, sitting in her chair looking at magazines. She can see I'm anxious though I try not to show it - I have so much I need to do! She's telling me to leave, she knows Dad will be there at some point. There is a recliner in her room, but she would rather sit in the wheelchair for some reason. I tell Dad we need to get her a recliner to have at home. She had said earlier that would be great - to have one at home. But that was earlier. Now she wants nothing to do with it. The food here is pretty nasty so Mom is eating a lot of Cheez-it's. I tell Dad maybe tomorrow he could bring her a burger and fries.

Mom is calm and wants to go home. I've been cleaning the hell out of their house, a little at a time, while Mom is gone because I can't do it while she's there or she gets upset. Dad tells me the therapist says Mom can leave tomorrow. We make a plan for Dad to meet Angie and show her around the house.

But Mom doesn't get to come home because they are finally concerned about why she is retaining fluid. Dad and I are both completely pissed off. Dad says she might be here another week and I tell him the twenty days is up April 15th - this is all medicare will pay for. You have to have stayed in the hospital three nights to even get the twenty days in rehab. Dad goes home and I stay with Mom. I tell her she doesn't get to leave tomorrow after all, and she takes it okay, but I know she won't remember the conversation anyway. I tell Dad that on Friday I'm going to pick Mom up and take her and Skylar to the park and then I'll bring her back. Dad says that's a good plan, it'll do her good to get out. I try to wait until they serve her dinner, but at 5:40 pm they still haven't and I have to leave. Dad remarks 'sorry shitheads.'

It soon becomes imperative that I find someone to weed flower beds at their house. I just can't do it due to arthritis in my hands. There is a teenage boy that lives down the street that might be interested in helping out with the flower beds. Angie is going to start Tuesday if Mom comes home on Monday. I finally finished cleaning the house so it is all ready for her to be released. There's always so much to do and take care of.

On Friday I take Mom and Skylar to the park. Skylar is happy to have french fries and run around the play area. It does her good to let off some steam. Mom really enjoys the Whataburger and fries we get and is happy to go to the park although it makes her pretty tired. Later that evening Dad tells me that they gave her a shower this morning, but it wasn't easy. Gina the nurse said she cussed them out and would *not* take off her underwear! Mom has always been extremely modest, and I can just imagine the hell she gave them for *wanting* to see her naked! I would laugh about it if I weren't so tired. Hey, at least she bathed, under duress.

They are weighing Mom every day and if it goes down that's good - it means she is not retaining fluid but if it goes up that is not good. I say surely they can't be pinning everything on that? How about some blood work or something?!

The next time I am with Mom, it smells like *shit* in her room. Upon inspection I find poop on the sheets and comforter. I am appalled. She has been sleeping in this?! What the hell are these people doing?! I make them change the sheets and I open the window to air the room out. I ask for a can of air freshener and the aide says they don't have any. How does a rehab/ nursing center not have air freshener for Pete's sake? Mom stinks as well and won't take a shower. I tell Dad to pull Gina aside tomorrow and ask her to make Mom take a shower because she smells so bad, like something might be infected.

The nurse that day does not win the friendly award by a long shot. I finally convince someone to make Mom shower, so they end up doing it about six in the evening. Which is fine. She's clean and the bed is clean. Because I was there insisting it get done. Otherwise, she would have slept in literal poop, in the bed and on herself. What a nightmare.

On April 8th Mom finally gets discharged. We all breathe a huge sigh of relief and try to imagine how to handle Mom at home. I think Angie will help a lot with the stuff Dad and I just can't handle. Like showering. Of course, Dad has his own issues with showering.

On Angie's first day she cooks bacon and eggs and takes Mom for a walk. Mom is happy to have the full attention of someone. That evening Dad says Mom ate all of her hamburger, but she went to bed at 5:30 pm.

Mom is happy to be home. She is loving sitting on the back porch while Skylar plays. We take some cute pictures of them together. She is calm and it's a nice change from the rehab center. The weather is beautiful, and Dad sits and smokes, happy that we're all there with him.

She has become fixated on Angie - we can't figure out if this is a good or bad thing. When Angie is there she seems happy, then as soon as she leaves she starts moaning and groaning to the point where Dad can't even eat his dinner. She has also woken up in the night a few times, talking loudly, then goes back to sleep. She sleeps longer and longer. Waking up at 9:45 am is typical, she used to be an early bird! She never stayed up late, maybe 9 or 10 pm, but now she goes to bed at 5:45 pm or 6:15 pm.

It's almost time for Easter. I pick Mom up and we go to Walmart to look for Easter basket supplies. We have a pretty good time. Easter is, barring Christmas, Skylar's favorite holiday. She loves hunting eggs. Especially at Granny and Grandpa's house. Grandpa hides all the eggs before we get there. Which of course means that Mama has to fill all the eggs and get them over to Grandpa the day before. All in all, it turns out to be a pleasant day, full of sunshine and laughter. Mom sits on the porch the whole time and smiles - we have the puppy with us and Mom can't take her eyes off her. Although she really doesn't want her to get too close. Skylar is happy with her haul of eggs and toys.

Dad is super stressed over the money. Angie isn't cheap, but definitely necessary. The stove needs to be fixed and he needs an electrician. He worries about having enough money to take care of Mom when she has to go to a care facility. Those places can run up to $6000 a month! To me that is insane, but that is the reality. Dad tells me that Mom wouldn't eat her dinner but came out onto the porch eating candy - he says she has no idea what she is doing, I say her taste buds have changed due to the Alzheimer's and she's craving sugar now.

I start at a Crossfit gym. I've got to do something about this weight gain and stress I'm under. I'm trying to take care of myself but it's hard, there is too much to do and too little time. It turns out that I really love Crossfit! But there's so many things my body won't let me do, like box jumps and jump roping. Burpees are impossible and anything that involves my neck is out. I have a lot of old injuries from riding and at least one fusion in my neck. But I do my best, and I have some fun with it. The trainer there is really nice, and I think I have a girl crush on her. Something keeps me coming back, and it sure isn't the weight loss, which is next to nothing! Hugely disappointing in that regard. At least I am finally doing something just for myself, even if it does take up even more time in the day.

One evening Mom is carrying on so horrifically - at 8:52 pm - that Dad calls me for back up support. He can't get her to go to bed, or do a breathing treatment, or go to the doctor. I ask what is actually the matter - she is having severe stomach pains (might be gas?) I go over and manage to get her calm enough to do a breathing treatment and go to sleep. Dad and I decide we'd better try and keep track of whether and when she poops. This is something you never imagine having to do for your own parent! It's just an awful scenario. She moans and groans a lot the next morning (I think she does this because she is angry - the mood swings with Alzheimer's are intense) but by evening she is fine. Drinks two beers and goes to bed at 7:45 pm with no issues.

At home, Skylar is crying because I won't let her mess with the dog while she eats, and please don't ride the tricycle next to where she's eating, in fact please get off the tricycle and sit at the table to eat. She is tired and overwhelmed. I hear her say loudly in her room "I just don't know why nobody will let me do anything!" Poor child, she is so mistreated. Ha!

When I tell Dad I'm so sore from Crossfit that I'm pretty sure I'm dying, he says "address for flowers?" I say "for my funeral?" and he says "yes." I roll my eyes at him over text and finally go to bed.

It's nearing the end of April now and Mom is more and more often confused. She is confused about everything! Where she is, her pills, her breathing machine. She also will say "there's a cat in here" when thirty minutes earlier she was petting and talking to the cat that she's owned for fourteen years. Dad says it goes on and on. It's totally heartbreaking.

On the last day of April there is a tornado warning. I tell Dad to put pillows in the pantry and get himself and Mom in there. He doesn't do it, though. Maybe he figures a tornado is nothing compared to the hell he's already going through. Luckily no tornado hits our little town and we are all safe.

CHAPTER TEN

The Status Quo

Summer 2019

At the beginning of May I have a horse show that is overnight. I take Skylar with me, and she is nervous because she's never slept in a hotel before. So she doesn't sleep much, and Dad is nervous because he feels like he doesn't have any back up while I'm gone. I tell him he can always call Tony.

The status quo appears to be Mom very confused on a daily basis, moaning and groaning and having some coughing problems at night. The doctor wants to increase one of her medications to help with the moaning and groaning. And it does. Dad and I are both relieved. She's now also on Spiriva and a double dose of Celex so the coughing is also much better.

One night Mom tries to go to bed in the room that is considered "mine" in their house, and another night she tries to go to bed in Skylar's room. She can't even keep track of where her own bedroom is. And when she goes to bed, she'll sit on the edge of the bed like she doesn't know what to do. I'll help her get in, pajamas are long a thing of the past, and she'll basically perch herself on the edge of the bed - like she can't pull herself more to the center. This is nothing new, it has been like this since before they moved to Pilot Point. But it worries me that she's going to fall out of the bed while she's sleeping.

Dad says she just isn't making any sense, not one word she says makes any sense. She will get angry, also, because she wants another cup of beer or soda, even though there is one sitting half full right in front of her. You basically have to put the cup in her hand to get her to drink it. She will be upset with Dad because he won't "take her... or get her." Nothing makes sense.

There is an appointment coming up with the brain doctor but I have to go to Ali's (my stepdaughter's) high school graduation and so I ask Dad if he can take her. He is extremely stressed out over this. I don't remember if he actually took her to the appointment or not. It's highly doubtful they made it there.

One day Dad tells me he "broke starch." I'm like what on earth does that mean? It means he took a shower and put on fresh jeans! I am very happy. I know he doesn't like to get in the shower because he gets so cold, but there is a space heater in the bathroom. He is so thin. There is only bone and strips of tendon and ligaments. Almost no muscle anymore. I think Angie must have convinced him that he was getting a bit rank. I'm sure she got the bathroom and shower all heated up before he went in there. I am relieved. One more problem solved.

We planned a graduation party for Ali, and I am worried what Mom will think and how she will be. Will she be able to handle it? We take an adorable photo shoot with Skylar and Ali - one graduating from high school, the other from preschool. Mom and Dad both come to Skylar's preschool graduation. Dad wears his best white tennis shoes and red long sleeved button-down. We manage to get Mom's hair done and dressed in appropriate clothes. I am pretty sure she's even wearing a bra! Two major events and they both go well.

Skylar's birthday is coming up soon. We are planning a backyard party at my house with her friends and all of us. My brother and his kids are coming for the party. I tell Dad I need the books "The Spirited Child" and "The Explosive Child." I am losing my mind trying to deal with Skylar's tantrums and fits. Dad says to buy them and tells me Mom is in bad shape (which of course I know but maybe it makes him feel better to say it out loud) - talks completely out of her head continuously - couldn't go to sleep with all these people here (there are no people). Asked fifty times when my nephew is coming - totally fixated on him coming. He says "I guaran-damn-T you if it weren't Skylar's birthday I'd tell your brother not to come!" My autistic nephew, David William, whom we call Ghostman, is seven and you have to keep an eye on him every single second. It's difficult to deal with but my brother does an amazing job with him. Skylar is difficult, but she's not autistic or learning disabled. It's just a matter of boundaries and getting enough sleep for her.

The party goes as well as can be expected. Skylar is thrilled with the attention and all the gifts. During the party Mom sits off to one side holding a pack of cigarettes. She doesn't engage at all and doesn't even notice when we bring the cake out. It makes me sad, but I have to concentrate on Skylar, so Mom doesn't get a whole lot of attention. She seems ok and not stressed out. She keeps pushing her hair back and smoothing it down. A repetitive motion. I wonder what she is thinking.

When we are at their house, Mom is content to sit on the porch and watch the kids play. I wonder if at this stage she is still consciously trying to hold herself together while there are people around or if she's beyond that. It's hard to tell. I think she still has some recognition that she is not as she should be or would want to be. It must be so frustrating, I can't even imagine her world from her point of view.

Occasionally I try to call Mom on her phone, to see if she can still answer it. Lately the answer has been no. But there is a day that I call and she actually answers. It's nice to hear her voice on the other end of the phone, like all is normal and there is nothing at all wrong. I still have a voicemail from her that I've saved on my phone. It's probably from a year or two ago, back when they were still living in Tyler and she still called me.

Mom will put four shirts on and pants but forget her panties. Dad tries to convince her to take a few shirts off. Sometimes successful, sometimes not.

I find lighters in random places. I always pick them up and take them with me or put them somewhere only Dad will know. I figure lighters are a dangerous thing to have laying around right now. She still knows how to use them!

She doesn't talk about the past. She doesn't talk about anything. You can't help but wonder what she thinks about. Her eyes are not blank; she's very much in the present. She knows us even if sometimes she says the wrong names. She

watches TV but does she process it? She surely doesn't remember what she's watched. I told her today about a book I'm reading called *The Tea Girl of Hummingbird Lane*. She and I used to read those types of books all the time. I do everything I can to have conversations with her. They're so one sided it's painful.

Everything is painful. To me and to her as well I suspect. Because I remember, and because she doesn't. She gets overwhelmed so easily, and Skylar is now at the point where she is realizing that there is something not quite right with Granny Susan. They both get frustrated when Mom can't do what Skylar wants her to do, or when she doesn't remember what Skylar just told her. Today Granny Susan kept getting up because she wanted to come see what I was doing. Skylar would pout and make her sit back down. Then she started walking back and forth in front of Mom – essentially acting as a sentry. I looked over and said what are you doing? She said, 'I'm guarding Granny Susan. So she can't get up and leave.' We all laughed but it was only funny on the surface. At least Skylar still absolutely loves her Granny Susan, if only for the undivided attention she usually gives her.

"

I just don't feel like a person.

"

Mom still gets sad; she still has emotions. Today there were tears in her eyes and I asked her what's wrong. Nothing she said, I'm fine. That's our standard response of course. But I pressed her and she admitted "I just don't feel like a person." The fact that she actually articulated what she was *feeling and thinking is astounding. I told her we love her and of course she's a person. But I knew exactly what she meant.*

We went out on the back porch, and I just sat with her. I took her hand, and she rubbed my fingers. Her skin is so soft. Mom has never been a person who enjoys touching, or hugging, or anything. We express ourselves with words. How important is it for me to try to physically touch her now? I want her to physically feel my love for her, but I also don't want to force her to do something that's uncomfortable when my intention is to comfort. She held my hand for a few minutes, and I pretended not to notice when she let go.

*Twice a week I make her dinner. She usually eats about five bites of whatever it is. She won't touch meat anymore – a new trend that started maybe a month ago. I give her corn on the cob and some potatoes. She looks at the potatoes but won't touch them. She picks up her fork and stabs it at the corn. For a minute or so she tries to figure out how to eat it. I hold up my corn and say gently "like this Mom." She is both grateful and annoyed, or so I think. It's very hard to read her now. She snacks all day but won't eat her dinner. Like Skylar. But Skylar is on the upswing of life and Mom is on the downswing. When she was in the hospital in March the doctor told me that when Alzheimer's patients forget how to eat – how to swallow – that's pretty much the end unless you put a feeding tube in. But Mom doesn't seem to be following the typical Alzheimer's curve. She **knows** us. She remembers people, she doesn't remember the past. I constantly ponder the question – how will this end? Because if she still knows who we all are there is no way I'm putting her in a nursing home. I just can't do that to her. She and I are so much alike – I can't imagine being in a nursing home myself so I sure as shit can't do that to her. What's going to happen from here? Always the million dollar question.*

As we leave tonight I give her a hug and make Skylar say goodbye. Mom smiles and says 'I love you too.' I still have that. I still have her loving me too.

I am struggling with Skylar. I am sure she can sense my stress and exhaustion, my fear and my anger, though I try to keep it mostly hidden. She screams at me and has unbelievable meltdowns. I can't vent to Mom any longer, so I try to vent to Dad but it's just not the same.

Mom starts giving Dad shit over a table she wanted to sell and now doesn't. I tell Dad Mom won't remember that table fifteen minutes after it leaves her sight. It'll be ok. Then he tells me Mom couldn't figure out how to open the paper on her Whataburger. I am continuously dismayed at how fast the decline is.

Then the shit hits the fan, almost literally. Mom has forgotten how to operate a toilet, how to wipe herself, and apparently can't tell when she needs to go to the bathroom.

In Dad's words: "Mom shit ALL OVER the toilet - floor - peed on floor by the door - shit on bed! Wonderful start for day!" I say that it might be time to start using Depends. Dad agrees immediately. I asked what Mom said about it. Dad says "I was in the garage - Mom said she shit everywhere - I ask if she cleaned it up or needed help - said she got most of it! Hadn't touched it." Dad cleaned most of it up but then Angie did the rest.

By 4 pm that day Mom is wanting to go to bed. That night, the same problem occurs. She has pooped all over the sheets and blankets. Dad has finally got some

Depends on her. I say it should help, but what if she just takes them off? At least maybe it will contain some of the mess. We also put a pad on the bed, but she still manages, somehow, to poop all over everything. This is horrific and we don't know what to do. The worst part is that Mom will say "I didn't do it, I don't know who made that mess!" And you have to get her in the shower to clean her up. I never wanted to see Mom naked but it's becoming a regular occurrence. Convincing her to get in the shower to clean up makes me want to bang my head against the wall.

Dad is trying to pay bills. He texts me "I can't even pay the damn bills without Mom wanting something! Shit!" I tell him it's the same with Skylar around. Dad takes Mom to Walmart and tells me - "Took Mom to Walmart as she was killing me to go somewhere. She was taking stuff off conveyer belt to put in basket before cashier rang it up! Good times!" Dad isn't good at this stuff. He has trouble being patient and I think Mom feels that.

I have to go out of town for a horse show and Skylar goes with me. When I check in, Dad tells me that Mom has once again pooped all over everything - even the wall around the toilet. I just can't imagine what is happening in that toilet room (separate area to bathroom) and I feel terribly bad for Dad having to deal with that constantly. Dad says the road is getting darker and darker. While at the horse show, Skylar gets a terrible ear infection so we can't come over for a while.

While I'm gone Dad gets up on the ladder to put up a new bird feeder. He asks Mom (who is watching) to hand him the new one which is on the BBQ pit by his foot. She cannot understand what to do. The simplest of tasks - it's a one man show he says. I tell Dad I understand. She asks to help when I cook but she literally can't do anything. She will attempt to crack an egg, and I will help her. Then she holds the eggshells in her hand and doesn't remember where the trash can is. She finally opens a cabinet door and almost succeeds in putting the eggshell in there before I intercede. She has taken to eating candy all day. But won't touch regular food. Another trip to Walmart - he says she took two packs of cigs, a paper towel and a magnifying glass with her.

Dad sends me a picture of Mom's burger on the table in the garage, without the plate. He had been wondering where it went. Mom is barely eating anything. Then Mom starts talking about Skylar "getting up on that thing." We can't figure out what she means. Dad cooks Mom a baked potato, but she only takes one bite. He is frustrated. She'll say she wants something and that it looks good but then she won't touch it.

I'm trying to convince Dad to try a muscle relaxer to help him sleep. I don't think he ever does try it even though I give him one of mine. He tells me that Mom went to bed at 3:30 pm! He had to get her up to eat dinner. She went back to bed at 5:30 pm then up again at 7 pm. She thinks it is morning because it is still light outside. This is getting bad. Really bad. I tell Dad I wish we had someone telling us what to do/what to expect. This flying blind is just awful.

There are some days when Dad is very quiet and doesn't text much. He says "just trying to get by day to day." I worry about him. We usually go over to Dad's on Sundays for dinner which I make. Dad loves these days. I feel terribly guilty if there's a show or something and I can't come on a Sunday. He plans for it all week long. One night in particular we had to leave early, straight after dinner, because Skylar was having a meltdown and he was so disappointed even though he understood. On August 19th I text Dad that I'm free!!! (Skylar started school, ha ha). I tell him I'm going to Target. Dad says "how did the drop off go? Lots of screaming, kicking, crying, moaning, leg hugging, trauma, Armageddon?" I said 'Nope! She soaked it all in, looked worried but didn't cry. Started playing with play-doh and I hot footed it out of there.'

We can't find Margaret the cat. Dad says he has looked everywhere. He looked up in the loft for her, but she wasn't there. Then he looked under every couch, bed, cabinet and closet! Mom is going to take this very hard. (Well, until she forgets about the cat which might not take too long). Last time they saw her was before Angie left for the day. I say I'm coming over. But then Dad texts and says apparently the damn cat was in Mom's room the whole time! Ha! Ha!

"

Our shared sense of humor remains intact for the most part. What else can you do?

"

Dad and I joke about making sure he hasn't kicked it yet when he doesn't answer his phone right away. I ask how's the cat? Still alive? Dad says "bbqing it for supper." Which really makes me laugh.

Dad typically goes about 4-4:30 pm to get dinner for himself and Mom. Whataburger is a favorite. Sometimes Chick-fil-a. One evening he got back with the food about 4:45 pm and Mom was already in bed. Dad had to get her up to eat. But at least she ate the entire thing - we've been having a lot of trouble getting her to eat anything of substance lately. But a few nights before Dad had gotten steak fingers and she wouldn't touch them. He says it's a crap shoot whether she'll eat or not. When she is outside with Dad on the porch she sets her Coke can down and says "I'm going downstairs for the good stuff" and walks back inside. Of course, there is not a downstairs in their house, nor in the one they lived in for twenty-four years. I wonder what the "good stuff" is in her mind. Wish I had some.

One morning I step outside and find a huge snake outside our front door! I tell Dad he has to come save us! He tells me to whack it with a shovel or a hoe. That's a **hard no**. I have to get a friend's husband to come move it. When it comes to snakes I am petrified. Dad tells me I'm a wuss! I tell him I was going to *shoot* it, but I was not going to *move* it while it's still alive. He says blowing its head off is a good idea. Apparently, it was only a rat snake. It was relocated and as far as I know is still living today. But not in my front doorway.

The final weekend of August brings some family birthdays. Mom is very confused about the fact that the "kids" are coming - my brother and his kids. She gets upset with Dad and even though he has told her fifteen times that they are coming the next day she says "you should have told me that!" as she gets into bed. Dad is annoyed but I gently remind him she just can't retain anything you tell her.

I am in charge of the birthday cakes. I get one for each of the two birthday kids, so that they will have their own cakes. My brother and I go into the garage to light the candles so we can all sing Happy Birthday. I have one cake and he has the other. I see him behind me as we walk into the house making a face and wobbling. I turn slightly and both our cakes drop to the ground. We look at each other silently, pick the cakes up and continue into the house laughing hysterically. We sing Happy Birthday. Mom has no idea what's happening. (The cakes are still edible - what a win!) We never tell a soul what really happened to the cakes that day, but we still laugh about it sometimes.

The thing I hate the very most is the way she carries unlit cigarettes around. She carries them everywhere. Like she knows they're part of who she was, but she doesn't know why anymore. I find them in all sorts of places – the bathroom windowsill, the floor of Skylar's room, her bedside table. She'll bring some along if you take her in the car anywhere. I always try to get her to leave them in the car instead of bringing them inside wherever it is we are heading. I am not entirely sure why I hate it so much. Maybe because it's a constant reminder that she isn't who she used to be. If she goes out on the porch and Dad lights one up for her, she'll take a few puffs but then she forgets it is in her hand. The ashes just fall to the floor as it burns up. Dad has to keep a close eye out because more than once she has taken a lit cigarette into the house and left it somewhere. She has

absolutely no idea what she's doing. I wholeheartedly wish that Dad would stop buying them, stop lighting them, and honestly, stop smoking himself. I think, though, that Dad feels this is still a connection to the past. Something he can still do for her. Like getting her a beer in the evening. That she'll forget she has and won't drink.

She picked up a pack the other day and looked at it strangely and then held it to her ear. What's going on here? I hear her say. She is totally confused by it. Many times I have found all the cigarettes out of the box and different little things stuffed inside. Usually trash but not always.

In my heart I feel so devastated for her. The reality that she's never going to get any better just eats you up. But where are the books and the people and the pamphlets and websites that tell you how it really is? What comes next? What should we be expecting? If the resources are out there, I haven't found them yet. Does Mom actually think about things? Does she have coherent thoughts? Does she understand anymore what is happening to her? I sure would like to know. It's still the elephant in the room. You still cannot face it head-on with her, even as her condition gets more desperate.

She wants to help me when I do the dishes or make dinner or clean the kitchen. I want her to help me, too. But she simply can't. She looks at me and says plaintively "can I help you?" or "I can do that – don't worry about that." She can't though. She just can't. Does she even know that she's asking to help do things she can no longer do? I have no idea what to say. I usually go with, no I've got it Mom, don't worry. But I know that isn't the point. I'm doing what she should be doing. I'm in her house doing her things. Not as a special treat but because she can't. And it kills me every time.

Sometimes she'll wander to the back of the house and after a few minutes she'll come back. I think she gets a little lost in her own house. What kind of internal struggle is going on in her head? Is there a struggle at all? If I knew these answers maybe I could find some peace. For a woman who used to think as much as I do, I can't imagine the inability to think. Is it peaceful, or is it distressing? Did it start as one and end up as the other? What is her daily reality? All these things haunt me.

I want to help you Mom. I want to help and I can't. We are on either side of a brick wall we can't reach through. The brick wall of Alzheimer's. Someday maybe someone will find a way to break it down. But it won't be in time for Mom. It won't be in time.

CHAPTER ELEVEN

Near Death Experience

Autumn 2019

The beginning of September is Grandparent's Day at Skylar's school. Dad puts on his best shirt and shaves the scraggly beard. I think Mom is even wearing a bra, but I can't say for sure. At the very least she looks good, only wearing one shirt and isn't carrying anything strange around. Dad looks dapper in his mustache, sporting his best Sam Elliott look and Mom is grinning ear to ear; it is a terrific day for Skylar who is so happy to have them there. I take some silly pictures of them all wearing the Grandparent's Day crown that Skylar colored and gave herself green hair for some reason. I notice that even though Mom is doing well, it is still extremely stressful for me to deal with it all. Crossing my fingers that it goes well, and at least it does!

Dad is due to have surgery September 16th for his leg pain. It's a vascular surgery, aimed at helping the blood flow to his left lower leg. He has already put it off once due to Mom's condition, but now he doesn't want to wait anymore. I am worried about the surgery for multiple reasons - how will it go? How will I cope? I'm hoping Angie will agree to come and stay later in the day to help with Mom. Angie says yes, she can do that.

Mom thinks Dad already had the operation and is constantly wondering how she can help him. When we all know she can't do anything. She really wishes she could, she knows she's supposed to be the one taking care of him. Mom starts talking crazy-talk - "I don't know if they're going to do it or not - they keep going in and out." We have no idea what she's on about. Dad says Mom's favorite statements are "I'm gonna need more stuff. I need to go get..." followed closely by "I wanna go... when are they coming?" She is driving him crazy by getting a hot soda every five minutes (and not drinking it) and also by obsessing over the pool and pool toys (which need to be put away). I tell Dad he needs to relax and enjoy his time in the hospital - which I know he won't - because it'll be like a mini vacation. But he'll be stressed and worried about Mom, upset about not smoking or drinking anything strong, and in a lot of pain. Well, hopefully less pain than when he went in.

On September 12th Dad spent three hours at the hospital for surgery pre-op. Mom has a cough/ congestion and it's getting worse. Dad is worried she'll be sick while he's in the hospital. Dad says you could take her to the ER and put her in the hospital for the weekend (he's kidding). And I say at least y'all would be in the same place then! He says I don't think your stress level goes that high and I say I'd end up there too.

I end up having to take Mom to the ER for what we think is pneumonia. Turns out no pneumonia, going home with steroids and breathing treatments. Lots of coughing. Dad and I talk about my brother coming to visit, possibly for Dad's surgery. Tony will take Dad to the hospital if David can't come. Dad is feeling very stressed. He says "I try to do one very critical thing for myself and it's so damn hard!"

Today was the third time Mom ended up in the ER due to a possible urinary tract infection. Thankfully this time they did not admit her. We have been successful in keeping her as hydrated as possible I guess, but the problem of her properly taking care of cleaning "down under" remains. For a period of at least six months Mom refused to shower. Or bathe. She would tell me she had done it and possibly she actually believed she had. But she had not.

*I was astounded today at how little preparation the hospital ER staff have for a patient with Alzheimer's. Because of Mom's unique situation where you LITERALLY CANNOT speak in front of her, I take to writing notes and cornering nurses in hallways. Everyone I meet has no idea of the fact that she has Alzheimer's or is not willing to admit they should know that already. They want her to sign things. Mom cannot sign things. They want her to understand procedures and tests and labs and x-rays. Way beyond her scope. They need to do a urine culture so they need to do a "quick in and out" catheter. From my stance in the hallway I can hear her crying out, terribly upset, why are you doing this? And the nurse saying you need to relax honey. Three times they tell her. I am dying in the hallway. **She Can't Relax!** She has no idea why you are molesting her! Because surely that's what it must feel like to her. The nurse comes out saying "We got it done. She didn't want any help." Basically rolling her eyes in annoyance. When I go back in* silent tears stream down her face and she says "we're not going back to Texas are we? I don't ever want to go there again. Never again." As she cries, I regret in that moment anything I ever did to worry or upset her. I wish I could take back my teenage bitchiness and my twenty-year old "I know more than you" ness. I bite the inside of my cheek, hard. She holds my hand tight, tighter than ever before and rubs my fingers. Finally the injury passes. I console myself with the fact that in a little while she won't remember what just happened.

Later she tells me "I just want to get up and do the things I want to do. I used to do whatever I felt like doing." She continues to try and get up the entire time we are there. I corner another nurse – she has dementia, Alzheimer's. She is going to be agitated and try to get up continuously. If you don't want her to do that you will need to give her something to help her relax. "I'll tell her nurse" she solemnly promises. I am aware nothing will change.

All these months later – five months after the first hospital admission – Mom is no longer angry. She can get agitated and upset, but she is not angry like she was. She knows she has dementia though she does not want to hear you say that she does. It's almost worse, in a way, because now that she's no longer angry she also is no longer fighting. As if there is nothing left to fight. We've crossed a line somewhere and there's no going back.She isn't cussing out the nurses and doctors but she's confused and sad and anxious. A nurse takes her out to get an x-ray. I look at Dad and he looks at me but we say nothing. There's nothing to say.

She's just talking crazy-talk. 90% of what she says makes no sense at all. Does it make sense in her head and she just can't verbalize it? Or is what is in her head complete mumbo-jumbo? There is no way to know. Is she a prisoner of her own

110

brain? I don't know. But we are all prisoners in her hell. We may not be experiencing the same thoughts and emotions she is, but we are all experiencing something. My main emotion is grief. Grief and utter helplessness.

Mom does shower now. Help came in the form of our lovely caretaker, Angie. She has relieved our burden tremendously. Anyone who tells you that caring for aging/ailing parents is not a burden is lying. IT IS. I'm not even going to say it's a burden I bear gladly because I would 100% rather have Mom back the way she was a few short years ago.

"

It's unfortunate, untenable and unbearable. It is what it is. We go on.

"

Dad asks if I can come over so he can go to Walmart. It is torture trying to drag Mom all around Walmart, as slow as she moves now. When I get there, I tell her we are going to change her pants. Amazingly she doesn't fuss. There are no panties, pull ups, nothing under her pants. I put some Depends on her. I just shake my head and sigh. Mom doesn't have a clue that there's anything wrong, as far as I can tell. She just doesn't remember how to dress herself or go to the bathroom anymore. Personally, I think the time is coming when we might need to find a place for her. The nighttime's are really hard on both Dad and me, as hard as we are trying to keep her at home it might not end up being a reasonable option. Dad insists we won't even discuss it until after Christmas. My brother is not able to come for Dad's surgery after all. He has the surgery on September 16th in spite of everything. Little did we know then that his life just changed tremendously, and not for the better.

The day after surgery I am at the hospital. My friend Kathy is with me. We are waiting for them to release him. Meanwhile he is worried that the back door isn't locked with the key and that Mom will go outside. I tell him I've got it covered and to stop worrying. Dad tells me it is extremely painful getting his dressing changed. I can imagine! I take a cheesy picture of him in his hospital gown, which I am sure he appreciates.

Once he is home I stay the night there, but a couple days later I go back to my own house. Angie is there and Dad is doing ok at night. I do have to go make Mom dinner before I teach my lessons because Dad isn't able to walk very well. Mom typically goes to bed by 5:30 pm now! She sleeps a lot, sometimes as much as fifteen hours at a time. I want to take Mom out shopping but she is slow and confused and I don't have the patience that day. She told Dad earlier she was going out on the porch to get some stuff. But she didn't know what she was supposed to be getting! Of course, Dad and I didn't know either.

On September 23rd Dad has a follow up appointment with the surgeon. I go to stay with Mom while he's gone. I find a frozen pizza that's been in the freezer for who knows how long. I give it to Mom for dinner. She says it is the best thing she ever ate! Dad says "I cannot believe you gave her that!!! I thought you got a fresh one! If she shits all over everything I'm calling you at 8 am!" Ha! I say it was *frozen* so it should be fine. I said you wanted me to feed her, and I did! Don't be picky. Dad laughs.

I did manage to get Mom out and get her toes painted which is a huge accomplishment these days. I can't get her to brush her teeth but at least she can have nice toes.

On October 1st I text Dad that Skylar has been a complete meltdown mess since 4 pm. I'm hanging on by a thread, I just don't even know what to do. Dad is worried about us and also says his incision is weeping again – it may be infected and his leg hurts. I ask if he's showered and cleaned the wound and he says no. I say that might have been important.

A couple days later - October 3rd - Dad looks like *death.* I take one look at his gray face, almost have a heart attack, and tell Angie I'm taking him to the hospital immediately.

When shit hits the fan, when stress has you wallowing in self-pity, when it's all you can do to keep breathing - what do you turn to to help you cope?

Dad went in for vascular surgery. He was nervous, I was nervous. He's the provider for Mom, who has dementia, and organizing everything so that he could get this surgery done was no mean feat. Mom cannot be left alone anymore so between myself, my brother, my husband, Mom's caregiver and my good friend Kathy we managed to be in all places at all times for everyone, Skylar and the horses included, while Dad was in the hospital and then for the first few days he was home. All was well.

Fast forward two weeks. Dad tells me he's not feeling great. He has a fever, chills and is throwing up. I think Flu. The next morning I come over to see him and I am shocked at how he looks. I take him to the ER right away. Once we get in the back, the people start swarming around him. I sit back and think to myself "Shit. This is not how it was when Mom came in. This is a bit concerning. Why are there so many people?" They are putting two IV's in - one in each arm. They are using an ultrasound machine to do it. They are taking blood and administering fluids and nobody is talking to me. Finally, one of the nurses (I think) tells me they are treating him as if he is septic. He is nonchalant about this so I don't really think much of it. We start getting results in - no pneumonia. Lungs are clear. For a man who has smoked a pack a day for sixty-five years this in itself is pretty amazing. Next - no flu. Well, I guess it's an infection from the surgery then? It doesn't look too bad, they tell me. Dad tries to tell them it hasn't been right since the surgery. Never stopped weeping, doesn't want to heal. They nod sagely. We need him to give a urine sample, they say.

We wait. Five hours later they admit him. I can't stay - Dad is alone in the hospital because I have to leave to be with Mom when Angie leaves for the day. At this point I don't really realize how close he was - how dangerous his symptoms were. Nobody tells me anything. I get one phone call from a case worker who tells me what room they are moving him to. I get no further results - no information about what is wrong with him. Dad is in no condition to text or call. Everything is eerily silent.

The next day after Angie arrives for Mom, and I've gotten Skylar to school and the horses fed, I finally make it to the hospital. He is bitching non-stop about how bad his neck hurts so I know he is feeling better. Over the next few days his discharge date keeps getting moved back and nobody ever bothers to fill me in on a diagnosis. I beg my brother to come - I need him to be with Dad. When he arrives he makes heads roll until he gets some answers. Finally a diagnosis. A staph infection and septicemia. What? I google it. **Blood Poisoning.** From the staph infection. From the original surgery, though no one will admit that.

Dad waited a very long time to have this surgery. Which was supposed to help with blood circulation in his left leg. This is what he got for his trouble. A near-death experience with a bacteria called Staph. Even now, weeks later, he is home and still very sick. He is on antibiotics which must be administered by IV through a PIC line every eight hours. Guess who gets to administer the late at night one? Yours truly. Skylar and I are having a never-ending sleepover at my parents' house.

Like I said, Dad has been smoking for sixty-five years. He is seventy-three years old. That's a lot of cigarettes. A lot of nicotine. A lot of reason for his veins to shut down. A lot of time to try and quit, and never succeeding.

Since he got home from the hospital, he has noticed that every evening around 6:30 pm he starts feeling really, really bad and is short of breath. Tonight he said "I think I figured it out. The wine, I think it is the wine." Dad likes a glass of wine every night - he enjoys it immensely. I say well Dad why don't you try not having it tomorrow and see if you don't feel this way? And he answers – 'I love that wine. I look forward to it every day.' And I point out that he's on a lot of medication and that if it IS the wine, then hopefully after he's done with all this medicine that he could go right back to drinking it every night. He shakes his head sorrowfully.

I understand. When life hands you lemons you drink lemonade right? It's why I can't give up the sugar I love.

*Why Dad wants that wine and those cigarettes. Why we do things we know are detrimental to our health. It's not because we aren't strong enough to quit. We are very strong people. We are stubborn and persistent and we can do **anything** we want to do. We have proved that over and over. When everything else is beyond our control and all we have left is the urge to self-sabotage, well. We do. Because it feels good in the moment. Because it's the one thing that lets us escape for even just half a minute. And mostly, because we are so exhausted from caring for everyone else, how can we deny ourselves the one thing that feels so good?*

I get it Dad. As much as I want you to quit smoking entirely, I totally feel where you are coming from.

CHAPTER TWELVE

Emotional Torture

October 9th. Mom cried today. For no obvious reason. Just tears pooling in her eyes and running down her face as I sat with her. I try to reassure her that everything is fine and that she is loved. I ask what is wrong, but she doesn't know. She's sad, I can tell. Alzheimer's is the worst kind of torture. You can't be sure what she is thinking, she can't be sure of the world around her. She can't communicate with you, and you know your words are empty and useless. It is soul crushing. I will never be the same person again after living through Alzheimer's. And I will live through it. Mom won't. There is a future for me, Mom's future is very short.

Last Saturday I spent feeling completely numb. Emotionless and drained. That morning I was at the house and Mom started groaning. She went out to the garage. I assumed she was getting a soda. She didn't come back in. I went to investigate and found her sitting in the garage with her pants down – and if you can imagine the worst thing that

could happen - that was what was happening. She was sitting on a stool, pants down around her ankles, literal shit everywhere. Bent over and groaning. She was distraught and completely disoriented. It was also thirty degrees outside, and the garage door was open. I had to get her inside, to the bathroom, into the shower and completely clean everything up, especially her. I was trying not to retch and also be sensitive and kind. She started to cry then too. She knows it isn't right. She knows everything is falling to pieces around her. She tells me she's sorry.

After that I couldn't get the pictures out of my head. I still can't. Probably never will. I never ever want to have to do that again. I told my brother what had happened, and he said, "we're at the end." The end of what? Her life? My ability to care for her? Her ability to function? The end of my sanity? I don't want this for her. It would be so much easier, I think, if she didn't know who we all are. If she was truly gone from reality. But she's not. She can't do many things – she can hardly do anything, but she still knows us. She knows this is not how life is supposed to be. She knows she can't do anything anymore. She knows.

Sometimes I wish, and I will admit it, that something would just happen to take her away peacefully. To end all our suffering. But at the same time how could I wish that? I love Mom. I don't want her to die. I don't want her to miss out on all the future things that are going to happen. To miss out on Skylar and her life experiences. I don't want any of this. I never wanted any of this. None of it is fair. Mom was a wonderful, good person. She certainly doesn't deserve this end to her life. Every day I am in a flux of emotions. Every day my heart breaks all over again. Every time Mom cries I feel completely helpless. What can I do? How can I help her?

I don't know. I don't know. I don't know. Do my own tears count for anything? Does anything I do mean anything at all? Am I doing anything right? Should Mom be in a long term care facility or should she be at home with us? She is basically incontinent. She doesn't remember to wipe. She doesn't brush her teeth. But if I remind her to do anything she gets upset with me. She doesn't get upset with Angie, but Angie isn't here all the time.

*Also, I don't **want** to remind her. I don't want to be Mom's caregiver. It's terrible for both of us. I want to live my life and have Mom be the way she used to be before. Before Alzheimer's. When I was just her daughter. That's all I want to be. Do we owe our parents this? This caregiving at the end of life? Because they've done so much for us, do we in turn have to give our lives completely over to them? How selfish am I because I don't want to?*

All I know is this. Alzheimer's disease is the worst thing that can happen to anyone. The absolute worst.

A few days later I am still musing on what happened in the garage. It is still very fresh in my head. I tell Dad, "the thing is, what if I hadn't been there? You were still in bed. She would've been sitting in the garage in thirty degrees with her pants down until who knows. And the garage door was open, for anyone to see her."

Dad says "Yeah it's a bad deal! Everything is a bad deal right now!" I still feel like he is in denial about how capable we are of taking care of Mom at this stage.

Skylar has been spending some time at their house. But Mom tells Dad that Skylar is driving her crazy. I understand, she is only five and has a ton of energy and imagination and needs constant stimulus and attention. But it still makes me sad that she would say this, she wouldn't have said it a year ago.

My heart is really hurting. I am at my parent's house once again and I DON'T WANT TO BE HERE. I'm basically babysitting because Dad had to go to the ER again. I brought Mom a breakfast burrito from Sonic. When she eats she makes these weird little moans and groans and I just want to stick a fork in someone's eyes. She'll take food out of her mouth and not know where to put it. She'll pick up her phone instead of her drink. She'll drink an old Coke instead of the fresh fountain drink right in front of her. It sounds awful, and petty, and mean but I am really, really done. I want to leave. Right now. I want to hide somewhere far away. I don't want to do this anymore. I don't want to watch Mom decline into such pathos. It smells bad back in her bedroom and I don't want to go investigate. I don't want Dad to have to deal with this anymore either. I just don't want there to be anything wrong anymore. And I feel terrible. In my heart I feel like a complete failure. Because I didn't know, and I didn't fix it, and I can't do anything about it. I don't know how to reach her anymore. I just want to be free again. But without feeling guilty about it. I'm tired. So tired. The guilt and the heartache and the despair is all too much. And even though there are people to whom I can vent, and I do, there is really no way anyone else can feel what I feel. Even my brother. He's too far away to experience the day-to-day living hell. Dad must feel all the same things I feel but we don't talk about it. It's like we just can't bring any of our darkness out into the light by talking about it. The darkness needs to stay

hidden, or it will envelop us. I am already feeling smothered by it. It's why I want to escape.

I got a book a few weeks ago about being the caregiver for someone with Alzheimer's. It was a totally useless book. It kept reassuring me that "I'm doing all I can" and "I am a wonderful person for being a caregiver." It went on non-stop about self-care and how I need to make time for myself because I'm such an awesome person for caring for my "loved one" until the end. Fuck. The end?! I can't do this until the end! And yes, I realize self-care is important, but the fact is self-care is not going to make me feel any better about this process. A bubble bath isn't going to take all the terrible feelings away. A brisk walk isn't going to clear my head or make me feel light-hearted again. None of this is going away! The book was stupid. I can't believe I wasted my money on it. It basically just pissed me off.

The nitty-gritty down in the dirt shit that goes on with a person who has Alzheimer's is not in any book I've found. And while none of them paint a rosy picture, the cute little stories that people tell don't begin to tell it like it really is. Figuring out how to get Mom to brush her teeth or change her Depends without her getting angry at me is what it really is. And her getting angry anyway, and me persevering anyway because the "diaper" is nasty and needs to be changed. Handling the abuse hurled my way because she's angry and frustrated and embarrassed. That's what it really is. The moaning and groaning nonstop while she eats and at other times during the day without her even realizing what she's doing is what it really is. The absolute inability to do anything you tell her to do is what it is. It's her watching TV all day and getting up and wandering around and going outside and you tailing her every move so nothing bad happens. It's her getting annoyed because she doesn't know *what she's doing but she sure as shit doesn't want you following her around asking what she's doing. It's remembering to give her all her pills every day and making sure she swallows them and doesn't stick them in a cabinet or under a magazine because she can't remember what they are. It's making a corkboard full of pictures so that maybe she'll know what time of year it is and remember who her grandchildren are. It's not having any idea what to get her for Christmas because she can't open a present anyway.*

*It's not having a clue what is **best** for her. Staying at home where we are all miserable? Or putting her in a home where she's safe, we think, but can't really know for sure because we won't be there all the time. She does not want any of us to tell her what to do. She's getting upset more easily now. Getting angry again.*

It's watching her tear magazine pages out randomly and wondering why. It's her sitting on a rain-soaked cushion on the back porch and then being distressed because her backside is all wet and she "didn't do anything." She knows people will think she peed herself. It's a different day and coming to terms with the way it is for her. Hanging out here all day for two days and not being able to do my job or be in my own house or live my own life. It's succumbing to the monotonous tasks of the very boring day and realizing that I can't change anything, and I can't make anything better than it is. At least not right now. It's remembering times past and wishing like hell we were back there again. Here's what it is. Drop your favorite, oldest, most precious Christmas ornament on the floor and watch it shatter. Pick up the pieces and realize that they don't fit back together again and even if you could make sense of them there isn't any way to repair it. Pick them up and hold them close to your heart and cry. Cry for what is lost, for what is never coming back. Cry for what is not repairable. Cry for yourself because you loved that ornament. And cry for the ornament that will never again be what it once was.

For some reason Dad's hand is incredibly swollen. We have home health to come to the house to do an x-ray on it, but it is not fractured. Before they arrive, Mom has wet her pants and Dad somehow manages to get her all changed, which I can't imagine how, seeing as he only has one usable hand. We have no idea what happened to his hand, but it is definitely the size of a small cantaloupe right now.

Because we are still having to do the PIC line antibiotics for Dad in the middle of the night, my sister-in-law, Shannon, volunteers to come spend the weekend with Dad and help out. Which is a nice vacation for me! And even though Shannon does a great job Dad tells me he misses me anyway.

While we are at home that weekend Skylar is trying to help me in the barn - I leave her for a few minutes to go down to the horse paddock aisle to throw hay and while I am down there she tries to put her pony, Corkie, in her stall by herself. Corkie ends up shoving the stall door into my little one's head while she is trying to feed her. I can hear the poor kid crying from where I'm at, and I rush back up to the barn. There is a nasty little hole in the middle of her forehead from the stall door latch that is bleeding profusely. We get it all bandaged up then she has to "rest" the day away on the couch while being brought all of her favorite treats and Band-

Aids. She did get a scar from that incident, which she still has today.

We barely make it through the week ... trudging up to the next weekend when there's another horse show to go to.

I should've seen it coming. Anytime there's a horse show coming up, or a weekend that is going to be very busy - it rains. Skylar gets sick. Something happens that requires emergency attention. My whole weekend shot to hell.

I am bleary eyed. At 5:45 am I was informed that someone was too sick to go to school today (It's not a school day). "You want to hear my bad cough Mommy?" Kid, I've heard it. I've heard it all night. And for Pete's sake go back to sleep - it's Saturday. "Noooo" she whines "I want to get uuuuupppp!" And because I know the whining won't stop until I do, I get up. Get her settled watching a movie. Can't go back to my bedroom because Tony is asleep from working the night shift and it's not like Skylar is going to let me sleep anyway. The dog is whining. Have to call Dad to tell him to get his medicine out at 6 am. Have to call him again at 7 am to be sure he's doing it. Was supposed to sleep there last night but didn't want to expose him to Skylar's germs.

It's 7:55 am and I've already fed the horses, given the cat endless treats, ripped at least five things out of the dog's mouth that she's not supposed to be chewing on, started the laundry, gotten Baby Girl Tylenol that she won't take - she has a 101.6 fever - and taken stock of my wreck of a house. I've already had one Diet Coke and am working on a Dr. Pepper. The horses have been in for three days and I'm going to have to turn them all out in the mud later. I need to do invoices and the lesson schedule for November. How is it already almost November?!

My brother is coming from Austin today to discuss with me and Dad what our future options are for Mom. Super fun conversation. Truly can't wait. Tony will get to escape at 3:30 pm and go back to work while I *possibly* help the kids get ready for the horse show tomorrow - I haven't heard that it's been canceled, and it probably won't be canceled until the horses are all back in the stalls bathed and prepped and the tack is all clean. I won't be able to teach in my arena for at least three consecutive sunny days and it's going to rain again on Tuesday.

Annnnnddddd Dad just called and informed me he needs to go back to the ER. Something is not right with the wound from his surgery. A hard ball that is getting bigger and is very painful, which the doctor dismissed yesterday at the appointment. I have not been impressed with this doctor. He just got the wound vac off yesterday.

Is there a plus side? I can't think of one at the moment. I want to wring my hands in despair and lay my head in the cradle of my arms and start drinking right now. I want to fix everything and it's all out of my hands.

Is God trying to tell me something here? Don't sweat the small stuff? Enjoy the teeny tiny positives in life? Don't strangle the dog for chewing up your boots or the cats when they won't stop walking back and forth over your keyboard? They are still God's creatures after all. God, if there was ever a time I needed you, my family needed you, to not only walk beside us, but carry us - it's now. Please let the footprints in the sand be yours. Please give us inspiration and strength and wisdom and faith.

Also, please bring me a house cleaning fairy and a wine membership.

Then Mom trips and falls while I am standing right next to her. Injures her shoulder or her arm - she can't tell me what hurts most. Mom just won't go to bed, either. I am staying at their house because Dad went from the ER to being admitted to the hospital again.

Dad and I both have a terrible night. Dad's blood pressure is incredibly high at 200, then 189, finally lots of drugs get it down, I stay up with Skylar who has a fever and won't take her medicine. Finally both Skylar and Mom are asleep.

I text Dad while he's in the hospital to tell him I love him, and I'll see him tomorrow. He gets out of ICU and into a regular room the next day. Predictably, Skylar's ear starts leaking blood and oozing.

Tony spends some time hanging out with Dad so I can take care of Skylar and Mom.

Skylar gets ear drops four times a day, antibiotics and Motrin. She is not a fan of the ear drops and it takes both me and Tony to get them in. She screams and screams and tries to run away. I cry just from her pain. I know how uncomfortable the ear drops make her feel.

Dad is bored and lonely and says he's ok, but I know he's worrying non-stop about himself, Mom, Skylar, me, my brother and his house and my house and everything else a person can think about while they're laying alone in a hospital bed.

Halloween is coming up and for a five-year-old, Halloween is a big thing. She has a unicorn costume - a frilly rainbow skirt with a horned headband that she is going to wear. It's the cutest thing. However, Halloween night I know I will be stuck at my parents' house "babysitting" Mom because Dad is in the hospital. I call up Miss Pooh who offers to come spend Halloween with us and help me out. At first the plan is for her to take Skylar the Unicorn trick or treating while I stay at the house with Mom. But I really want to go. I don't want to miss it, and I am torn. We don't have any good trick or treating neighborhoods around us, therefore we have to drive somewhere, and it can't be too far away. Miss Pooh and I come up with the solution to wait until Mom goes to sleep, then hightail it out to the car to find a nearby neighborhood. I am anxious as hell, but our plan actually works. I drive the car while Miss Pooh walks with Skylar to each door. We are gone for about an hour and make it back while Mom is still asleep. Mission accomplished!

Dad finally gets out of the hospital on November 1st. We have to hire a person to stay the nights and weekends when Angie isn't there. I just can't do it all anymore. The first person we get is named Margaret; she was hired through an agency. We paid the agency and they paid her. It is a twenty-four hour at a time type of deal. She makes dinner, cleans up the house and caters to Mom and Dad's needs. Margaret sleeps there one night so she is on call if anything happens, then a different person comes for the next night. We do this a few weekends until Dad feels strong enough to cope again. I spend time researching memory care facilities. I am extremely sad but also extremely stressed and I know the time has come. Dad doesn't want to do it but realizes that as sick as he's been lately, we are at the end of a short rope of options. Once I have a few picked out I'll take Dad to visit them with me.

I spend a lot of nights sleeping at their house to help out and so someone will be there if they need anything. Dad is not eating much. His regular doctor gives him medication for appetite, but I am pretty sure it doesn't really work.

We've been looking at memory care facilities this week while Dad is up to it. Dad and I checked out two on Monday in Denton and Wednesday I went and looked at two more in Frisco. Two of the four places have been kicked out of the running already. I have two more that I haven't seen yet.

People say, "oh you'll know when the time is right to move your mom." That's pure bullshit. It's never going to be the right time. She loves Dad, and she is comfortable at home. She knows us all by name still. How do you broach the subject of moving into a whole other place? Sure, she can bring her cat (a pet friendly place is non-negotiable) and we will furnish the room with stuff from her own life, her own things. But still, she will not be with Dad every day. How will she handle the transition? Will she feel like we are being terribly mean and shunting her away? Will she even know the difference? Will she get used to a new place? Will she enjoy being cared for so completely? Having new people around her, and new things to occupy her time? Will she blossom with the attention? Or will she go downhill again? It's impossible to know. Her brain is dying but physically she is doing fine. How long until she loses what is left? There are too many questions and not enough answers.

I bet you can't imagine how much a memory care facility costs per month. How do people cope that do not have any savings? I can't even fathom putting her in a place that is "less" than these private care and private pay places we are considering. One of them was $6600 a month! And that wasn't even the nicest place. They also were offering a "special" of $4500 a month – lock that rate in for two years! Well hell, let me run home and say "HURRY UP MA we gotta take advantage of the move-in special! Grab your things and let's go!" What total crap. This is the same place where the Director took me into a room that was locked in order to show me yet another gathering place that looked like all the others. The reason the room was locked was because this lovely young lady was doing music therapy with a very old resident. The Director proceeded to tell me very loudly – over the music – what the room was used for. The guitar playing music therapist kept stealing glances at the Director. I'm sure they appreciated the intrusion.

I wonder what Mom went through when she was having to move my Granny Judy from her house in Austin to an assisted living place in Tyler. She started out in a little house in an assisted living community, then had to move to an actual assisted living building before finally being moved to a nursing home. There may have been another move in there. I wish I had paid more attention. I especially wish I had paid attention to how Mom handled telling Granny Judy about each move. Granny Judy did not have Alzheimer's – she had a type of dementia called Lewy-Body syndrome. Different, more entertaining certainly because Lewy-Body makes you hallucinate. Granny Judy also did not have my grandfather. He passed away long before I was born. Did that make it easier? She was used to living alone, the only person she had to depend on in the end was Mom. Because Mom did not have the best relationship with her mom growing up, was there a disconnect there at all? I do know how hard it hit her when she missed being with Granny Judy by ten minutes when she *died. I can still hear her voice on the phone when she called me shortly after. I know how Mom suffered over her death.*

I pray every day about this situation. I pray for Mom of course, but I also pray that I will not get Alzheimer's. The odds are stacked against me, but I'll fight it. God knows I won't ignore the signs and symptoms if and when they come. I pray that Skylar will not agonize for one minute over what to do with me. I will do everything I can to make advanced directives regarding my care. If nothing else this process has taught me to be prepared, to think ahead and to definitely not ignore my health. I pray for peace for Mom and for Dad. In the end I hope that Skylar does not have to deal with this same situation but if she does, I hope that she knows that I want her to live her best life. Surround me with my stuff, my books and my pictures and my bottles of wine and I'll be just fine.

On a sunny, cold day we go to visit the facility in Frisco, we'll call LW. The person in charge of "selling" the space is enchanting. We both enjoy her a lot. She is very respectful of Dad and earns his trust. We think it's a really nice place and the cost is *only* $5500 a month. The bedroom is very big, private, and there is a private bathroom as well. We visit a couple other places, but Dad is impressed by the LW facility and that's the place he chooses, with my agreement. Luckily for us, Dad is on full disability payments from the military otherwise we would not be able to afford this kind of setup. Many people out there just can't afford a private pay facility. But I will say right now, and many times later on, it's the quality of the people and care, not the quality of the facility that matters!!! And we will definitely find that out in the next nine months.

The weekend before Thanksgiving I am at a horse show in Tyler, which is a three-day end-of-year show. Mom has an accident in the house again and there is poop everywhere. Because I am out of town, Dad gets Tony to come over and help clean up and put new sheets on the bed. I feel terrible. Mom is confused - accuses Dad of just wandering around the house and wants to know if he "had a good time." She can't imagine who did "all that" - it wasn't her. Happens about once a month lately, Dad says. This is what is spurring me to move her to a memory care facility. We just aren't equipped to handle this. Mom also was "talking on the phone" (to no one) and said she was in Austin, and they should come over! Tony says he has PTSD now - I know I can't ask him to do that again. But he does go back when everything is cleaned up to help make the bed. I couldn't ask for a better husband. I tell Dad to make sure Mom's hands are washed as I know there is likely to be poop encrusted under her fingernails, as I have a vivid memory of taking her to Whataburger and she kept smelling her hands and saying something stinks. I finally figured it out and took her to the bathroom to scrub her hands, which she shockingly let me do for once. Not a fun moment.

Dad is home but not doing well. Wearing a wound vac again at first, but finally that goes away, and he doesn't have to sleep with it anymore. He's pretty ecstatic about that. Mom continues to have accidents, which one of us gets to clean up and help *her* get changed and cleaned up as well. Usually, I try to get her to remove one or more extra shirts she is wearing. It is all just so depressing. Extra shirts, poop under her nails, wearing Depends. Can't even clean up when she's watching or she'll get upset. I wonder if I will ever recover from all this.

Right before Thanksgiving Dad starts having issues with his blood pressure and is told he needs to drink more water, but then on Thanksgiving Day he is weak and sick, can't even get up out of his chair. He is transported to the hospital by ambulance. I have the last picture I ever took of Mom and Dad together at their home - he is attempting to walk with a walker, and she has her hand on his back, attempting to help. It's a terribly heart-rending picture.

CHAPTER THIRTEEN

Christmas

December 2019

In early December, Dad is in the hospital again and I can't remember why. He calls me a lot, needing help. So now I am trying to take care of Mom at home when Angie can't be there, run my business, be there for Dad and be a parent and a wife. December 4th is when we move Mom to LW. We don't tell Mom what is going to happen, it feels like subterfuge, but I don't want to distress her any more than is necessary. We had ordered a bed from Amazon which was delivered and set up by the maintenance men there. Angie takes Mom out to get her nails done and to get lunch while my friend Kathy and I take what furniture and things Mom needs from the house to the room at the facility. We decorate it nicely and we even take the cat and her litter box. Angie brings Mom in, and she exclaims how lovely it all is, but you can tell she has no idea what it's for. I tell Mom she's just going to stay here while Dad is so sick. It's the biggest lie I've ever told her, and I feel extremely deceitful. I hate what I am having to do. It's around 2 pm in the afternoon and I've got to leave to pick up

Skylar from school. Mom is sitting in a chair, and I tell her I have to go. She turns to Angie and says, "You're not going are you?" Angie says she will stay awhile. I have a huge lump in my throat as I leave her there. That's the hardest thing I've ever had to do - leave Mom in that room. Leave her there and not take her home with me. I know it's for the "best" but who's best? Mine? Hers? Not Dad's... he will miss her being at home with him even though it's really difficult to take care of her.

Dad is moved to a rehab place in Frisco so that he can be nearer to Mom, and I can see them both easily. One night not too long after he arrives, he starts texting me... meet jeep...meet jeep... Which I finally figured out means "need help". He is sick and dehydrated and can't figure out how to call me. It is 9 pm at night but I jump in the car immediately to drive the forty-five minutes down there. No one answers the phone when I call over and over. He has been calling out, asking for help from the staff for hours! Apparently, they have been ignoring his cries, and I am PISSED. I arrange to move Dad immediately to a new place. I am not having this - staff ignoring him when he cries out in pain and needing someone. They say he still has clothes in the laundry - I say I will buy him new clothes. They can't even locate half his stuff. We are out of there the next morning. I won't stand for him being mistreated, regardless of what they think he needs, if he calls out for hours and no one comes to see what's wrong... that's neglect and abuse. I let my brother know what is happening as he works for the Health and Specialty Care System of Texas and I'm sure he can make some heads roll over this.

Alzheimer's has a terrible finality to it. Her brain is shrinking, dying off, but her emotions remain intact. It's like everything has been taken away from her except her ability to feel. And that sucks. She can still be angry, frustrated, scared, annoyed, and mostly sad. She's in this wonderful and caring environment now where she is well taken care of and yet she's terribly sad. She isn't at home, she isn't with her husband, or her children or her grandchildren. She's in a brand-new environment that would be daunting for the most astute of us. Encouraged to embrace a whole new lifestyle full of people and activities and food that she isn't used to. In a place that has all her stuff in it but isn't actually her home.

And I can't talk to her. I can't just check in. It is a huge adjustment for me as well. I want to know how she's doing; I want to know if she's happy most of the time and if it's just for me that she shows her real feelings. I want to know how she's coping; I want to know if she's enjoying meeting new people or if she hates it. But most of all I want **her** to tell me. And she can't. I can't just call her on the phone and get her to dish on all the gossip of the memory care place. She isn't capable of answering her phone anymore though if you actually did get her on the phone she can fake her capabilities really, really well. But if I call the activities director, who is actually very nice, am I annoying her? Am I being a pain in the ass? I just want to know how she is. The answer I'm going to get is that she's doing fine. Which may or may not be the truth. Because Mom certainly isn't going to let on that she's NOT fine. Not to them. Only to me. And only when I get to come visit. And I feel as if the memory care staff are

135

going to tell me she's fine, no matter what may actually be happening.

Forty-five minutes away may not seem like a lot, but it's certainly a lot when you want to go every day. Is it in her best interests for me to check on her every day, or is that just making it harder? If I don't come, does she think I've forgotten her? Does she even recognize that I didn't show up that day? Or does the time simply run together until I do show up again? Based on her reaction when I walk in that door, I think she is well aware of the length of time I've been away. Even if it's only a day or two. Which, in fact, two days is the longest I've gone without going to see her and that's only because Dad's health issues forced me to focus on his needs and care instead of hers. And in the moment that I explain that to her she totally understands and is worried about Dad and wants to be sure he is ok. But how long does she retain that? Not long enough I'm afraid.

Forty-five minutes is a long time to think about things. I wonder, Why? Why did she get Alzheimer's at such a young age? Seveny-three isn't young but it isn't ninty-three you know? Granny Judy didn't get diagnosed with Lewy-Body syndrome until she was eighty. That's another type of dementia. And she lived until she was eighty-eight, a lot of that time in assisted living - you could still call and talk to her. Even if she did tell you that there was a man upstairs peeing on her bathroom carpet through the vent every time you talked to her. She really believed that. Turns out the AC unit was leaking through the vent, onto her bathroom rug. I believe now that Mom was showing symptoms of dementia probably as young as sixty-three and we all just were not aware.

Was it the smoking since she was a teenager? Was it the drinking beer every night? Was it the lack of exercise?

Certainly not a lack of education. She was a librarian for goodness sakes. She read insatiably. Just like I do. She was a storyteller. She used her brain!

Did her tragedy riddled teen and early adult years contribute to her early mental problems? Was it the fact that her own father was bi-polar and her mother's side of the family has a long line of dementia? Was it a low-testosterone problem? A depression problem? How much could we have done for her if she had clued us all in?

Was it the chemicals in products that we use every day? Was it pesticides or sunscreen or tampons? I want to know. Was it hormones, or lack thereof? Who knows these answers? If I were younger my whole career may have been different. I may have wanted to pursue the answers to these questions I care so achingly about. I could have been a great researcher. I'm seriously into facts and detail checking. I'm insanely curious. A medical researcher – why not?

And what are the things I am doing or not doing that could lead to Alzheimer's? I've already purchased the Alzheimer's Prevention Food Guide. I make sure I exercise. And I'm easing into more natural products, from tampons to milk to deodorant. But I still love Diet Coke. Part of me is curious to see if I continue to drink the diet drinks will I actually get Alzheimer's? And will that be the main reason? I think it is really impossible to know. I could give up Diet Coke entirely and **still get Alzheimer's**. It's not an absolute. Nothing is absolute.

So what do we do now?

For Mom all I can do is take care of her and love her the way she is. There is no going back. There is no cure. There is nothing more to be done. We don't even go to see her neurologist anymore. What's the point? It upsets Mom, and they can't do anything for her.

137

And for me? Well, I'm hoping and praying that I have enough of Dad's side of the family blood in me. The strong, healthy, sharp Thomas brain that won't give up on me. And I'll be living the best life I can while we wait and see. I'll try not to dwell on it at any rate, and I will be watching for the early signs – so that I can help myself as much as possible. So that my husband and my daughter don't have to handle what I handle with my mom.

It's all I can do.

Kathy and I take Skylar and Ali to the Polar Express train adventure. I am trying hard to do normal things so that Skylar doesn't remember only the bad things about this time period of her life. The train ride is a success, and Skylar lights up when Santa comes on the train and hands her a bell. We each got one, so we still have three polar express bells to this day. We also got hot chocolate in keepsake mugs and sugar cookies. It was definitely fun, although bittersweet since it was no longer Mom taking these adventures with us.

Mom seems to be doing well at the memory care facility. She seems happy, happy when we are there visiting and I am receiving pictures of her making crafts and gardening with her new friend. I'm not sure she has any idea what she's doing but she is smiling at least. Skylar and I take a bracelet making set when we go visit, and Mom is thrilled we are there and happy to sit at a table with us, but she can't figure out how to put a bracelet together. Still, it is close to being a good time and it seems like she is being well taken care of. Skylar likes to push Mom up and down the wide hallways in her wheelchair and enjoys it immensely if I let her sit in the wheelchair while I push her around. They have a doll crib with a doll and baby stuff for the residents. Mom has no interest in this set up but Skylar has a grand time playing with it all. There's also a rocking chair so you can "rock the baby." When my brother comes to visit a few days before Christmas she cries when she sees him.

At some point Dad comes home but then almost immediately he is in the hospital again. He has been telling doctors and nurses that his left foot hurts but apparently no one believes him and doesn't bother to look at it. Finally, at the hospital it is discovered that he has the staph infection in a wound in his foot, in his heel. He is transferred to a hospital in Ft. Worth for treatment by a NEW doctor, which I am grateful for. While at the ER, before the transfer, I am in tears begging him not to leave me alone. He holds my hand and tells me he'll be alright. But he is still there a few days before Christmas Day and when we all troop in to visit, he is very happy to see us but very tired and out of it. He later tells me he doesn't remember us being there at all. We can't stay long as my autistic nephew just can't handle being in that tiny room for very long.

My brother and I just spent our very first family Christmas together, alone, without our parents. It's something I wasn't prepared for. With Mom in memory care and Dad in the hospital it was just us and our four children. I made the kids wait until my husband woke up on Sunday morning before we could open presents. It just felt too weird

not to have another adult there. Like some sort of bizarre plot twist in a time travel movie.

Overall we had a good time. We did go visit my parents and the kids opened gifts from them that Grandpa paid for but never saw. My brother ordered them, and I wrapped them, and the kids gleefully tore into them, unaware and unconcerned of what emotional price I was paying. We went to Babe's chicken one night and ordered pizza the next. No traditional Christmas dinner was planned nor cooked. No cookies were baked, and no pies were devoured. My nephew watched How the Grinch Stole Christmas four times. I've had "wa hoo wa hoo wa hoo wa hoo something something Christmas day" stuck in my head ever since.

The two girl cousins, Amy and Skylar, had a great time until there was a misunderstanding over a stuffed unicorn and both girls were in tears and tired of each other. I was done drinking and ready for bed before my brother was, which we were probably both disappointed by but there's only so much I can handle before I need to escape. I'm still recovering.

Today is Christmas Eve. Tony and Skylar and I went to see Mom and took her gifts for Christmas. Her room at the memory care center is always fairly destroyed when I arrive. She spends her time moving her possessions around, packing them up and stuffing them in bags and cabinets. She is clearly confused by her surroundings at the best of times. I tried to decorate her apartment with all the things she loves best: pictures of her and Dad, pictures of me and David and all her grandchildren, things Dad made for her and things that belonged to her mother. My grandmother loved yellow roses, yellow roses were all over her house, especially on these fancy plates. There are big plates and small plates, gold rimmed plates and plates that should be hung up and plates that sit on fancy holders. There are cups and saucers, too. They're all *beautiful and they're all extremely old. And precious to Mom. Oddly, I feel absolutely no nostalgia for these things except for the fact that I know Mom loves them.*

Today I found a broken saucer. Did she drop it? It's split clean in half. She had shoved it back in a cabinet and I found it there and sadly pulled it out. Oh no! I cried to Tony, look! I was devastated. Mom couldn't tell me how it happened. She told me not to worry about it; she seemed very unconcerned. And as she was sitting there with Skylar right next to her, she asked, "Where is Skylar?" I looked at Tony, and he looked at me and neither of us said anything at all. She opened one of her gifts, a shirt, from me and told me she loved it. Later, when we were getting ready to go, she said, "Oh I don't need that thing." Referring to the same shirt.

We took her to Whataburger for lunch. She was overjoyed and kept repeating "this is just incredible" and "you are so sweet to do this for me." But at the same time, she was very worried about being in the truck and absolutely unsure what was going on at any time. When I took her into the restroom, I noticed that once again there was a wet spot on the back of her pants. She also told me that the place smelled but I am pretty sure it's just that she gets stuff under her fingernails. Because she can't remember to use toilet paper and gets confused in the bathroom. This is why she's in memory care, this more than anything else. It just guts me to realize that it will still happen, even with the best of care. You can't tell her, either. But she does let me wash her hands this time, which is a small miracle. I scrub them clean and we head back to the table.

Like the saucer, I am broken. I can't enjoy this season. I am sad and angry and not yet ready to relax about it all. I wish Dad was at home, I am not sure if that would have made any difference, but it would have been nice to have him with us at our Christmas celebration. The thing that tears me up most, about the broken saucer, is that Mom wasn't concerned about it. What was once precious to her has been forgotten.

Sometime, in the not-so-distant future, my brother and I and our children will all be just like that broken saucer.

CHAPTER FOURTEEN

Just Before Covid-19

January - March 2020

I'm used to texting with Dad pretty consistently, but he is extremely ill while in the hospital and doesn't pick up his phone much. He is miserable and lonely, and I really feel for him. I do talk to him on the phone, and I try to visit as much as possible. Then he is moved to another rehab place (where Skylar once again excels at pushing him around in his wheelchair when we visit) and finally something goes our way! We are able to get him into his own room at LW, which is where Mom is – this is a tremendous improvement for me and our family. At first, Dad is confused a lot, and I think he is dehydrated. We move his recliner in and everything that will make him more comfortable, including his coffee machine as there is a tiny kitchen in his room.

January 22nd, I bring him and Mom Whataburgers which they devour. Dad is finally doing better. He gets to have dinner with Mom now they are in the same place. Tony and Skylar and I try to go as often as possible, but it is forty-five minutes away and that takes up the day pretty well.

I have to go pick up Dad to take him to an appointment on January 27th. We have to go to the vascular doctor to find out why Dad is in so much pain all the time. Of course, we don't get any answers while we are there, but more tests are ordered. Dad rolls his eyes.

Dad tries to have all meals with Mom, but he is dependent on the workers and more often than not he misses it because they don't come get him which makes him really mad. He is not strong enough at this point to move the wheelchair on his own very far and the dining room is really far away. Then the director says that Dad can't eat with Mom anymore! We are incensed. Dad says he has been setting a perfect example - I raise hell with the people there. This is not acceptable. Then we find out that Mom said she didn't want to eat with Dad because he's mean to her. I tell Dad Mom doesn't mean it - she was also in tears because she hasn't seen him. Mom doesn't even know what she is saying - how can they not investigate that further before just saying Dad can't eat with Mom? Just another example of their inadequacies. I am beginning to lose my patience.

On January 30th I take Mom out of LW to go to lunch - we go to get pizza. Mom is absolutely thrilled but hardly eats anything. She drinks her entire Coke, though and it's nice to spend time with her and pretend that everything is normal. We also go to Hobby Lobby. I don't realize then that this is the last time we will go to Hobby Lobby together. There are a few more lunches out together but little do I know that COVID-19 is coming... and our days out together are short.

Somehow on February 2nd Dad fell out of bed - I do not understand how this happened and why he wasn't

144

able to get up. I guess he is just super weak still. I don't know how long he sat there until somebody helped him up. That night I went to watch the Super Bowl with him. We discuss moving him home and hiring a caretaker. I talk to Angie about being Dad's caretaker because she doesn't have a job yet after having moved Mom to LW. Dad would *love* Angie to be his person. He really enjoys her. And she's a person in the house to keep him company.

Dad has a lovely foot doctor, Dr. Jacoby - who comes regularly to see him at LW, and also later at home even though her practice is in Plano! She is truly a great doctor and a lovely person. The wounds are terrible on Dad's foot and are really slow to heal. I don't know what we would have done without Dr. Jacoby. The wounds are from the original staph infection and Dad has to constantly wear a soft boot on his left foot. He even has to sleep in it. Dr. Jacoby is doing everything she can to help these wounds heal.

It's February and my Aunt Patty has been staying at LW in Dad's room. Somehow, she convinced them to let her even sleep there in his recliner. She is an invaluable help as she can get Dad wherever he needs to go and help him with everything he needs. But Mom is jealous of Aunt Patty. Mom says Dad is being a jerk and she doesn't want Aunt Patty there at the table. She says Dad is too busy for her because his sister is there. Dad says he and Aunt Patty have been especially nice to Mom. BUT. I tell Dad to have a few meals with Mom by himself. Mom needs to feel that Dad is there just to spend time with her, without his sister.

Aunt Patty starts to tell me the care there is inadequate to say the least. These people just don't care, she says. I am not ready to hear it - I've mostly seen good care when I am there. She says, "But what about when you're not here? Trust me, it's not good. Not quality care. These people are just here to do a job and that's it." I come to eat with Mom and then plan to see Dad after. But I can't find a person to let us out of the memory care part! It is locked - everyone is locked in at all times. Including me, apparently. It is so aggravating although I understand that the staff can't be everywhere all the time, and they don't want residents just exiting through the doors since they are all suffering from some type of dementia. However, it seems to me there would be a better system. When you find yourself locked in somewhere you don't want to be. It doesn't help that the memory care space is very large, and you have to walk around a lot to even locate a staff member.

I've been reading the book "The Opposite of Fate" which is a book of musings by Amy Tan. It turns out that Amy Tan's own mother died from Alzheimer's. Which I must have read before, because I'm certain I've read this book before, but I did not grasp it at the time. This time, when I got to the part about her mom's death I sat straight up in bed and read very closely. Still, it didn't reveal a whole lot. She died four years after her diagnosis. It hits me, though, how closely Amy Tan tied into my mother and I's relationship. Along with other famous authors such as Alice Hoffman and Maeve Binchy and Lisa See, to name just a few. Mom and I were continuously and forever connected through our love of books and reading.

She loved the survival stories – survival against all odds such as "Into the Forest" and "Into Thin Air" – the Jon

Krakauer story. She loved books about China – Chinese mothers and daughters which is where Amy Tan comes in – "The Bonesetter's Daughter" and "Saving Fish from Drowning." Perhaps her favorite book of all time was Barbara Kingsolver's "The Poisonwood Bible." She and I must have read that one at least three times each. One of the characters was named Adah. Which means "a beautiful addition." I told Mom I was going to name my daughter that someday. Of course I didn't, but I didn't forget either. The name is still special to me, as is the book. I saw that book today while at my parents' house and I snapped it up – to take it home to my own library so as to keep it forever in my heart and in my mind.

I also saw "Still Alice." A story about a woman diagnosed with early onset Alzheimer's. A story that was made into a movie that I couldn't, wouldn't watch. Starring Julienne Moore I believe. We both read that book a long time ago, before all this. Anyway, I saw that book and I left it there on the shelf – I am not now and may never be able to read that one again.

I brought home some books, but I was dismayed by the ones that were not there. Did we get rid of them? Did she? I looked and I couldn't find them anywhere – only her most favorite are left, along with "Still Alice" which makes you wonder why she held onto that one. And for a moment I got lost in her world. The world where she no longer understood where she was or what she was doing. And I felt her there, with me, as I let my heart mourn. When she stopped reading, I was surprised, but I didn't push the issue – you don't push the issue with Mom. She'll cut you off and shut you down and get angry. Which I always avoided at all costs. I was a big fan of keeping the peace. I also remember when she stopped reading People magazine. When I asked her about that she said, "oh I just don't know any of those people anymore." I thought she had just lost interest. Looking back, I wonder how many years has it been exactly,

147

since she stopped reading? Why didn't I do anything? I should have known, known that she didn't really prefer watching TV to reading – it was just easier. A way out of explaining that she could no longer retain what she read. Even as far back as Harry Potter, she would tell me she didn't like those books because she couldn't keep track of all the characters. Of which there were a lot, so I thought that was the honest truth and there was nothing more to it.

Mom will never really be gone from me. I miss her voice; I miss talking to her every day. But every time I read a book that we both loved she is with me again, reading alongside and holding my heart in her hands.

On February 17th I am notified that Mom fell, hit her head and is in the hospital. I hightail it to the hospital but she's not there. Discharged at 2 am but nobody told me. I go to LW. She's in the dining room. The communication from this place is abysmal. Mom has fallen several times at this point because she is unbalanced, the place is too big and there aren't enough staff. She tries to get out of bed, and she falls, she tries to walk to the door of her room and she falls, she tries to walk down the hall and trips on her own feet. She has lost several teeth, and her face is constantly black and blue. I raise hell and tell them I want to be notified the instant she is injured, not once she has already been at the hospital, alone, for hours!

Not long into March it appears that Mom has fallen at LW again! They call me immediately. They have sent her in the ambulance with the EMT's and I talk to one of them on the phone. She is going to get x-rays on her knee and head. And a CT scan. Mom has a massive bruise on the left side of her face and left eye, and she is in a lot of pain. I would swear that something in her face is broken. She's got a neck brace on and can't move her head very much. I just want to cry big elephant tears when I see her. She is so happy to see me but winces with every movement. She doesn't understand what is happening, so I stay with her.

We order Life Alert for Dad. Dad is very insistent that it is ME who takes him to the doctor for information on his upcoming leg surgery. This is a very critical appointment. Dad will go back to LW for rehab after his surgery, but the plan is that he comes home March 31st. Dad is very concerned about his truck which has been parked at LW for months now. Dad wants Tony to pick it up and take it home so that nothing happens to it.

This is the beginning of COVID. The store shelves are EMPTY when I go. I am even more worried about Mom. Will they not let me in to see her? I don't know what is going to happen, but nothing is looking good at the moment.

Aunt Patty ended up staying with Dad for a long time at LW, days turned into weeks! They weren't happy, but they started the lock down after she was already there and she refused to leave! Dad goes in for his procedure March 25th. I am glad she is there.

Right now I'm saving time and gas by not being able to drive to visit my parents but that is simply replaced by extra worry because I cannot see them. For people whose parents do not have medical issues this may not be a big deal - for me it is crucifying. Mom can't even have a decent conversation with me so all I can do is have five minutes with her by video chat whenever I don't miss that call. I know that every day is one

day closer to her not remembering who I am. And I'm missing this crucial time with her. And while I'm super angry and sad about this I am also not willing to risk her health and the health of the others around her. She wouldn't survive Corona - I know this. The facility is on lockdown and no one except staff and medical personnel are allowed in but this certainly doesn't guarantee that the virus will not be brought in somehow. And here's the worst possible thing - if she does get it and is admitted to the hospital I won't be allowed to see her there either. I can't even begin to imagine Mom in a hospital, confused and sick, and I'm not allowed to be by her side. The worry is overwhelming.

And Dad. Dad is already in the hospital again. Having had three or four surgeries in the past week alone, for the vascular problems in his leg. I have lost count. His new doctor is amazing, I know this even though I have never met him, because he saved his leg. It was weeks, maybe days, away from having to be amputated. Dad's nickname is Bullworker, and he has a bit of a following on Facebook. I am grateful to everyone that has posted words of comfort and support. I know he reads them. I am not allowed to visit him there, and I will not be allowed into the rehab place either. However, I am hoping against hope that I will be able to transfer him from hospital to rehab thus getting to spend some time with him, if even just for as short a time as that. I imagine that the rehab place will take good care of him, but again, the coronavirus is an ever-ominous threat, and I am worried. My aunt has taken up residence in his hospital room; after refusing to leave once she brought him in, and thus she is now trapped. If she left for any reason, they would not let her back in. I am exceedingly grateful to her. She is a Thomas, after all, and persistence and damn cussedness runs in the family.

CHAPTER FIFTEEN

COVID-19

April - July 2020

I received a phone call today from LW. It was Charity, the Director of Nursing of the third floor which has both "extended care" and "memory care" patients. This woman is very sweet, and I am grateful for her. She says to me that she's in her office and that the Executive Director is with her. I am immediately more alert. I know it can't be good.

"I just want to tell you of the incident that happened yesterday afternoon" she tells me. "Your Mom was locked in a room with a male resident." Excuse me, what?

Thinking back, I don't remember the exact things she said after that but the gist of it was that Mom had decided that she'd like to keep the company of males, only. And if you try to separate her from her "friends" she becomes upset and angry. Aggressive even. Mom has apparently (according to Charity, who must know a lot about Alzheimer's and dementia patients, I assume? I hope) latched onto males because Dad is no longer around. And she wants to be with him, so she is substituting for him.

Well, she was locked in a room with another resident. My immediate thought was "Uh, they have locks on their doors?" Yes, indeed they do. It is the right of all residents, memory care included, to have locks and keys to their rooms to safeguard their belongings. I am astounded. Mom doesn't have a key. I am certain of that. Mom wouldn't have a clue how to use a key. This male resident must not be nearly as far along as Mom is in his memory problems. As I was listening to Charity, I was somewhat astounded, somewhat amused and somewhat thinking "why are you telling me this?"

The situation was quickly resolved as it appeared that by the time Charity got to the room after having summoned the Executive Director the door was unlocked again. Now this all happened yesterday. I heard about it today about 2 pm. It appears to be policy that they let me know what happened. And I can't help but wonder if I am supposed to do something about it. Somehow, I feel responsible. As if I could have a stern talking-to with my mother and tell her she must never, ever do this again. Later, upon reflection, I had another thought. What if a man takes advantage of her in some way because he does still know what he is doing, at least somewhat? That scares me. I know the facility does the best they can with keeping track of where everyone is, but it's not a lockdown situation. They are free to move around.

The falls Mom have leave me feeling extremely worried. An anxiousness deep down inside myself because I am helpless. I cannot do a thing. I wanted to talk to Mom so they Facetimed with me. She does not understand how to hold the phone, so they help her. Today, she couldn't focus on me. Usually, she sees my face and she lights up. Oh, I'm so glad to see you! She'll say. Not today. Today she said hello and we talked a little bit, but I never got the feeling that she wanted me – like she always has before. I never got the bright eyes, I never got tears or a real connection. She said I love you when I said it to her. I'm not saying she didn't recognize me – but it felt like there will be more, not fewer, of these types of conversations. I told her to behave herself and she laughed. She did not ask after Skylar. I asked if she had talked to Dad and she said no. It was just.... somehow hollow. She did not want to be on the phone long.

I bet that I'll never get to take Mom out for another lunch. I'm guessing it will be months before I see her in person again. How desperately I want to hold her hand, wipe away her tears. Hug her before it's too late. I can feel her hand in mine. I held it for a long time in the hospital that night. I stroked her fingers and she squeezed mine. You wouldn't think that an evening in the hospital like that could be a blessing. But I'm afraid that it was. I'm afraid that it was.

I feel like she's been locked away. Like they used to lock away people in institutions for mental or emotional or physical handicaps. She seems so remote from me, and from everything she should be doing and experiencing right now. There is a depth of anger in me so deep - so deep that I might drown in it. I never knew it was possible to feel anger so deeply within my soul.

The reality is she is not locked away. She is where she needs to be for her own health and safety. But reality doesn't mesh with my feelings about it. The fact is - I cannot take care of her. I was not trained for that. I cannot maintain any semblance of a "normal" relationship with her if I am cleaning her up after an accident or constantly re-directing her actions or helping her eat with a fork. My heart breaks enough just being with her and not being able to hold a conversation.

They call me, they do. At night when she's so upset that she can't breathe. I talk her down off the ledge time and time again. I tell her she's loved - so much - and I tell her everything is alright and then I tell her stories about her granddaughter and the horses and whatever else I can think of that will make her heart smile. I wait on the phone while she takes her medicine she was refusing earlier. I wait until she can breathe again, I tell her I'm drinking wine and that she should be too. She laughs and says, "that sounds good!" I make it a point to bring her a few beers the next time I come to see her. I tell the caregivers to be sure to open it and serve it to her over ice - she can't do it herself.

They call me during the day with video conferencing. I am desperate not to miss these calls. I wish they were more consistent, but I understand that they are busy and doing their best. I'm glad to see her face, even for just a few moments. I'm glad to hear her voice. She still sounds the same as ever. I have an old voicemail she left for me a few years ago and the entire reason I have not got a new phone is that I don't want to lose that voicemail.

She should be here. Enjoying this beautiful sunny day. Gardening, or cooking something new to try. She should be playing with Skylar and laughing and rolling her eyes with me at her sassiness. She should be sitting on the back porch *and watching the squirrels and birds and appreciating life. She should be there when I go to see Dad. She isn't.*

Would it have been easier if she had died from cancer or such? From an accident? Something quick? I don't know if it would have been because that isn't the way it's happening. Instead, Grief hangs over us all, unrelenting because in a way it hasn't really started yet. We are all just holding on. Waiting for the inevitable. For a future where we have to learn to live without her entirely. A future where Skylar gets married or has babies without her grandma to witness it. Where she graduates from high school or wins a champion ribbon in a horse show. Maybe joins the swim team. There is no telling what Skylar will do - but it is absolute that her Granny Susan won't be here to bear witness to it.

That is what makes me the saddest of all. I know we can't go back. Back to swinging in the hammock in the back yard in Tyler, chilling out drinking a beverage and shooting the breeze with Dad while Mom makes my favorite meal. Sitting at her table with her in the evening discussing everything from books we are reading to the mysteries of life. We can't go back to the everyday phone calls and the advice and love she gave me every day. It's the future that we will miss most of all.

She's not locked away, I know this. She's safe, she's healthy and I've got to believe the people there really care about her wellbeing. All the same, she's "locked away" from my everyday life. And I find that impossible to bear. Sometimes I take my anger out on my husband, sometimes on Skylar. I try so hard not to - I know it isn't fair. My husband understands. Skylar doesn't. I hope someday she'll understand that it was very difficult to have a Mommy with a constantly broken heart. I hope she'll forgive me.

And I don't want you to worry Mom. In all the important ways - I'm holding on tight to you.

Dad starts to mention that his throat hurts sometimes. He eats a lot of ice cream. He says it hurts most in the morning and then gets better. We don't think much of it really. At the end of April Dad comes home from LW. He is so done with the place and so is my Aunt Patty. She has consistently been telling me that the place isn't as good as I think it is. That it's the people that make a place nice and these people are just there to do a job. They aren't careful and they don't care. Maybe one or two of them do but most of them do not. I realize later on that she's totally right but at the time I still think Mom is where she needs to be.

Skylar makes a bird feeder out of a plastic milk jug, a bunch of sticks and some blue paint. She brings it to Grandpa as a gift. Together they hang that bird feeder on a tiny tree in the backyard. The bird feeder lasts a long time, til one day it is blown away in a storm and we pick it up, crushed and ruined. I tell Skylar she can make another one. But it isn't the same, and she's not convinced. It's a life lesson, that things don't last forever, no matter how special they are.

Dad and I are very unhappy that we cannot go see Mom. They simply won't let anyone in. We have to be content with video calls, which we are not. I end up cutting Dad's hair and whiskers with my horse clippers because no barber shop is open and he's looking pretty gnarly.

Once he's home, he immediately starts complaining about his hip hurting. Aunt Patty goes home although she is very worried about the staph infection coming back. That we have to do the antibiotics consistently. I tell her not to worry, that we have this under control. And we do, of course. Taking care of Dad is my top priority at the moment. Skylar loves to spend time with Grandpa. They'll sit in his chair together - she's so tiny she can perch fully on the arm of the chair - and look at his phone together. She flits around the house eating powdered donuts and fruit snacks, playing on her train table which is purposefully located in the living room so she's close to Grandpa. They go outside on the porch a lot. Grandpa watches while she swings and plays in the playhouse. She has a little blue car she can drive, that she inherited from her cousin Matthew. She zips around in that, often putting Dusty (Aunt Patty's tiny dog) in the passenger seat. She is living her best life and is a pretty happy (but still dramatic) kid.

In the middle of May two bad things happen. Mom has another fall and has to go to the ER. Without me. Without me. I can't bear it. I can't think of her hurt and confusion. She doesn't know what COVID is. She just knows that I am not there. She is ok and goes back to LW without me by her side.

And then, my baby colt Bo dies from colic. After a terrible storm I find him in the morning, losing his fight already and I have no idea how long he's been lying there. We finally manage to get him up and into the hay barn, with lots of pain medication administered by my local vet. The vet shakes his head at me. It's too late he says, there is nothing we can do. He wouldn't make it into a trailer, much less the journey to a clinic. So we put him down. Right then, right there. And we bury him on our property. He was only eleven months old. My dreams of him are over. I am wrecked.

*Life right now is so uncertain, so unbearable and shitty. But bear it we must. There is no other choice. And I must be the one to be strong. For Skylar, for Dad, for Mom, for me. You've heard it before but I'm telling you right now that when the Devil told me I couldn't withstand the storm I almost believed him. I wanted to shake my fist at him and rage "you Mother **EFFER** - give me back my Mom! Give me back my life and my sanity and my confidence!" And then I realized. He's not the one.*

I have never in my life given up on anything. Not when things were as bad as I thought they could possibly get, not when I lost the first baby, not when I was told I would lose Skylar, too. I had faith I would get through it, I bore my parents' pain, especially Dad's when he cried for baby girl #2. I told him it was going to be OK - instead of him telling me. I laid my head in his lap, and I told him it was going to be OK. And it was. God saved Skylar - and he saved all of us, too.

Everyday I fight depression so hard it threatens to swallow me and Skylar up with it. I fight, I struggle and I lose a lot. Depression is no joke when you're right in the middle of it. The meme's and "words of wisdom" that implore you to "choose happiness" - that shit doesn't fly when you have severe depression. If I was in any way capable, I would certainly choose happiness. Wouldn't we all?

It's a Sunday night and I'm in the bath. Her bathtub, in her room – in the house she lived in for only a year. Still, it has her essence – her clothes I can see in the closet, her bathrobe hanging from the hook by the tub, her shampoos and conditioner to turn frizzy hair straight. I use the last of the bottle of bubble bath – her favorite scents, vanilla and patchouli fill the room. I breathe in. I try to relax; I try to calm my troubled heart and head. After I get out of the bath I go into her closet and try to imagine her there, choosing her own clothes, her own shoes. I try to remember when she'd be in the bathroom with her coffee putting her makeup on and getting dressed in the old house. When the doors were shut and she didn't want anyone to interrupt her, much less help her.

Don't think about the fact that she started to wear the same clothes day in and day out. That she stopped wearing pajamas. That she would put three or four shirts on one on top of the other. Don't agonize over when you had to pack up some of her clothes and had to throw away so many of her pants and underwear due to stains. She was so proud. She would not want you to remember that. She would be mortified if she knew you had noticed. Don't dwell on how you looked at the bras in the drawer and dismissed them. She wouldn't wear them anyway. You considered the socks and decided against – just another slip and fall waiting to happen. Bare feet or shoes are best. She was never a fan of socks anyway.

I look at all the things in her bedroom and bathroom. These were her things. The stuff she picked out for her own and enjoyed. The ornamental birds, the tiny doll bench at the end of her bed, the yellow rose antiques she inherited from her mother. I can't stand thinking that she will never see these things again. And if I took them to the place she's at – I can't call it her home – would she remember them? Would she look at them vaguely and say oh how nice! Or would she say oh! Yes, I remember this. I loved this.

When they call me through video conferencing, she is so happy to see me. But even so she can hardly figure out how to hold the phone so that I can see her face. A lot of times she puts her thumb over the picture, as if she is stroking it. As if she would stroke my hand if I were with her.

Because of COVID-19, I haven't seen Mom in person in over two months. I haven't held her hand or hugged her. She seems happy most of the time. A week or so ago she fell in her room and had to be sent out to the ER because she had split her lip and hit her head. I knew she would be terrified. The lovely ER nurse that answered the phone when I called told me "I know how hard this is for you. My story is different, but I have a story, too." The EMT's had made her aware that Mom has Alzheimer's. I didn't need to panic. She let me talk to Mom on the phone - twice. She got her a Coke to drink when I told her it was her favorite thing. She thanked me for telling her. She kept Mom close to her, and I am so grateful. It seems so rare to come across such kindness, but I believe that one thing COVID-19 has done is to make us ALL more grateful for the nurses and doctors taking care of our loved ones. They may not have the same story, but they know your story is so personal and important to you. This nurse didn't try to dismiss my feelings; she helped me process them. How many nurses do you know that have ever done that for you, in such a heartfelt, caring way? Her name was Gerri. I am exceedingly grateful that she was the one that was there, in that place, at that time.

Mom's cut is healing; she no longer has a vivid red mark across her upper lip. She has a friend, John, that she was sitting with today and having a "wonderful time." Those were her words. She could not tell me what she was actually doing, but the fact that she was enjoying herself was balm on my troubled soul. I miss her. They were having holiday cookies and just talking I was told by the Activities Director. The best caregiver I've known there, Seema, immediately took over taking care of Mom's precious cat when I was no longer *allowed in. I didn't have to ask or worry about it. People step up, you know. People go above and beyond their call of duty. God has sent angels to watch over Mom while I can't be there. Today was a dark day for me, for more reasons than Mom's situation. But at my lowest point, when my heart was weeping, that call came through and I was able to see Mom's smiling face. I can no longer tell her that I am upset, that I miss her, that I need her to comfort me. I don't want to cause her anxiety, so I don't tell her about my colt that died, I don't tell her that I often feel impotent as a parent. I don't spill my rage and hurt onto her shoulders anymore. I don't tell her that I never thought I'd have to raise my child alone, without her, and that it sucks.*

Nobody listens like your mom listens. So I think I will tell her. I'll go down past the pond and choose a paddock, choose a pony, and I'll vent and weep and rage. And I'll listen. I'll listen to what she would have said, when she was able. I'll feel her close by and I'll be comforted by her touch that whispers like pony whiskers on my arm. And in the horse's soft nicker and gentle nuzzle I'll know who is listening.

I'm pretty sure she'll be there.

Susan Wade Thomas

1

2

3

4

5

6

7

8

9

David Lee Thomas

10

11

12

13

14

15

16

17

18

19

David Lee and Susan Thomas

20

21

22

23

24

25

26

Thomas and Tullos Families

27

28

29

30

31

32

Photo descriptions are at the back of the book

CHAPTER SIXTEEN

COVID-19 Continues

Dad is depressed. He sits in his chair all day watching the Weather Channel or Westerns then starts drinking about 4 pm. Maybe sooner. Goes to bed each night by nine. Dad routinely has three large whiskeys and three plus beers. He is as skinny as a stick and takes a lot of medication. I honestly don't know how his body absorbs all that. He swears he uses a small glass that I have never seen. He sends me a picture of it. It doesn't look particularly small to me. I ask him to please try and cut back, not least because he's unsteady on his feet and I don't want him to fall at night when no one is there.

Dad is not smoking right now because of the leg surgery he had. The doctor has told him that smoking will undo all the good the surgery did. Dad is not convinced. It's been months and he's getting no relief from the cravings. When you've been smoking for sixty plus years one day without will feel like a hundred. There will be no relief, and he knows it. He gets angry easily, because he's unhappy and nicotine deprived. Not angry with me, or his Fu-Fu (what he calls Skylar), but just angry at the world, angry at his situation and Mom's.

Pretty soon the nights start coming when Dad is drunk and falls in the house. He will never admit that he was drunk. He always "tripped." Yeah, because you were drunk, I think to myself. He has a Life Alert cord he wears around his neck. My husband has to go over and help him get up. Life Alert will automatically call 911 and get the firemen there, so Dad usually tries to call us first. I suggest a service dog, but he nixes the idea. He doesn't want to take care of a dog. Dad tells me he's in pretty bad shape and wants to talk to me about it. I brush him off, telling him he's doing great, he's just depressed. I think that my heart and soul can't handle him telling me he's not doing well. I just can't face it. He's lonely as hell too and I know that doesn't help. I tell him I cry a lot, and I sleep to escape. He does the same thing. I tell him I want Mom just as much as he wants his wife. He says that when she was still here, he was so busy taking care of her that he didn't have time to feel bad. I try to convince him to get some counseling through the Veteran's Administration (VA) but he won't hear of it. He's very stubborn. He's absolutely convinced nothing can help. I suggest hypnosis but that never happens, either. I know at some point he will start smoking again, when he can't handle one more minute and can't distract himself, or it's too early to start drinking or go to bed.

Sometimes the facility tries to FaceTime me so I can talk to Mom, but they never give me any warning, and I'll miss them if I'm not looking directly at the phone. This makes me mad! Why can't they leave a message, try again? Why can't they send me a text - hey are you available? What's a good time? I guess it's a spur of the moment thing, they only think about it when they are with Mom. And I suppose they are doing their best but it's super disappointing to miss those calls.

COVID is keeping us from seeing Mom and it's killing me and Dad. I finally get to go see her on June 16th, but they say I can't give her a hug or touch her. If I do, they will ask me to leave! I want to tell them to go to hell but instead I just covertly hug her when they're not looking. I get an adorable picture of the three of us (Me, Mom, Skylar) and send it to Dad. It makes him happy, and he also gets to schedule a time to go see Mom.

At the end of June Mom is admitted to the hospital for a bladder infection and I make a huge stink because LW does not bother to tell me. In fact, they tell me she is in her room resting at nine am when I call to see how she is. The EMT's had called me the night before to tell me they were taking her to the ER but that was the last I heard until I called LW this morning. At four pm the hospital calls and tells me she was admitted. I'm sorry, what? I will go to the hospital first thing in the morning. I can't go in the evening because Tony is working, and I have to take care of Skylar. They would never let Skylar into the hospital with COVID going on.

A bubble of despair sits on my chest. It's heavy and it's making its presence known. If someone looks at me sideways - or doesn't - it's going to explode into rivulets of tears down my face. This bubble welled up out of nowhere; I've already had one explosion today. In my bedroom, dark and deep, where no one could hear or see it. But apparently my grief and fears want an audience because it's back, and larger than ever.

My husband sits down with me on the couch and just like that the bubble pops. Skylar doesn't know what to do when this happens, she wants to cuddle and pat my arm, but she is shooed into the playroom because "Mommy is sad." Mommy IS sad. It's the type of sad borne out of an inability to fix what's wrong. Mommy is used to fixing what is wrong.

What do you do when you no longer have control? How do you watch your loved one wither and morph into something you don't recognize, and which doesn't recognize you? I'm not sure, I tell my brother, that she knows exactly who we are, but she knows we are important to her. She knows she loves us. She knows she wants us there. She does not call me by my name.

She is in the hospital, and I am sitting by her watching her sleep. I have moved a chair so that I can finally hold her hand, after three months of not touching. I rub the soft spot between her thumb and forefinger. The corners of her mouth are turned down and there are tears at the edges of her eyelids. Her chin is a mess of black and blue from where she fell. There is some dried blood around her mouth. I notice long hairs on her chin and upper lip that I know she would be mortified by if she knew they were there. I am struck by an urge to pluck them for her, but obviously I do not. She has gained weight, and her arm is a bit swollen from putting the IV in. She wakes up and looks at me briefly. She is calm and for that I am grateful.

Mom has been in the ER and then in a hospital room since Wednesday night at 11 pm. It is now Friday at 8 am. I talked to the EMT that transported her to the hospital and was assured the hospital had all my information and would call me. I heard nothing further all night long. When I called the facility where she lives at 9 am Thursday morning, I am assured she's in her room, resting. I am relieved and go on

170

with my day. Thursday afternoon at 4 pm a phone call tells me she has been admitted to the hospital. From .... where? I ask. From her room? What is going on? No, she was never brought back to the facility. She was in the ER until 1 or 2 pm today when they finally admitted her.

She was in the emergency room ALL ALONE FOR SIXTEEN HOURS?! Horrified, I immediately called the ER she was taken to and the person that answered was actually Mom's nurse. What on earth? I ask. Why did no one call me? I had no idea she was there by herself! The ER nurse said that they did not have any phone numbers. And you couldn't call the facility and get my number? "No," he said. "I didn't bother to do that."

Y'all. Have you ever felt so enraged that you could jump down that phone line and rip someone's F&#$&%# balls off? Not to mention that Mom has been at this hospital before and I am absolutely **certain** that there are phone numbers, somewhere, for one of us at least.

You didn't bother? I slowly state, just to clarify what he said. "No," he said coldly, and "I can see this conversation isn't going anywhere so can I just transfer you to the third floor where she is now?"

I get that he was probably pretty busy but seriously WTF. She has Alzheimer's - I am sure the EMT told them she has advanced dementia. She was all alone in a place she did not recognize, could not speak for herself, and did not have anyone to advocate for her. She must have been absolutely terrified. That nurse took advantage of the situation and knew that Mom could not understand and could not speak for herself, and he decided she would not remember and therefore was not AN ACTUAL PERSON who needed a family member. To top it all off, I also found out that one visitor per person is actually now allowed at that hospital so I could have *been there with Mom the entire time. Actually, physically present.*

I. Can't. Even.

I called my brother. He promised me that he would "do what he does." Heads will roll and if that nurse isn't fired I will be surprised (and pissed off.) I am usually all about forgiveness, and making mistakes and people being people and screwing up. Not this time. In no way does that nurse NOT deserve to be fired. He clearly did not care about his patient. Her emotional needs were not considered. He did not care when he was speaking to me, he simply wanted to pass me along and get me off his back. I simply can't believe this is the same hospital as last time, when the nurse Gerri lovingly took care of her for so many hours. But all people are different I suppose, and that goes for nurses too.

There are so many things that are wrong here. Mom is finally back in her room, with her cat, whom she does know is named Margaret. I believe she is probably doing as well as she can be. She was not actually injured from either her fall, or her prolonged stay in the emergency room. She doesn't actually know what happened - she insisted that she "didn't do it." Whatever it was in her mind - she was sure she wasn't at fault. I can hear her, in my mind, and I know she was scared.

There is so much more I could say about being with her in the hospital, and how she was, and what my thoughts were. About how we finagled the system and got Dad to meet us in the lobby so he could see her and hold her hand for five minutes before I took her "home." I have so much to say. There is so much that I feel. But grief is the top emotion, and grief is what causes the bubble of despair. I am supposed to be Mom's advocate. I was denied the opportunity to be there for her, and I am filled with anger.

So today I am a mushroom - hiding in the dark and hopefully gaining a little strength by being alone so that next time, next time, I can be there for her in all the ways that matter. I am her advocate. I am her daughter. She is not alone, no matter what that ER nurse thought. She has people. SHE HAS ME.

The next morning after I see Mom, I make a plan for Dad to be able to see her, too. Who knows when we will have another chance. I ask for, and receive, permission to take Mom back to LW myself. I have Angie bring Dad to the hospital when she is discharged so that he can be with her for a little while. I take a really cute picture of them together holding hands in the hospital lobby. It's the first time he has seen her in LW alone, without me. She doesn't understand. She has no idea what COVID is. I hand her over to an aide and walk outside, tears streaming down my face.

Dad's hip pain is getting worse and worse. It makes a terrible clicking noise now when he walks. It's bone grinding on bone and it sounds just awful. He finally makes an appointment to have a screening done for a possible hip replacement.

In July, Skylar, Tony and I head out to visit Skylar's godparents in Nevada. Skylar hasn't ever officially met them since the last time they saw her she was an infant getting baptized. We are not letting COVID stop us even though we have to wear masks on the plane. It was crazy that Tony and I had to keep masks on unless we were eating and Skylar, being only six, did not. I have since learned that the strain of COVID that was making everyone sick was airborne and was spread most easily by people talking, not coughing or sneezing (Malcolm Gladwell's book The Revenge of the Tipping Point). So even just Tony and I talking to each other would spread the virus if we had it, unless everyone else was at least six feet away. Which I think, on any normal plane, the seats in front of and behind you are not actually six feet away. Maybe they should rethink how they squash people in like sardines... anyway I am rambling away from the point.

Of course, the day we leave Dad ends up spending several hours in the ER for high blood pressure, which was over 200! He went in to see Cassie (our Nurse Practitioner) and she gave him a pill which didn't work so he had to go to the ER as his blood pressure was at stroke level. They did an EKG and blood work and gave him another pill. It finally went down enough for him to go home. Being a thousand miles away and I couldn't be there for him really hit hard. I was so glad he had Angie, I can't imagine how he would have coped if he had to endure all that alone.

Angie took Dad to see Mom, where he had to stay behind a window, but at least they could see each other. COVID is a nightmare when your mom has dementia and doesn't understand anything. It must be so confusing for her. Why can't her husband touch her? But bless her heart, she doesn't know to ask any questions or to get upset. She just accepts it for what it is. She is so glad to see Dad she smiles non stop.

The next day Dad has to go to the hospital again; this time he goes to a heart hospital and gets two new drugs and a new doctor. The blood pressure thing is scaring me, especially as I am in Nevada and not at home to help. Dad is anxious for me to be home, although he's happy we're having a good time and getting a vacation. I know he's lonely without us there. We plan to go over on Saturday and Sunday evenings to cook dinner for him. The reception in the mountains in Nevada is terrible; we can text, but the phone calls won't go through. I let him know when we've made it home to Dallas and he's much happier that we're back in Texas. Skylar had a blast in Nevada, as her Godparents have their own swimming pool and she was introduced to the world of Playmobil. We also got to see the Las Vegas strip, albeit in the daytime, in the heat.

Mom's birthday is coming up. We order a gorgeous flower arrangement for her, to be delivered to LW. Dad goes to visit for her birthday and takes a card, cupcakes and a fountain drink. Mom is very happy to see him but has no idea what to do with the drink. She is thrilled to be made a fuss of though and everyone at LW tells her how beautiful the flowers are!

Dad ends up in the ER again for his blood pressure and he is not happy about it. They do a cat scan and give him more drugs. Dad buys a new, more reliable blood pressure cuff so he can monitor it better at home. Finally sees a cardiologist who tells him that the Meloxicam he was taking for pain caused the whole problem and even though he had stopped taking it, it took a while to get out of his system. Secretly I think the drinking probably isn't helping either.

I have been struggling hard lately with the situation with Mom. The question is - am I being spared or am I being

robbed? Spared from watching her sink even further into decline, should I be grateful I don't have to watch it or experience it every day? I don't have to brush her teeth or clean her up. Should I simply be happy when I do get to see her? One thing I know is that she is not being spared. She is living this terrible reality every day, and she doesn't even have me or Dad there for comfort. And when I think of it like that, I feel robbed. Because she's being robbed of our company, our comfort. She's being robbed in her final months, maybe a year or two of spending all her last moments with her family. If I had known Coronavirus was coming, I would have thought twice about putting her in memory care. I would have hired a full-time caregiver and kept her at home. So now I'm angry. I'm angry all the time.

I am not allowed to go into her facility but if she goes to the ER I can come in and hold her hand and hug her and nobody says I can't. So even though she fell again on Friday, I am grateful for those few moments I had with her physically. She saw me come in - she raised her head and reached for me before I even said a word. I'm here Mom, I'm here. I smooth her shirt, I tuck her hand into mine. I look into her eyes. We are both wearing masks, but she yanks her off and I see her face - where her cheek is swollen to three times its normal size. Will she need surgery? Mom has never had surgery in her entire life.

I lay my head on her chest (facing away) and she tries so hard to talk to me. "I'm glad you're here," she says. And it was enough. But now, in my house and with some perspective I am worrying about how much pain she must be in. For her, it wasn't enough. For her, she doesn't know where I went or when she will see me again. She only knows what is right in front of her. I hope and pray they are giving her pain medicine every six hours. It's the weekend so I can't really check on her. None of the regular personnel are there. I will go in the morning. I will go even though they won't let me in. I'll make someone talk to me. Tell me how she is. Do all the memory care residents have someone to advocate for them? I hope they do. I've given the Director of Nursing this idea of having family members send in pictures and then they could be displayed on a screen, and they could all see and talk about each other's families. I think it would be so good for them. Many of those residents no longer have cell phones. Mom can't just go check Facebook or get a text from me. She has no outside contact if I can't get in there. She doesn't know if Skylar had a birthday party or rode a new pony. She doesn't know how much Dad and I miss her.

This morning I woke up in a very bad, very angry mood. I should have known right then to just go back to bed. But there are too many responsibilities, you know. Horses to be fed and lessons to teach and Dad to think of, not to mention Skylar's needs. I know I let her down a lot. I will wish one day that I had all this time back.

And then I couldn't hold it in anymore. I started to cry and in trying to explain to my husband exactly what was wrong I finally said it was like I just keep stepping backwards off a ledge and Mom is no longer there to catch me.

And there it is. It's grief. Grief is my problem. Every day I step off that ledge. Every day I fall. I cannot seem to stop myself from stepping off. I can't get a "new" grip on reality. Reality was Mom always being there. Always being my rock, my shield, my wingman and my back up singer. There was never a day in my life that I didn't know she loved me, and while I know this is still true, I can't just call her anymore. She can't give me advice or offer to take me shopping or to lunch. She can't say hey I will come visit this weekend to help out because you need a break. I can no longer go to their house in Tyler just to escape when things get tough. She is still here but she is not here for me.

This evening when we went to Dad's house to have dinner (which I cooked - damn I miss Mom cooking for all of us) I decided to take a bath in her bathtub. When I surround myself with her things her spirit comes to me, and I can pretend that we are back in Tyler. That she is reading her book and that Dad and Tony are waiting for me to get out of the bath to play dominoes. That tomorrow morning we will make French toast for breakfast and then we will go shopping. That in this space, in this moment, she is here. She is here.

I ask God to let me dream about her, the way she used to be. But it doesn't happen. Any dreams I have with her in them are always sad and frantic and anxiety ridden dreams full of grief. Grief that I have no idea how to process. How long will it go on? Will life ever be livable for me again? Will I allow myself to be happy? Will Dad?

"

How do I go forward when all I want to do is go back?

"

I step back, I stumble and I fall. Mom, please be there, please pick me up again. How do I go on living without you? How do I go forward when all I want to do is go back? No matter how strong I am, how strong everyone thinks I am - I am nothing without her. I am Grief. And that's all I can be for a while.

CHAPTER SEVENTEEN

A New Start

August - October 2020

I have been really struggling with my right foot lately. I know I have plantar fasciitis plus a weird little lump on the top of my foot. There is also a permanent swelling on the inside of my ankle. I have been seeing Dad's foot doctor, Dr. Jacoby, and she wants to try a cast for four weeks to see if everything will heal on its own. She knows a boot won't cut it, I will not wear it consistently enough and I will walk too much. With a cast, my foot is trapped and can't move! I agree to try it. It is very hard to walk as much as I do, ride, and teach lessons when you are in such serious pain with your foot.

On the other hand, Skylar, my friend Kathy and I are supposed to be leaving for a brief beach trip, which I had promised Skylar we would do. The doctor and I agree to wait until after the trip to put the cast on. We are headed to Gulf Port, Mississippi. It takes about nine hours to get there, and we manage to do it all in one day, with a just turned six-year-old! I'm impressed with myself, but my foot is on fire by the time we arrive. It is, of course, my right foot, and I'm the one driving.

While we are gone Dad has to get some teeth pulled and he is very worried about it. I don't know how these things always happen when I am not there! He is preparing for the hip replacement surgery he'll be having soon. Every night he texts me that he is very tired, in serious pain and going to bed. I feel so bad for him. He tells me "I can't believe that after all these years of very "manly" things - tractors, cotton pickers, ploughing, helicopters that I'm in such bad shape." I tell him that all that is probably what caused the problems he's having now. I find it interesting he didn't mention the army, well except for the helicopters.

We have a good time on our little vacation and Skylar is enchanted by the ocean. There are no large waves there so it's relaxing and laid back, and Skylar can play to her heart's content in the water. We hunt seashells and walk up and down the beach. We are staying in a cute little house, but the train track is directly in the front yard! Really close. We are able to walk a couple of blocks to the beach. We also visit a train museum and shop endlessly for souvenirs. Once we're back, I spend some time with Dad, ordering gifts for my brother's kids, who have birthdays coming up. We plan to celebrate at the house with Dad, my brother and me and all the kids. Dad tells me he really appreciates all my help, and I tell him "I love shopping! Especially with other people's money!" Ha! And I like wrapping gifts and organizing birthday parties, too.

A few days later Angie's father is close to passing away and she has to travel to be with her family. Dad is distraught that she is gone even though he understands she had to go. Her father manages to hang on for now and Angie returns after a few days.

"

To lose her without her actually going anywhere - it's terribly unjust.

"

Depression has crept up on me. Through the years I know I've suffered from that word. But in the last two years it's crawled his way in and just won't depart. If I can pinpoint it, it must be when I learned Mom has Alzheimer's. It all goes back to that. To watch her falter, then flail, then just wither is more than anyone should have to bear.

In these COVID times, with the facility she is at, I have not been able to see her or spend any time with her. She is more distant from me than she has ever been. I have no idea of her day-to-day-ness. Nobody tells me anything about how she is doing, if she's eating, if she's sleeping, if she tries to talk about us. I hear Nothing and Nothing has angered me.

A week from Monday I am moving her to another facility. A much smaller place with only twelve residents total. It's like a home, where everyone is together much of the time. Where the residents can go sit outside on the front porch as much as they want. Where the director will get her a cheeseburger from McDonald's if she desires one. Where there is plenty of nature - birds, horses, trees and flowers. A gazebo just outside her window. I've ordered the cat a cat tree to put beside the window.

There is no locked door to keep people out... or in. Only the front door to be locked at night as you would anywhere you live. Her bedroom is across from the kitchen - where the residents and caretakers gather to help cook if they like. The meals are all freshly made and made to order. There is only

181

one floor and very little space for her to trip and fall. There are games days and activities for all - families invited. Now, of course there are still COVID restrictions. But the truth is I can go and see her anytime I like, I can take Skylar. Dad can go every day if he wants to. She'll only be twenty minutes away.

I am worried, of course, that the move will be hard on her. She's been where she's at for nine months. She's gotten used to it. But I haven't. I need her close to me. I need to see her and be with her. And of course, how would I know if she's happy? Certainly, nobody is telling me she's not. Why would they? When they try to FaceTime so that we can see each other more often than not I can't even hear her, and she can't hear me, due to all the background noise. They give her the phone to give her some "privacy" while she talks to me, but she can't even hold the phone so that I can see her face! It aggravates me so much I stop bothering.

I'm looking forward to the move. I believe it's the best possible outcome for all of us. Skylar asks me all the time when is Granny Susan coming home? It's the hardest thing in the world to tell her she's not. At least now she'll be able to see her weekly!

And maybe my old companion Depression will let up a little. Maybe he'll go on a vacation. If I can feel like Mom is truly settled and happy then maybe, just maybe, I can be happy too.

Dad's surgery gets postponed because he tripped on the rug and fell, scraping his elbow. Dad is distraught and depressed. I am not very kind (which I later regret) and tell him he was slurring his words when I talked to him, so I know he was drunk and that's why he tripped and scraped his elbow. The surgical center people won't do the surgery because of his history with staph infection - he'll have to wait until the scrape is healed and new skin grows over. He says he'll be more careful with the whiskey but when I say it needs to be no whiskey at all he doesn't respond. He just says he is hurting and going to bed. Goodnight I tell him, I love you.

At the beginning of September Angie's father dies. She has to leave to be with her family. Dad's days are long and lonely though I try to be with him as much as possible. We are making plans to move Mom and making arrangements for my brother to come. He will stay with Dad so that makes Dad happy.

We lease an ancient white pony for Skylar to ride. Her name is Lily, and she is the sweetest little thing. I am happy Skylar finally has something that she can really learn on.

I plan to go make Dad pancakes (one of his favorite things) for supper on Friday evening. I have been pretty sick, but I think it is allergies and not anything worse. Dad tells me he has been throwing up in the mornings. I ask him if it's gotten any better and he says a little bit. I tell him he needs to go see Cassie, our local NP. Why is he throwing up? He's not sick with a virus or anything that we can see. It worries me, but we both have so much else to worry about we don't think too much of it. We probably should have.

In all my life I never had a need to learn to cook. Mom was a great cook, and she loved to do it. She made fabulous meals for every get together and always made too much. Thanksgiving, Christmas, Easter - it was always at her house, and she was the host. Cheese balls, dips, chips, veggies, fruit salad, it was all there ready to snack on before the main meal even began. She used to make this absolutely phenomenal Brandy Dip for fruit that I simply couldn't get enough of. She modeled it after the stuff you get at La Madeleine with the strawberries, which probably doesn't have actual brandy in it, like Mom's did.

We used to make fudge at Christmas. All kinds of fudge. We passed it out as gifts. maple walnut, regular chocolate, mint chocolate, peanut butter, I can't even remember all the types we tried. She taught me to make it so that I can do it in my sleep and that's a tradition I will always have in my heart. We laughed so hard when one time she forgot to put the sugar in... she was stirring and stirring and getting all sorts of irritated - why isn't this turning? she fumed. I looked over - well Mom it sure doesn't look right, did you put everything in? And that's when we discovered no sugar! We simply laughed, threw it away and started over. Mom and I loved to go to Hobby Lobby to buy all those little containers to put the fudge in. We loved Hobby Lobby, period. In fact, on the very last outing I took her on - in February - we went to Hobby Lobby. I pushed her around in her wheelchair and she had a great time just looking and looking.

When Mom discovered how much I love almond extract she made an entire recipe up just for me. She took lemon cookies and turned them into almond cookies. They even had almond frosting on them. They made the largest batch   of cookies you've ever seen - like forty-eight cookies or something insane - so it would have been sweet of me to share them with everyone.... but I didn't. Her chocolate pie was to die for. I used to request that, along with twice-baked potatoes every time I came home to visit. And Dad would make chicken on the Big Grill just for me, even though everyone else wanted steak.

Mom had this way of cooking that was so like Julia Child - just flinging flour and shit everywhere and not caring one jot about cleaning anything up until later. I don't know if I was amused or horrified but I definitely have a habit of cleaning up as I go now. She would have large flour handprints on her black pants that she almost always wore - I think she had about twelve pairs of black cotton capris. She didn't care about the flour - she'd just shrug and smile and keep going. She had a wonderful habit of cussing as she cooked. You'd hear her muttering "shit!" and "fuck!" as she fiddled with something over the stove or as she tried to maneuver something into the oven. Her fridge was a haven of things long forgotten about. "Mom! What's in the sour cream container in the back here?! Is it actually sour cream?" Hell, I don't know! She'd reply. We cleaned out her cupboards once not too long ago and found canned goods from the eighties -- no lie.

Mom is short - so she had her library stool that she kicked around the kitchen in order to reach things. I have that stool in my kitchen today. It was a bittersweet moment when I took that from her house and put it in mine. I remember she used to have this yellow plastic tea pitcher that she'd toss some Lipton tea in - without measuring - and then stand at the sink sighing while the water ran full blast into the pitcher. It was such a "moment" for her. I wish I still had that pitcher.

Mom made me anything I wanted - even as a kid. French toast was my favorite breakfast, and I'd stand watching her flatten it into oblivion with the spatula. Why do you do that

185

Mom? I asked one day. I don't know, she shrugged - I've always done it. So now, of course, I flatten my French toast with the spatula. Maybe it makes it taste more like bacon grease, I really don't know but I still do it. And I think of Mom every time.

There are so many memories of Mom in her kitchen. In Harker Heights - where I lived as a kid - the eating area was in the kitchen, and she used to sit at that table and smoke and read way into the evening. That's where I'd find her if I needed to talk to her about something. That's where the wall phone with the long cord was, where the kitschy trash can she found at Canton First Monday Trade Days was, and the wire mesh basket that hung from the ceiling that held the potatoes. That wire mesh basket used to hang in the kitchen in Tyler, too, and finally made its way to my own kitchen. I also have the seventies spice rack that is dark brown with faded and peeling pictures of all the spices on the front. I actually use it, too.

There are some things you just can't let go of. In my mind Mom will always be in her kitchen. And I'll always be there with her, talking and laughing and eating and smiling and living and loving her.

In the meantime, I am completely fed up with LW and I can't wait to move Mom to the new place, which is a very small "home" named "Just Like Home" in Whitesboro which is about twenty minutes north of my house. The people there are lovely and it's very small, so Mom won't have to walk very far to get anywhere. Again, she will have a private room and bathroom. I feel in my heart that this will be a much better situation than LW. They even agree to let the cat move with her! We set a date of Monday, September 21st. However, things get really heated up at LW between me and management and I move up the date to September 14th. The facility absolutely would not let me in, until I finally just barged my way in and said "I am going to go get my mother. We are leaving." I told them they could call the cops if they wanted, but my husband is a cop and I don't think it would get them anywhere. They said nothing. Just looked on as we moved Mom and all her things out.

My brother has driven up from Austin and between him, Tony and myself, we get Mom out of there. Mom wasn't in her room. When I walked into the dining room of LW, she was just sitting in her wheelchair doing nothing and with no attention. I quietly said, "Mom, Mom I'm here." She looked up, stretched her arms out wide and whispered, "Where have you been?!" I cried then. I will never forget that moment for the rest of my life. She wasn't angry or sad, just so happy that I was finally there. I, on the other hand, have never felt such guilt in my life even though I know it wasn't my fault.

We go back to her room as I explain what is going to happen. Mom, we are moving you to a new place. A place where I will be allowed to come see you whenever I want. A place you will be better cared for. A place where Dad can come and sit with you. I promise it will be so much better. She is ecstatic to see my brother and while she doesn't fully understand what we are doing, she couldn't be happier to be surrounded by her family. She watches as we pack up her things. We have her cat, Margaret, in a cage by her feet. Every once in a while, the cat meows and Mom looks for her. "Where are you sweetie? Are you ok?" Mom, she's here, right by your feet – see? In this cage. She is going with us, don't worry. Mom looks down and acknowledges the cat but soon the information is lost again.

The place Mom is going to does not have a locked door. There are only twelve residents who can come and go as they please. It is in the country with thirteen acres and horses across the street. There is a huge, covered driveway with rockers and chairs. The residents love to come outside but they don't go far. Everyone watches out for each other. Some of the residents do not have memory problems but everyone there is treated just the same. No one is behind a locked door meant to keep them in and everyone else out.

Mom and I drive to the new facility, singing songs along the way. It astounds me that she cannot hold a conversation, but she can remember the words to, and sing, any song that she knows. She is having a great time, and I'm just happy to be with her again. We purposely stop at Whataburger where Dad with his caregiver is – we say hello across the car windows. I'm not entirely sure Mom realizes it's Dad – she's pretty intent on eating her hamburger one piece at a time. She takes it all apart and eats each piece by itself. She makes a huge mess, just like a toddler would. I have to remind her to take a drink of her Coke. She no longer runs her tongue across her teeth to clean them while she's eating – an action we all do without thinking about. I find it difficult to be with her while she's eating because all the things she can no longer do are exemplified. I try to avoid mealtimes. I don't want to be hit in the face with her inadequacies.

The room at her new place is so much smaller that we have to leave some of her furniture on the trailer. It doesn't matter though. Even though the room is small I am sure the care will be better. The dining and multi-use room is only a few steps away. You can always find a caregiver – at the old place I would wander the halls looking for someone and never find anyone. The men are busy trying to put together a dresser. So I take Mom with me when it's time to go pick up Skylar from school. She's been in the car a lot today, but you can tell she doesn't mind – she's just happy to be with me.

When we get back to the room my brother has to leave. Skylar and I take Mom into her room so she can finally see it. She seems pleased with it. She plays with Skylar who is hiding behind the shower curtain. Mom laughs when she jumps out and says Boo! The time has come to leave Mom there, but I feel reassured that the staff will care lovingly for her. Her room is nice – cozy with all the pictures of family and roses that she loves. I notice that all her expensive toiletries are missing. I didn't buy this Suave shampoo. I would never buy that. Mom uses John Frieda! I am appalled as I realize that her shampoos and lotions and soaps have been taken – stolen – by someone at the old facility. Chances are it never made it up to her room from when I had to drop it all off at the front desk in enticing Target bags. I am burning with rage but there's nothing I can do. I'll buy it all again so Mom will have HER stuff that she's always used and loved.

That night I sleep better than I have in a long time. Mom is closer to me, and in good hands, and I'll be able to see her again soon. She won't think that she has been forgotten and abandoned. She will know that I am still here, still loving her, still her champion and her advocate. She will never again have to say, "where have you been?"

I am here, Mom, right here with you. Always.

The day after we move Mom, I go to Just Like Home to see how she's getting along, and she is settled in a rocking chair on the front porch just smiling big! She is so happy, which makes my heart feel so glad and joyful. I try to keep her smile in my mind all day, I just know we made the right move. Mom now gets to enjoy a lot of time outside on the porch and she is just glowing with the change - she is so happy now. She always loved sitting outside on the porch with Dad and watching the birds and wild animals. She was a big one for gardening in her day (flowers not vegetables) and I'm thrilled she can get just a tiny bit of this back. One day the facility asks me if I'd like to plant some flowers in the pots they have on the porch. So I wheel Mom right beside me, I dig the holes, and I have her put the flowers in and cover them up. She is delighted.

Less than a week in, the cat is causing issues and can't stay at the facility. They love her, but she is terrified, throwing up everywhere, and wanders into the kitchen, where she absolutely is not allowed to be. I end up taking her to Dad's house, where she is content with a lot less people and more room to roam. Mom never notices that the cat has gone.

When Dad gets to go see Mom, she is delighted that he is there. She doesn't call him by his name, but she says "I love you" about ten times. Dad and I ponder, does she know him? Seems likely. Does she remember his name? We are not sure. Dad is hurting and discouraged. I try to keep his spirits up by teasing him with "how many more sleeps" he has until his surgery.

This is a trick I use with Skylar when she's looking forward to something. Dad doesn't seem amused.

The hip surgery finally happens and is successful. Of course the surgery itself causes pain, but with time that should fade and he should be much better off than he was before. However, he can't smoke and can't drink and that makes him extremely grumpy. We talk about the logistics of Aunt Patty leaving. She needs to go home for a couple of days but wants to come back - I don't want her to have to make unnecessary trips so I tell her I will stay with Dad a few days though I have to leave for the weekend again, for another horse show.

Dad has physical therapy at home, and he is struggling but I know he's doing his best. He wants to get more mobile so he can drive himself places - to see Mom, grocery store, liquor store. Right now he can't get in and out of his truck.

Now that I can go see Mom whenever I want, I FaceTime Dad so he can see her, too. Of course he does go up to see her in person, but I am very happy that we can do both so easily. Mom is reveling in all the attention. She loves the new place and is always smiling. We sit out on the front porch a lot, under the eaves and just enjoy being outside. She went outside (with me) maybe three-four times the entire nine months she was at LW! They *never* took the residents outside or even opened the doors onto the patio. Fresh air can do wonders for the soul and Mom is breathing it all in. One day an ice cream truck comes, and all the residents get ice cream. Mom is still using a walker some of the time, and an aide lovingly walks her out to the truck to pick her ice cream out, then sends me a picture of Mom holding it up triumphantly. It's so sweet.

Dad tries to be patient, but he wants me and/or Skylar and/or Tony to come be at his house all the time, when Angie isn't there. I totally understand but it's super hard to juggle his need for companionship with Mom's needs and Skylar's needs and the horses, too! I still have to teach lessons and go to shows and make money. I feel so torn all the time and guilty as hell that I can't do everything and be everywhere all the time.

CHAPTER EIGHTEEN

Just Keep Loving Her

November 2020 - January 2021

Dad likes to text me mid-morning if I haven't texted him yet. Here I am! Still alive! I joke that I didn't hear from the EMT's last night so I figured he was ok. He laughs and says, yes, they know me! (And in fact they do. A couple years later I run into a few of them in a gas station and they ask after him).

We talk about me spending a night at his house once a week or so, just so that I can get a break and actually sleep. Both of us know that Skylar won't allow this but it's a nice thought. If I can make it happen I will. I have my own bed at Dad's house - I might as well put it to some use!

Finally, Dad is ready to start driving again. He practices getting in the truck only to find that it won't start as it hasn't been used in so long. We call on Tony to come jump it and get it going again. Dad is very happy to tool around town in his truck, just being out on his own again. He drove down to Whataburger and was very pleased with himself.

We (Skylar and me) are looking for a pony of her own to buy. We find one in Ardmore, Oklahoma named JPH Bruno Mars. He is a small Welsh pony, only three years old. But he is super cute, and Skylar does well on him. We will take it slow, put the pony in training and start off on the lunge line. A few days later I pick the pony up and drive him to the school where I pick up Skylar as well. Everyone is excited to see a pony in the pick-up line! Skylar is bursting with pride!

A few nights later Dad falls again - trips on his walker - and the EMT's call me. They say he is bleeding, but Dad insists he's fine. I ask how many drinks and he said just one. I wonder to myself how big that "one" was. It hurts my heart to know how much pain he's in and that's why he drinks so much. At least he's not a violent or mean drunk. Just gets tired and goofy. When he was younger and drinking with my uncles, they used to pull stunts like putting a toilet out in my Grandma Margie's (Dad's mom) front yard which just horrified her and made the rest of us laugh like crazy!

We find out from the x-ray later that he cracked a rib when he fell. Which I feel like must be incredibly painful and I am hoping he doesn't drink too much on top of the pain pills that they gave him. Aunt Patty is on my case about convincing Dad to "stick to beer." I tell her that if I could've done that I would have done it already! We know she's just worried about him, too, but I can't control how much or what he drinks.

The next week is Thanksgiving and my brother and his "troops" are coming.

I take my horse clippers up to see Mom and try to do something with her hair. They don't have a salon at the facility and no way to take her anywhere. Eventually (after COVID is mostly over) I get my own hairdresser, Darla, to come up every couple of months to do Mom's hair. This time, though, when I get there, Mom had been crying for some reason. I don't know why. She was happy to see me though and I trimmed the sides of her hair up and all the curls in the back. And I clipped her chin hairs! Her teeth frustrate the hell outta me. They wouldn't be so broken if she hadn't fallen so much. And I can't take her to a dentist. The one time I tried (back when she was at LW) they told me they couldn't do anything because of her condition and Mom announced that she "had to poop" when we were waiting for the dentist. She didn't, of course, it was just something to say. Still pretty mortifying though! I think that they just weren't willing to help because of her condition. But maybe they were right, and it would have been too stressful for her because she wouldn't have understood what was happening.

Strangely, we have a tornado warning the weekend after Thanksgiving! In Texas! In November! Crazy. One of my horses starts colicing the next day - horses can't handle barometric pressure changes very easily. The shift in weather will cause them to get upset stomachs. And horses can't throw up so it's a very dangerous situation when it happens. So much going on and I just can't seem to get a break. I thank my lucky stars we found Just Like Home because I don't have to worry about Mom so much, I know they are taking the best care of her.

I end up having to take the horse to the vet hospital and leave him there for them to sort out. Skylar wants me to take her to see Granny Susan so we drop the horse off then head out to Whitesboro. Mom is overjoyed to see us as always. We spend a few hours with her and take a bunch of pictures next to the Christmas tree they have up. One of our favorite things to do is to take walks down the country road with me and/or Skylar pushing Mom's wheelchair - we like to visit the cows and horses and just see the nature that she missed out on before. We can't do that today, though, as it is too cold for Mom. Instead we hang out inside the building for a while, taking pics and reading stories. Skylar brings her coloring pad and markers and tries to share with Mom. Mom takes a marker and a sheet of paper but frowns and looks over at Skylar's paper. She doesn't know what to do with it. Interestingly, she is still holding the marker correctly. But she can't make it do anything.

I always tried to get Dad to stop by my house and hang out but he never would do it. I think he was afraid of bothering us. He is very proud of himself that he can now drive to Brookshires, get out of the truck, get a buggy, shop and pay and then get back in the truck. Compared to this time last year, this is tremendous improvement! It makes me happy when he can do things for himself as he so obviously wants to be self-sufficient.

I make Mom's fudge every Christmas time - it makes me feel super close to her. I make some for Dad and some for the staff at Just Like Home. They love it! I love bringing them things to show how much I appreciate all they do for Mom. I have a lot of fun shopping for gifts for them all for Christmas. I wish Mom could shop with me, but that's no longer a possibility.

Tina, Mom's favorite worker there, calls Dad and tells him she's having a rough day. She tells him to bring her some beer! I laugh, they really know how to make Mom feel better! I told him to bring a 24-pack and let them all share! Dad does take a 6-pack up there, they put some in the mini fridge Mom has in her room, so she'll have some when needed. I don't blame them, alcohol makes me feel more relaxed, so why wouldn't it work for Mom? I don't know what all medications she is on but hell, if she enjoys it still then why not? Mom of course is very happy to see Dad and very happy about the beer! She'll never remember that it's in the little fridge, but I know that Tina will see to it that she gets some, sometimes.

Two weeks ago, Mom's hospice worker called me. "Julie. Your mom can't hold her head up. She isn't talking." I'm on my way, I tell her. I'll be there in twenty minutes.

Mom did not have a stroke, which is what we all thought at first. When I got there, she was in a wheelchair with her head propped up by pillows. She was doing a strange jerking motion with her whole body and didn't seem to realize I was there. Her eyes kept closing.

We finally all decided that she was just very, very sick with chest congestion and so that made her very weak. The doctor was called, and he prescribed antibiotics and a steroid. Within a few days Mom was back to her regular self. The jerking stopped with the removal of a certain "calming" medicine she had been on. Such a relief!

But in the midst of the medication changes something else has happened... Mom has become more aware again. I feel like she was possibly being over medicated at the previous place. In many months she had not said she "wanted to go home" or that she "wanted her husband." She had not been combative very often. She was recognizing Dad and me, but it was fairly understated most of the time. Occasionally she seemed to not realize who I was.

But since Mom recovered from her illness and the "calming" medication was removed (replaced? I am not sure) Mom has been **much** more aware. The other night about 7:45 pm they called me because Mom was feeling worried and anxious. She actually talked to me. She said she just wanted to talk to me because she was a little scared. I told her I missed talking to her at night and I especially missed playing Words with Friends with her. Do you remember playing that game Mom? Yes! She said. I miss it too. I was stunned. We talked a bit more and then she went back to bed. I guess she had been up wandering around when she was usually asleep. She didn't communicate perfectly but it was so much better than it has been - I just couldn't believe it. I even texted her caregivers and asked if I was crazy for seeing such a remarkable change!

Today Mom was combative with her favorite caregivers, Tina and Nikki, and didn't want to get out of bed or take her pills. This has happened more often in the last two weeks than it had in the preceding nine months. When I arrived, they told her they had a big surprise for her. She had been crying all morning. She comes around the corner and sees me and her face just completely broke down. She grabbed me and hugged me and just cried. My heart shattered in that moment. "I'm here Mom. Everything is ok. I promise." But that perfect recognition, while extremely painful to watch, is a glimmer of the Mom I knew "before." And so I'll take it. I sat with her for a while and then we went out to get a Sonic drink. We drove mostly in silence, just holding hands. Mom starts to eat her hamburger but soon forgets about it and it *falls to the floor. I give her one of Baby Girl's small stuffed ponies to hold. She rubs its fur for a bit then tries to eat its tail. If that doesn't show you how an Alzheimer's patient regresses to toddlerhood, I don't know what would. I gently take it from her and say, "can't eat the pony, Mom."*

As I was about to leave I told Mom it's ok to cry sometimes. And she said thank you in such a small voice. Then I said, "it's ok to cry sometimes but not all day, so pull your shit together Mom." She laughed so hard. She knows that's what she would have said to me. We both laughed then and I know she was doing better. I left the little pony with her.

*I told Tina that I just didn't know what to do for Mom. That I hate hearing about the bad times but that of course they need to tell me. She said to me, **"Just keep loving her. That's all you can do. Just keep loving her."***

No worries, Mom. As if I could ever stop.

I tell the caregivers that when Mom gets upset in the evenings (sundowning) that it might be better to let her eat her dinner in her room, that all the activity in the dining room might be overwhelming her. I tell them that both Mom and I have always liked to be alone at night, reading and drinking beer (or wine in my case). I love that they listen to me and are willing to try whatever is needed for Mom to be relaxed and happy instead of worked up and sad.

I buy Mom a small CD player and audio books for Christmas. She loves sitting and listening to them. I am pretty sure she can't really follow along with the story anymore, but it is still comforting to her. I buy The

Secret Garden and The Book Thief. I know the staff will fix it up for her whenever she needs or wants it. I also make her a little photo book of her family, all our names and ages. They tell me she hardly ever puts that book down. That she is constantly turning the pages and looking at the pictures. Which I can attest to, as the pages soon get slightly worn and sticky. We read books when I am with her, like Where the Wild Things Are and Riki Tiki Tembo. Books she used to read back when she was in charge of the children's area of the Copperas Cove Library. She was such a good storyteller. She had amazing voices that she could do. Skylar has inherited the ability to make crazy voices! They both amaze me! I also give Mom chocolate and new pajamas for Christmas which she loves. They have little cardinals all over them, which is her favorite bird.

I finally convince Dad he needs a shower, again. I tell him home health is going to send over an aide to help him do it. He says we'll give it a try. I think after this is when Angie starts helping him shower. He has the shower and he says it went well so I am encouraged by this. He's bound to be feeling a lot better! It's always nice to be clean.

Dad sends Mom a humongous flower arrangement for Christmas. All the staff are in awe of it. It's really beautiful and Mom is very proud of it! One night they send me a video of Mom singing along with the carolers that came to visit and I break down in tears. Just to hear her voice like that! And knowing all the words! They say that singing is something that the Alzheimer's patient can do a lot easier and for a lot longer than having a conversation. Muscle memory maybe?

Dad comes to my house on Christmas Eve, to spend the night and do Santa with us on Christmas morning. Skylar is very excited to have her beloved Grandpa at her house for Christmas. In the morning, I get him situated in a recliner and he sits and watches Skylar open presents. I have the cutest picture of them together, where Dad is helping Skylar get a new toy out of a box. I am so glad he came and spent Christmas with us. I know it made him exhausted, but I will treasure this memory.

My brother and his kids come for a visit the weekend after Christmas. We try to have a good time even though Mom isn't there at the house. It's really hard on us. Dad and I try to figure out what the difference is between stuffing and dressing. I still don't know. My brother has had a metal beam made with replicas of all the stickers Dad had put on the beam he had in his old shop at the house in Tyler. Dad is very pleased with it and gets a little misty eyed. He misses the place in Tyler so much. David says he'll hang it up in the garage for him.

I make an appointment for Dad at the neurologist because his tremors are getting worse. He can barely hold a pen or his cup of coffee. I have taken to writing all his checks for him, which he signs.

And just like that January 2021 comes.

Some days are easier than others. Some days that compartment that holds my love for Mom stays shut, hidden behind a stronger piece of me. But all too often I find myself looking at the door to that bit - the bit that is shattered and

laying all over the floor in a million tiny pieces that will never, ever be put right again. If I am feeling strong, I can look at the door and acknowledge it without opening it up. I can feel my love for Mom and just feel warm and happy knowing that she's there - somewhere - still there inside of me.

Then there are the days where all those broken pieces overwhelm me, and I **have** to try to put a few of them back together. I sit on her old bed at the house where Dad still lives and her essence is so strong that I can feel her sitting next to me. She takes my hand. I lean my head into her shoulder. The tears fall and she wipes them away. I can hear her voice. Her sweet, beautiful voice that I pray I will never forget. She's there and I'm nowhere. I'm lost among all those shattered pieces.

She's on a different medication now and it's making a world of difference. She's so much happier and more alert. When I go to visit, her whole face lights up and the first thing she says is "I love you so much." We hold hands, and we sing silly songs like "There was an old lady who swallowed a fly," and watch her favorites on YouTube like "Hallelujah." Her old spark is there and I savor it. But then I ask her to look at the phone to see a picture and she says Oh, I see it. But she's not focusing on the phone at all. Even now, even now she has the presence of mind to know what I want to hear and to say it. Even now, she tries to hide her illness. Even now she doesn't want to be helped or patronized.

I read her stories from the past, like Stone Soup and Leo the Late Bloomer. She loves this. She takes the books from me and endlessly looks at the pictures. It is so obvious that her hands were meant to hold books. I think this might be the part of herself that she misses the most. The books. The endless parade of books in our lives. I let her keep the books so she can look at them as long as she wants. I order more children's books that I can bring her. We have finally found a connection that should have been obvious to me all along.

I miss the days gone by more than my heart can possibly acknowledge. I miss the way she was, the way she was my champion always. I miss talking to her about all the wrongs and all the rights in my life. I miss the way she was just there, just always there - at her table, reading her books, playing on her phone, watching TV. I always knew where to find her. I miss the way she almost always put me first - maybe selfish, but isn't that what most moms do? I miss how she was always thinking about me.

That compartment of my heart that is Mom - it might be ravaged with loss and regret and grief but if I can just push aside all that I might find that all that is left is the memories. The love she had for me. I can see her there, behind all the pain and she is happy. She is young again and walking out with Dad. And all her best days are ahead of her. She's exploring Europe with her military wife friend Brenda. She's heading up a library and excelling as a storyteller. She's got that crazy white cat, Gertie, at her heels and she's even younger now - sitting on the back patio with her beloved dog Fella and the sun is shining and she's waiting for her daddy to play with her.

It's getting late. Every day is one day later for Mom. Every day she is one more day further away. And so, while I can still reach her, she will consume me. She will be and have All of Me and that is ok. That is the way I want it to be.

Aunt Patty and Aunt Diane come to visit Dad. To keep him company, presumably. I think Dad prefers to wallow in his lonely misery if Tony or I (or my brother) can't be there. Not that he doesn't appreciate their concern, it's just a lot for him.

I buy Mom one of those "warmies" - a cat that is orange and white. You warm it up in the microwave and it smells like lavender. I don't know if they ever warm it up for her, but she loves it just the same. In fact, she adores it, and wants it with her all the time.

Mom has had a wingback chair in her room that I love. The old blue chair that I fought to keep in the house we moved to her new room. But it isn't practical (plus the cat had thrown up on it multiple times) so we buy her a recliner at the staff's request. It is an electric one that moves up and down so that they can get her in and out of it easily. A very good buy and Mom seems to love it. Dad has found that if he sings "You Are My Sunshine" to Mom she will sing along with him. I think this is so sweet!

Around the middle of January Dad falls out of bed somehow. He lays on the carpet next to the bed for a long time. He is so weak that he can't get himself up if he falls down. Luckily, he does have his Life Alert around his neck, and they call the EMT's who come to help him get up. There's a lockbox outside the front door of Dad's house with a house key in it. The EMT's know the code at this point! Dad is very discouraged about his lack of mobility and weakness. I feel terrible for him, but I don't know what else to do. At least he has help in the form of the EMT's or me and Tony when he needs it. We try so hard to really be there for him. My brother says that no man in his family has ever lived as long as Dad has, and Dad doesn't know how to "be old." Dad's father, James Dalton Thomas, died of lung cancer when he was just fifty-nine. The men all worked hard farming and then died rather young. That's a hard life - farming. He died a year after I was born. I never knew him at all. In pictures, my Grandpa JD did not look fifty-nine, he looked more like seventy-nine when he died.

Dad and I talk a lot about what he's having for dinner - considering it's the only meal he will eat all day. He likes to have ice cream for breakfast, and something like cake if there is any. He'll snack sometimes but mostly starves until dinner (not for lack of food in the house!). He wants to know what I'm going to make him or buy him for dinner. We talk about tacos, pancakes, key lime pie, cherry pie, chicken wings from Brookshires, and a million other food items. He sends me recipes for things he wants me to cook for him. I try to get at least one thing cooked for him a week. Otherwise, he eats a lot of chicken - from Brookshires or Chick fil A. He eats Whataburger. But that's about it. He's not a fan of Mexican food which is something the rest of us love to eat. He likes tacos but only the hard-shell ones. He thinks Tony is crazy when he eats the soft tortillas with his taco meat! He tells me that when he was a kid, he and Grandpa went fishing a lot so that they didn't have to eat salmon patties on Fridays. They always had fish on Fridays. I told him that was disgusting and he said, "you ate what Mom cooked! No other choices!" Dad is trying really hard to eat healthier. I buy lots of fruit cups for him and Skylar.

We are still battling COVID related issues. Skylar's classmate tested positive, so we are all on virtual school again, which Skylar hates and refuses to do. It's a serious test of my patience to get any schoolwork done at all. When she's at home, she just wants to play! We end up having to make a diorama of a giraffe habitat, which is slightly fun and mostly exhausting. It's pretty cute in the end and at least we did what we were supposed to. She has to read the "book" on giraffes out loud to the computer camera so we can send it to the teacher, and she is not a fan of this. There's a lot of 'ums' and looking away and fidgeting and staring at the camera making faces. I think it's pretty hilarious myself, if not incredibly frustrating while we are doing it!

January 25th is Mom and Dad's wedding anniversary. I buy a cake and some flowers and Dad and Skylar and I go to Just Like Home to surprise Mom. I am sure she has no idea it's her anniversary, but she is thrilled to see us, nonetheless. They sit on the small couch together in the front room, where Tina has set up a table and she brings them their lunch so they can eat together.

On the very last day of January Dad admits that he should never have had that vascular surgery on his leg. I remind him that he was *adamant* that he get it done. We had no idea what a shit show it would turn out to be. We both admit that we are each suffering from severe depression. It's not a fun conversation. I try to convince him to sell his truck and get a car that is lower to the ground so that it is easier to get in and out. This doesn't ever happen, of course.

CHAPTER NINETEEN

Just Trying To Thrive

February 2021 - May 2021

It's a very cold month, not a lot is happening, but Dad and I take turns going to see Mom. Mom loves it when I bring Skylar and looks at her like she is enthralled with this little child - but I think she doesn't always recognize who she is. It's awfully hard to take care of the horses in this weather, so I'm not in the best of moods. Dad is wanting comfort food, chicken pot pies and baked potatoes. That's easy - I can do that! On the other hand, he didn't tell me this before I went to Walmart on Monday, so I am annoyed that I have to go back to the store. Everything annoys me these days!

Skylar's school closes for a couple of days because of the bad weather. School has already closed multiple times because of COVID, now the weather. I am getting fed up!

We've got some visitors in the form of ducks on our pond, which Skylar and I are pretty excited about. Dad says "Damn! Mighty good eating - fried." I tell him I'm horrified and he chuckles.

I tell Dad about my overwhelming sadness - I probably shouldn't lay it on him but it's getting tougher and tougher to function like I need to. I just want to sleep and stare out the window.

I hang up the phone with a medical billing department and I go stand in front of the fire. I stare into it for a few minutes until my husband asks what is wrong. I am overwhelmed, I respond. A few moments pass and the darkness descends once more. Why is it, I ask, that it's times like these that I start to think about Mom, and miss her so hard? I don't know Babe, he says.

But I do. What do you do when you are overwhelmed? When you need to talk to someone? When you need advice or a listening ear? You turn to your mom. You call her up and it's like a warm hug coming across the wires - or airwaves now I suppose. Her very voice is a calming balm. The way you instantly know she'll do whatever she can to help. The way she says I love you. Nobody ever loves you like your mom loves you. Nobody can listen in just the same way. Nobody knows you better than you know yourself, except her. You know what you need? She asks. A long, hot bath and some time to yourself. Everything will be alright - you will get through this, you always do.

Her presence in the house Dad lives in is strong. Her bedroom is unchanged for the most part. Her closet has clothes and shoes lined up. Boxes of pictures, wrapping paper and the old Wade Family Bible are there as they should be. A candle from my Granny Judy's funeral. An old doll and her leftover aura are there. Her bathroom drawers hold makeup, hair products and her electric toothbrush. Some old creams and eyeliner pencils gather dust. Sometimes I look in these drawers, but the only thing I have thrown out is some expired medication and a bottle of face cream that smelled bad.

I wonder about the headboard that was left in the old house. I think it was very firmly attached to the wall and that is why it was not brought to the new house. I put her favorite yellow rose plates, cups and pictures - the ones that have not been broken - into the small wooden cabinets that belonged to her mother. I dust the pictures of her grandchildren; of my wedding and the blue glass vases she loved. I hang up some paintings and embroidery pieces I find. I am not deterred by the fact that she will never live here again. It's still "her" room and I want it to be perfect.

I am still wracked by guilt over the way we moved her out. It was December 2019. Dad was very ill, and I could no longer cope. Her caregiver and I devised a plan. She would take her to get her nails done, then drive her over to visit Dad in his skilled nursing unit. My husband, my friend Kathy, and I would pack up her things and take them to the place we had selected in Frisco. When we brought her upstairs and showed her her room she was, of course, very confused. Angie, the caregiver, stayed with her a long time. We told Mom she only had to stay there while Dad was in the hospital then she could come home. A lie that continues to haunt me. I remember when I had to leave, she asked Angie if she was going to stay and Angie said, "I'm not going anywhere." But I have such terrible guilt imagining the fear Mom must have felt when Angie did leave late that afternoon.

How could I have done that to her? How could I have left her there? I thought she was in good hands, and I thought it was the best thing for all of us. But over and over again I look back and wonder if I did the right thing. I still can't believe that I did. I was overwhelmed. I couldn't cope. But what *about Mom? She was overwhelmed, confused and scared. Dad was too sick to have a say. People now will tell me that she doesn't remember any of it. But does that make it right? I don't know. I don't know how to move on. I don't know how to let go of that pain. I know she's in the best hands possible now and that offers a modicum of relief. But somewhere in the distant past I promised I would never do that to her, I promised she would just come live with me when she got old. We joked about just taking her out with an Uzi if it got bad. She said she'd rather that than end up like her mother, my Granny Judy.*

And yet, here we are. A million times worse than my Granny Judy ever was, and a million times harder because Mom and I were so close, whereas she and her own mother were not. I promised Mom I would take care of her. I promised.

And I feel like I lied.

Skylar competes in her first ever horse show all by herself on her new pony Bruno. She places third in a 'flat' class (not jumping) out of about ten kids and she's so thrilled with herself. I have to admit I'm ecstatic as well, I have been dreaming of this day for years. My kiddo finally being able to horse show on her own! She competes in the trot poles classes and gets a fifth and a sixth in those. It's a cold day and after her classes she snuggles up with her *'blankie'* and I am reminded how young she still is. She's whiny and tired but I still have other students to teach. I send the videos to Dad because obviously he couldn't come watch. I wish desperately that Mom could focus on the videos long enough to enjoy them, but I know that's a lost cause. Mom will never know how this particular dream of mine finally came to fruition.

Mom is doing as well as can be expected during this period. We keep in touch with the caregivers, because it has now snowed and we aren't driving north in this. Tina makes sure to call Dad on Valentine's Day so that he can say happy Valentine's Day to Mom. He can't go up to see her because of the snow and the ice on the roads. Mom wasn't very "with it" and was pretty confused, but she was happy to hear Dad's voice, I think.

Then things get worse in the form of no power at our house. The water in the barn is all frozen up. Skylar and I go to Dad's house for the night because he still has power. Tony makes a fire and stays at home, but by the next morning he's pretty frozen. It's pretty damn miserable for sure. Now this is some nasty weather, with no power and no water for the horses. We have to attach a hose to the washing machine faucet in the house, open the back door, and fill up a large bucket that we have on the back of the tractor. Then we take the water to the barn on the tractor, very slowly. It's a process. We also have to clean all the stalls. Usually, we have heat lamps in the barn, but with the power out we don't even have that. The horses themselves let off some heat so as long as we keep the barn doors closed, they are ok. Skylar and I amuse ourselves by throwing ourselves down in the snow and making snow angels. We find bunny and other animal tracks. She is learning what it really takes to have horses! There are times, like now, when it just isn't much fun at all. We end up bringing Daphne the "barn" cat inside the house which thrills Skylar. But we have to hide her in the office so the other cats don't get upset.

Dad thinks I'm going to be able to get him fresh pineapple and fresh strawberries at the local store. Dad, I say, it's February. There isn't going to be any fresh fruit in our tiny Brookshire Bros store in February. You'll have to make do with canned. Once the snow and ice thaw we have broken pipes in the house (luckily on an outside wall - water goes outside the house) and in the barn. Life's the shits at the moment. If it's not one thing it's another.

We finally get out to see Mom. She is doing just fine, no more falls since we moved her in September! Considering she had *nine* falls in *nine* months at LW. I feel that this is a strong indicator of the difference in care!

Angie finally gets to come back to work, and Dad is a happy camper. She makes him bacon sandwiches, and he probably talks her ear off all day.

Dad and I talk about the vacation I am taking Skylar on August first through fifth at Moody Gardens resort in Galveston. I tell him I need a break from reality. He tells me that sounds familiar. He really doesn't want me to go by myself but other than Tony or Ali, I really don't want to take anyone else and neither of them can go. Dad reminds me that he and Mom used to go to Moody Gardens all the time for a big wood-working trade show they had every year.

Before February is over Dad has fallen again but is ok. He managed to get himself up. I think the Life Alert program is the best thing we ever signed him up for. We used to laugh at the commercials - probably everyone did - but I swear it has saved his life.

When I ask Dad what he wants for his birthday which is March fifth, he tells me "a jug of whiskey would be nice." I roll my eyes at him. I tell him, sure Dad, let me contribute to your negative state of health by intoxicating you more. I do buy him a fancy chocolate cake with chocolate covered strawberries on it, though, which is his favorite. It even says "Happy 75th Birthday" on it. I buy him a large print of a cotton field to hang on his wall in his living room, which he loves.

Lori, the Director at Just Like Home, calls me as I am leaving Dad's house one day and tells me that Mom isn't doing well today, but they think it's from the COVID vaccine she got the other day. I head up there and Mom is asleep, she doesn't seem to be in pain - just nonresponsive. Not eating or drinking. The next day Mom is doing better, smiling and trying to talk to me. We are very relieved.

I take Skylar up to a tulip farm here in Pilot Point and we get a whole mess of tulips for Mom's room. I, having spent three years in Germany and traveled to Holland as a child, am not impressed by the tulip farm. It's nice, and it's pretty, but it isn't Holland. Skylar has a good time though and picks tulips incorrectly before I can stop her and show her how to do it. I take some cute pictures of her with her tulips in the basket. It's a nice sunny day and I feel like I am doing some bonding with my child, which we don't have time to do very often.

Dad and I both end up with sore throats, and I tell him it's Skylar's fault! Bringing home nasty germs from school! I don't know at this point that Dad's sore throat is telling me a lot more than I want to know.

Dad is very excited that he now has an Amazon account on his phone and can order things for himself.

He's even more excited that he knows how to use it. He tells me he ordered an American flag for his flagpole, got blades for Tony's lawnmower and got a hat. I say, but did you EAT? He tells me he ate ice cream pie and chili - very strange combination but at least he ate. He also had peaches and cornbread. I tell him he needs to eat even when Angie isn't there. He says he will try and I say, *"There is no try, do or do not."* I am not sure he laughed, but I did. Dad also orders himself another whiskey glass that he saw and liked. I am afraid we have created a monster with the Amazon account! Dad, I say, slow down!

Dad buys us a new fridge for our "drinks" fridge in the laundry room because both of our fridge's go out at the same time. You just can't get better luck than that. We still need a hot water heater too. Things are not looking like they are on the up and up anytime soon. I start balancing Dad's checkbook for him, something he used to do for himself all the time but hasn't looked at it in months. It takes me hours, but I finally get it to within $150 of the current bank balance which I figure is the best it's going to get right now. Dad never signed up for online banking, so balancing the checkbook is still an important task.

Dad and I take turns going to see Mom so that we don't end up going on the same day for the most part. I try to go at least two to three times a week and so does Dad. Mom doesn't say much but she is always really glad we are there.

One day Dad makes an appointment with the local funeral home. He and I go up there to discuss burial and funeral arrangements for when the time comes. The room with the sample caskets is creepy. The funeral director is nice and appreciates our dark humor. Dad picks out solid oak caskets for himself and Mom. My brother says they'd better be solid oak and good quality - or Dad will sit up in his and call it a piece of shit. We all laugh about it. I assured him they are made in the good ole USA (a requirement for Dad) and that they looked pretty nice to me. It isn't easy or fun to make these arrangements, but Dad and I power through. He once told my brother that he did not want the song Amazing Grace played at his funeral as he was never lost nor blind. We know already that they will both be buried at the Central Texas National Veterans Cemetery just outside Killeen, Texas. They will be buried in the same plot, one on top of the other. Dad wants to be sure all his arrangements are made before anything happens to him - he puts me and my brother on his bank accounts, and he also names us as beneficiaries of his life insurance policies. Knowing that we will take care of Mom no matter what, he knows it will be easier on us if those policies are in our names. Dad has left nothing to guess work. He has thought everything out carefully and meticulously planned for his eventual demise.

Skylar is six now and has been showing her new pony, Bruno, in the trot poles classes at the shows. I always send Dad pics and video, and it is the cutest thing ever. She is doing really well on him, earning lots of ribbons and smiles from everyone around her. Dad can't get out to the shows, so he is happy looking at videos. I try to tell Mom all about it, and I even arrange to bring Bruno and another pony to Just Like Home so that everyone can meet the ponies. It is a big hit, and I get excellent pictures of Mom in her wheelchair petting Bruno! Bruno mostly minds his manners but is very curious about all the people and just a little bit pushy. The other pony, Corkie, just wants to eat the grass and not be bothered!

Easter is coming up soon and we talk about doing an Easter basket for Mom. Skylar has a great time helping me put it together. We find a little chick that chirps if you set it on the palm of your hand. Skylar loves this thing! Dad and Skylar and I all go out to Mom for Easter, and I take pictures of them all on the front porch.

Dad is dying for a smoke, but we cleaned them all out of his house and he doesn't have any. He is pretty weak and depressed lately but smoking is just going to make everything worse. I want Dad to get stronger and better. I am worried about him. In the middle of April he falls again, and I am notified by Life Alert. I keep trying to get him on the phone and he finally answers. It is midnight and I have no idea what he was even doing out of bed. But as usual, he is ok for the most part.

I take a video of Skylar reading about deserts for school and send it to Dad. He's very impressed. Dad tells me that when he saw Mom today that she was doing good, said more words than he's heard lately! She was very talkative and that's a great thing.

There's a tornado warning at the end of April. I call Dad and tell him we are in the closet waiting for it to pass. Dad is still in his chair, waiting to be blown away, I guess. He doesn't seem to be worried. He has been doing a lot of exercises with Angie and I know he's tired. But I would prefer him not to get swept up by a tornado.

One of the ladies at Just Like Home sends me a short video of Mom shuffling along with her walker in the hallway. They are trying so hard to keep her as active as possible, walking for as long as possible. I love to see it, but I also notice how much she has physically deteriorated in these past few months. She is missing more teeth, somehow, and her face and hands just look different. I buy Mom a bird feeder to have outside her window. It's probably a little late for something like this, as I don't think she can focus on the birds, but maybe she will hear them chirping and see them a bit and be happy.

Skylar wants to have a tea party with Granny and Grandpa, so we load up all Skylar's play food and dishes, and we pick up Grandpa and go to see Mom. I'm quite sure Mom has no idea what is going on but as usual she is just happy we are there. The caregivers provide a long table and tablecloth in the front room, and Dad and Skylar sit on the couch. Skylar is wearing her best party dress and sets the table and passes out the tea and cookies. She is using an old Beatrix Potter tea set that I had when I was young, that I hardly ever used. And she has brought her fake ice cream set complete with a shaker full of sprinkles! I got some adorable pictures, including one of Grandpa sipping his tea with his finger out. It is hilarious what grandparents will do for their grandchildren. Everyone has a great time. Mom even pretends to eat her ice cream.

Mom finally gets her hair done at the end of May and it makes a tremendous difference to how she looks and probably feels as well. It is her best friend, Panchita's, birthday and we make a little video of Mom saying Happy Birthday for her. Mom doesn't really know what she's saying it for, except that I told her to say it. She laughs after, and I send it along to Panchita -

I worry that she will see how far Mom has deteriorated and be upset but there's nothing I can do about it.

Dad is making an effort at drinking less. He sends me pictures of glasses half full and left for the night. He tells me that lack of alcohol is seriously affecting his sleep. I tell him he doesn't need to sleep for twelve hours a night anyway. Dad records the Kentucky Derby and the Preakness Stakes so that we can watch them together at his house. He asks if he can buy me some wine, but I have lately moved on to hard seltzers - White Claw Black Cherry is my favorite. Skylar likes me to drop her off at Grandpa's so she can "supervise him" while I go running errands. She hates being in the car and loves spending time with Grandpa so it's a win-win situation! I am happy to leave her with him; it makes my life a lot easier.

At the end of May Tony and Skylar and I take a trip to Branson, Missouri. Even though Skylar and I hate the drive (six hours) it is so beautiful there that we are glad we did it. We have a few days planned with things like going to see *Jesus* at the Sight and Sound theatre, going to the Titanic exhibit and going to a little zoo they have. At the zoo Skylar and I get to hold all sorts of baby animals, including a baby kangaroo! We also go to a dinosaur park and Skylar loves that. I send Dad all the pictures I can so he can feel like he's involved. I talk to the caregivers at Just Like Home almost every day and I know Mom is doing well. Dad is glad we are getting a break, but he also can't wait for us to get home. I know he misses us.

CHAPTER TWENTY

Birthdays

June & July 2021

Skylar wants to go to The Cheesecake Factory for her birthday dinner. This kid adores cheesecake. Dad doesn't want to go but he is willing to pay for it. So Tony, Skylar and I head to the zoo and then we meet Ali at the restaurant for dinner. I'm sad Dad didn't want to come; I can barely get him to leave the house these days. I am sad that Mom won't know anything about it. I can describe it in great detail to her, but it won't amount to anything. But I am happy that Dad has agreed to foot the bill as it's a very expensive place. He'd do anything for his Fu-Fu.

I bring Mom a chocolate shake from McDonald's one day and she sees it in my hand and immediately reaches for it. For the drink, not for me! We all laugh and I am glad to see Mom still recognizes one of her favorite things. The caregiver Tina asks her if it's good and she says, "real good!" Then Tina says, "I love you" and Mom responds with "Well I love you too, but I don't know what you're talking about." We all get a good chuckle out of that one. Mom is also having spasms from the drugs she's taking - Dad says he does the same thing. Their bodies jerk a little every once in a while. I've seen it too and wondered what it was. Lori, the director of the facility and the RN there, is keeping an eye on it.

Tony is taking Skylar to karate lessons and Dad buys her the cutest little pink karate outfit - she looks absolutely adorable in it. They can't wait to show Dad what she's learned. Karate only lasts a few months though before they get too busy to go. Skylar also finally learns to ride a bike without training wheels - this is a milestone summer for her!

For Father's Day I make Dad a banana cake complete with Nilla wafers which he absolutely loves. Dad gave it a "double damn cake was excellent!" review.

One day I notice a lump on Dad's jaw/neckline. He says it hurts. We start making moves to get it checked out. It's something I haven't noticed before. His complexion is also very wan. He almost looks yellowish.

Tonight, Dad asked me what I want for my birthday. My immediate answer was - "I don't know, Dad, everything I want is so expensive." We have always been gift givers. We like to buy for other people, and we like to give presents. Even as adults the gifting didn't slow down - just became more expensive and less quantitative. At least from my parents down to us kids. We, my brother and I, also like to give meaningful gifts to my parents and our kids and everyone. We shop, we think, we ponder, we wonder, and we muse over what to give. What, what will cause the most joy? Which of us can give the most appreciated gift? Yes, it's a challenge

and almost always my brother wins. I have a good memory, so I remember what people want and like. My brother, however, has imagination and also the creative ability to do interesting things. I am always awed by what he thinks up.

As I think about what I want for my birthday, what I really, really want (besides world domination. I mean peace. Of course) there are things that come to mind.

Obviously, I would like Mom not to have Alzheimer's. I would like to know why my daughter insists on acting like a puppy even though she is now seven years old. I would like to know where my hairbrush is and why I never find it on my first circuit around the house and which of my daughters has taken the detangling spray and where they have put it. I would like there to be less laundry. I would like to find whatever the obscure button is that makes me lose weight and do I have to stop drinking wine to accomplish this?

I would like to wear my new Ariat jean shorts I can't fit into. Same for my swimsuits. I would like to have a day where pain doesn't enter into everything I do. I would like my cat to stop yowling at me nonstop and for the kitty litter I order to actually come on time. I would like to go to church and not feel anxiety at the very thought of it. I would like to spend an evening on a front porch swing I don't yet have drinking wine with Tony and listening to country music while Skylar plays in the front yard - probably acting like a puppy.

I would like to sweep my floors and have them stay clean for a day. An hour. I would like a bigger desk because for some reason my husband has the bigger desk even though I do all the financials and business stuff. I have five books I have yet to read and even though I read every single night before bed I would like to still be able to discuss them with Mom and also have more time to read.

*I would like to get rid of this damn king size mattress that is taking up space in my garage. I would like to spend more time with my friends. I would like to talk to God and ask him why, **why** do things happen the way they do? Just a conversation, like sitting down and having a drink on a pier by the lake with Him. I would like to know when life gets easier and if we ever get to where we really want to be. I would like to have access to unlimited hay (for free) and to be able to clone Skylar's precious, amazing pony so that every little girl can have one. I would like never to have to say goodbye.*

As I come back down to reality, and as far as my birthday goes, I suppose some new clothes would be nice. Maybe a dinner out and a cupcake with a candle. A sweet card from my husband and something handmade from Skylar. Dad picking up the dinner check and actually coming with us. Those are the things that could possibly happen. Those are the things I will treasure and be grateful for. And spending an hour or two with Mom. Even though she won't know it's my birthday. I'll tell her anyway and she'll love that I'm there with her. She'll pat my arms and hug me, and she'll know who I am. And that's enough for me.

Dad falls again and I am frustrated. But then my brother comes to visit. He explains that the "one glass" of whiskey Dad is drinking each night is like four shots. And Dad weighs like 125-135 pounds. He's like a ghost. Every bone sticks through his skin, he looks emaciated. This is nothing new. He has looked like this for a long while, but I start to wonder if it is even worse than it has been. I keep trying to convince him to EAT but he says he isn't hungry. He only ever wants desserts and fried chicken.

Dad is having all sorts of testing. Angie takes him to get a PET scan. We are all worried that the lump on his neck is cancer, but Dad refuses to talk about it. He wants to wait to see what we are really dealing with. I have no idea how he is really feeling inside, he is definitely keeping it close to the chest right now. I think I am in denial because I just go on like nothing is happening, nothing is wrong. I think that if he does have cancer, we will do chemo and everything will be just fine.

"

I also try not to think about it.

"

Dad continues to have issues with falling and the EMT's coming to pick him up off the floor. He is too weak to get up by himself. One night he falls in the kitchen and lays there all night. He has peed all over himself too. When I find him I think he hit his head because he tells me he's only been there a few minutes but I can see it has been hours and hours. I don't know what to do at this point except keep trying to stay the nights there. Also, he has stopped taking showers again so the body odor is really bad. I try not to get too close. He says it's just too cold. He doesn't want to get wet because then he can't get warm again. I sigh. I know we can heat that bathroom up to *Hell* settings, so I'm not sure if that's the real reason or he's just too damn tired or too damn drunk to care. He ends up falling asleep in his chair and then tries to get up to go to bed and falls down is what I think.

I had a dream the other night that Mom had died. And when I went to the hospital to see her, I learned that she really hadn't died at all. That they had taken her off of a medication she was on and the result was that she was completely back to normal. Her old self. Before Alzheimer's. I was astounded, and so very happy. It wasn't a sad dream at all. I was able to be with her and talk to her again and have her talk back. I don't remember if we actually said much at all during the dream, but what I do remember is just such a feeling of peace and calmness.

I thought about the dream all the next day. I carried it with me. I told Miss Pooh about it. I wondered what it meant. I thought that maybe it was referring to the deep-seated fear I have that Mom is really ok inside her head, and she just can't tell us. That she's trapped, so to speak, like those people we hear of in vegetative states whose brains are actually ok, but they are paralyzed and not able to communicate. I realize there is virtually no chance that this is the case with Mom but still the thought of it haunts me. The fact that she has lost control of bodily functions, eats with her hands and has forgotten how to clean her teeth with her tongue while she's eating means that her brain really isn't working at all. But still I worry. Because I know that if this were the case she would be truly, truly miserable.

The last few weeks have been tough - Mom has cried and been teary on several visits. Including one time when I FaceTime'd her and she cried because she couldn't touch me - she was able to communicate that enough that we figured out what was wrong. Her whole face lights up when she sees me, and she immediately reaches for me, so I know that FaceTime really isn't a good second option if I can't get there. In fact, that day I was so unnerved by her tears that I dropped what I was doing in order to drive out to see her.

And the time before that she cried as well. Teared up a lot the entire time I was there. I think always that her tears are not just tears because she missed me, but also because she so desperately wants to tell me something and can't. A few days later her nurse, Roxie, put her on a new pain medication and that seems to have made a difference. Maybe she was in pain. Maybe when she saw me she thought "here's Julie - she'll be able to know what I want." And then frustration because I didn't.

There's no shortage of pain and guilt and sadness and rage within me. But as I sat with her one day a week or so ago something new crept in. A sliver of acceptance. It snuck in across the floor and slithered its way up to where I sat, her hand in mine, and touched my heart. She was dozing and I was quiet, sitting there watching, and I felt it. And I was glad. Acceptance means I can see her now in a new light. I can appreciate the beauty that is still there, the way love still radiates from her eyes. I can be more still when I'm with her, not always trying so hard to do something, but just to sit, and be quiet and hold her hand.

Mom doesn't care if I fill the birdfeeder up with birdseed. She doesn't care if I walk her around the building or down the street - although she does enjoy it very much. She doesn't mind if I don't bring a new book to read. I don't have to find a new way to reach her. Her hand in mine, the joy in our hearts is enough.

Miss Pooh said maybe the dream meant a release from pain and a newfound peace. She was referring to when Mom actually does pass away. But maybe, just maybe, we're already there.

In July Skylar has a horse show that is local. Tina brings Mom to see Skylar ride. She has to lift Mom in and out of the vehicle. I am amazed that she can do this. Honestly, Mom has no idea where she is, but she definitely enjoys the sunshine. Skylar loves on her and is excited that she's there. I don't know it at the time, but this is the last time that Mom will actually leave the facility. It is just getting too hard to transport her anywhere. The most we can do is take a walk down the country roads around the facility. But the important thing is that she did get "to see" Skylar ride her pony at a show, and we will have the memories and photos of that day.

On Mom's birthday in July she gets her hair done again and Tina dresses her up in a lovely black shirt, and puts some make-up on her. She looks so good and so happy. She truly loves Tina. In fact, if you are one to believe in past lives then you have to believe they have loved each other along the way sometime before. The connection is so close and so real.

Mom's best friend Panchita has come to see Mom for her birthday. Skylar and I decorate the front room of the facility with flowers (roses, Mom's favorite), a cake and plates and napkins. Skylar insists on putting an "It's My Birthday" pin on Mom's shirt. Panchita brings Mom some gifts, including a pennant from the place where they used to go to Summer Camp each year - Camp Mahaba. Mom feels the felt and smiles real big, as if she remembers. I have no idea if she remembers Panchita or not, but the love in that room is very real. Plenty of stories are told. It is a great day for all of us.

At the end of July Dad finally gets his face shaved and his hair cut. He looks so much better.

CHAPTER TWENTY-ONE

Better Days In Hell

August 2021

At the beginning of August Skylar and I took our vacation to Moody Gardens in Galveston. She brings her Breyer horses and the first thing she does when we get there is beg to go to the beach. So we take the horses and she immediately plops them in the waves and starts playing. This is not like the beach we went to last year, though, in Gulf Port. That beach had no waves and was shallow. Galveston has a lot of waves and is darker. Skylar is a little intimidated. After about ten minutes (at which point I had finally gotten my chair and everything set up) Skylar says she is done and can we go back to the hotel. I remind myself she is only seven. I groan and growl but we pack up and go back to the hotel where she immediately asks if we can go to the pool. So I throw a swimsuit on and we go. She is innately happy there and wants to stay in the water nonstop. I do have to buy her some goggles though, as we didn't have any to bring. She jumps in, climbs out and jumps in again about fifty times.

We went, at one point, to the Rainforest Cafe for dinner, where they had a "jungle tube ride" and a build-a-bear store. She got a cheetah which she named "Teena" after Mom's caretaker Tina. The jungle ride was a lot of fun even though she was terrified at first!

Back to the hotel pool where we order icee's and she practices her front flips endlessly. She is a little fish and can't be tamed. She informs me she does not want to go back to the beach. So basically I spent all this time and money on taking her six hours away to a nice hotel with a large pool. I probably could have found that a lot closer to home and saved a bunch of money too.

We did end up going to the "pyramids" they have at Moody Gardens, like the rainforest one which is the only one I can remember. We rode some type of ferry boat as well. I was worried about Dad the whole time we were gone, and he was very anxious about us being there alone.

One thing I was very worried about was that Dad was going to have another surgery on the Wednesday after I returned. We had to be sure he was off the blood thinners before the surgery. Who could take him off them? We spin around and around for a full day before my brother gets the answer we need. No more blood thinners as of Tuesday, a week before the surgery. At ease, I order another drink from the bar and go back to baking.

Once we get back Dad basically stops texting me. He gets very sick with pneumonia and is admitted to the hospital. Aunt Patty comes to help out and to sit at the hospital with him.

WEDNESDAY AUGUST 18, 2021

I stand by the side of Dad's hospital bed as he tries to open his eyes. He doesn't see me. His breathing is at best raspy and at worst like he's drowning. The sound of him gurgling will be my constant companion tonight. So far today he's had his lungs deep suctioned at least once, been on oxygen multiple times, and has been in the OR for a PEG tube so he can get some nutrition, at last. He hasn't had any food in seven days. He can't swallow on his own. He can barely talk. His mouth is so dry his tongue must feel huge in his mouth. He's been sleeping most of the day, seemingly painlessly, thank goodness. Yesterday he thrashed and tried to leave the bed and couldn't make sense of anything and hallucinated like he was on LSD. They finally gave him a fentanyl patch to ease the pain. He settles down completely after that.

Dad does not have COVID. He doesn't even have COVID related pneumonia. Dad has cancer. The tumor that has invaded his throat, which started in his left tonsil, has grown so that he can no longer swallow. It is pressing on his carotid artery, which we assume is causing his confusion. It was found in lymph nodes on both sides of his neck. The pneumonia that put him in the hospital was caused by him aspirating on something because he was having trouble swallowing. But we didn't know. He didn't know.

We were pretty sure a throat cancer diagnosis was coming. A couple of months ago Dad fell in his home and was sent to the ER by the EMT's. There they found nodules on his

lungs during a typical chest X-ray. He was referred to a pulmonologist who ordered a PET scan (positron emission tomography). A PET scan is often used to detect cancerous cells in the body. The lung doctor let us know that the nodules in his lungs seemed harmless (for now) but that he detected "something" in his throat which needed to be checked. So we made that appointment and waited anxiously for the day. Emotions ran high with all of us, one minute we were thinking lung cancer is definite since his own dad died from it, and the next we're dumped into throat cancer territory. All unknowns to us, as my brother and I have not ever really experienced knowing anyone with cancer.

A week before the appointment Dad falls backwards and hits his head on the fireplace. He refuses to go to the ER although the wound is deep and bloody. Somehow, he lost his balance with his caregiver standing right there next to him - and she was unable to stop him from falling. He seems ok, though, so we all take a deep breath and just move on. We are all super concerned at this point about his confusion and his lack of balance. We discuss endlessly and come up with no answers. We talk about cirrhosis, we talk about dementia, we talk about urinary tract infection. Home health runs tests and rules out a UTI but it takes a full week, and we are all irritated with the delay.

The morning of the appointment arrives, and Aunt Patty and I load Dad up into the car. Dad is worried, of course, though he won't talk about it. At least not with me. Dad and I have zero ability to talk to one another about things we are deeply concerned about. I believe it's just us trying to protect the other one. We just don't talk about the bad stuff. I want to talk to him about it, but I'm met with a shake of the head and a "let's not talk about it until we know what it is." And since I'm also afraid of the answers I easily let it go.

Apprehensively, we wait in the doctor's office. Before he comes in an assistant pulls the PET scan up on the screen. I go over to look at it. I see bright blue spots, multiple spots, all over his throat. The biggest one is right where the tonsil is. I know immediately what it means but I keep my mouth shut. When the doctor comes in he does not acknowledge the cancer. He feels Dad's neck, he looks in his throat, he says "yes, we need to do surgery to take this tonsil out." He doesn't use the word cancer. He says we can do the surgery on Wednesday. None of us ask the question. We leave feeling drained and discouraged.

And then we are told he needs multiple "clearances" before a surgery can take place. As we pace the floor and start making phone calls and appointments and with a heavy blackness over all of it, Dad has a seizure. He's been sitting outside on the porch - something he hasn't done in a while due to feeling so poorly - and Angie is helping him come inside. He sits down on his walker seat and she is maneuvering him into the house when he goes stiff and his eyes roll back and he starts to shake a bit. She calls his name and gets no response. She says his name again, and he responds "yes" but without making eye contact. She's about to press his Life Alert button when he finally looks at her and stops shaking.

Home Health is called. They say we need to take him to the ER. It could be a brain bleed from the fall against the fireplace last week. I cancel my evening plans, load Dad up and we head out. At the hospital they check out everything. Ironically, they do another chest x-ray. Dad is very dehydrated. They admit him, but after a few days of everything under the sun they cannot find a reason for the seizure other than dehydration and low vitamin B12 levels. At this point surgery on his throat has been delayed a week.

Now we spend every moment on the phone trying to get the cardiologist to agree to give consent for the surgery based on the records from the hospital. It's not like we can take him to the appointment. Finally, the cardiologist signs off. Now another hurdle - Dad is going to rehab. Surgery cannot happen while Dad is in rehab. He has to be discharged first.

Dad does okay in rehab - he's alone a lot but he seems to be coping. He's going down to the dining room for meals (assisted of course), and he's eating well. He's watching HGTV non-stop until all my enthusiasm for the channel has been thoroughly squashed. Not only is it on every single time I am there, but whenever I call him, you can hear it perfectly in the background, as it's so loud. Turn that shit down, Dad, I tell him. He likes the one with the two redheads - Mom and daughter. "The mom is bat-shit crazy," he tells me. "And the daughter ain't bad to look at but she's pregnant in every other episode."

On Monday he's released from rehab and Skylar and I go to pick him up. We stop at McDonalds and get fries, which he eats in between coughing spells. The coughing is terrible - a dense, dry attempt to get something up. It's a good thing I have a towel in the car as eventually he has to spit everything out. I am wondering what's up as I haven't heard this strange coughing before. He hacks and chokes all the way home. Aunt Patty is due to arrive again later that day and I happily let her take over as I am one hundred percent exhausted.

On Tuesday Aunt Patty takes Dad to his pre-op appointment which apparently goes fine, and I am told that Dad has to be there next morning at 6 am. Oh geez! This means a 4:30 am wake up call for me, which honestly isn't that bad - horse show mornings call to me. I love the sky at that time of morning, and the stillness and the chill (well not

234

in August). Like nothing at all has happened yet and anything is still possible.

A couple hours later I hear that the surgery went well, and I return to take them back to the house. Dad is tired of course, but functioning. We are optimistic. The biopsy results should be back by Monday. Aunt Patty can't get Dad to eat that day, though, and every time he takes a drink he chokes and coughs. We think maybe just soreness from the surgery, maybe swelling? We don't know yet that the tumor has basically shut off his esophagus. The epiglottis is not able to function properly so anything that goes in, goes into his lungs. These are details that we are unaware of as yet.

By Thursday Aunt Patty is really concerned about the congestion. We get a call in to his doctor and procure some antibiotics. But when the home health nurse comes later in the afternoon she tells us his oxygen levels are way too low. She says we have to take him to the ER. He is extremely congested and not getting enough oxygen. Aunt Patty takes him as I stand by at home.

This is when they stay in the ER for nine hours before they get a room. This is when we find out a whole lot of things we didn't know. Like he has bacterial pneumonia from aspirating his own saliva. Like his throat is basically blocked. Like he's not getting enough oxygen because he can't breathe properly. Like things are way worse than we thought.

That was a week ago. So much has happened while Dad has been in the hospital, but on the other hand nothing has happened at all. We learned on Friday that Dad's cancer is called squamous cell carcinoma. We all rushed to google it. It's just a type of throat cancer that is currently located in the tonsil. Nobody has ever said that there is more than one tumor, or spot, even though I am SURE I saw more than one on the PET scan. It has been called tonsillar cancer, throat *cancer, and glandular cancer. I was told that the glands are continuously excreting cancer cells. That it may not have spread to the lungs but then again it may have. The nodes are too small to do a biopsy on. I don't really understand, seeing as how the lump on his neck is clearly visible. Thursday through Saturday was spent trying to beat the pneumonia with antibiotics, watching HGTV and wondering about nutrition as he is not allowed to have anything by mouth.*

Sunday I am with him for an hour - I try shaving him with a battery-operated razor I have just purchased at Walmart. I don't know what it is meant to shave but it certainly isn't hair. We bemoan the lack of functionality in today's electronics. Dad suddenly looks at me and says, "Do you know what's wrong with me?" I say, "Well you have pneumonia, Dad." He responds with "well that beats the hell out of cancer." I swallow hard and say, "you have that, too." Dad just looks at me and then looks away, eyes closed. We don't say anything more about it. I saw the pain in his eyes, though.

Sunday until Wednesday was spent watching HGTV and waiting for the PEG line (feeding tube) to be placed. As each day came and went Dad got weaker and weaker. Clinimix was given (lipids and fats) through an IV but no protein. By Tuesday when Dad was thrashing around and hallucinating - he didn't even look at his phone. He didn't want to talk to me, as if he just couldn't make sense that it was me that was calling him. Aunt Patty texted me Tuesday night and told me there were days in Hell better than today. I've never heard or seen Aunt Patty in tears, but I imagine she might have been.

We had no idea what was coming.

I arrived Wednesday morning, August 18th, to be told that Dad had gotten a pain patch of Fentanyl. He was sleeping peacefully. Still no PEG line, though. Aunt Patty had done all she could. She has to leave to go get a COVID test before her long-planned cruise. Not thirty minutes later they come to get him for the PEG line operation, finally. I can't sit still so I wander around the waiting room reading everything on the walls. Finally, I am told Dad is in recovery and I should head back up to his room.

Dad has done well. Aunt Patty and I are ecstatic at the thought of the PEG line. Surely this will solve so many problems. Dad will get stronger now. We are optimistic. They tell us he woke up in the elevator and talked to them for a minute. Aunt Patty leaves again, to go on her cruise. I know she doesn't want to leave him, but I tell her we will be fine. I am going to stay by Dad's side. I will sleep here. And so I do. Every few minutes the alarm goes off for something. I swear all I have to do is take my glasses off to try and get some sleep and the alarm will beep. Or Dad will start moaning. He doesn't do this because he is in pain, he does it just because he can. He has always done this - even back when I was staying with him at home I would have to go in his room and say "DAD. What the heck with the groaning?!" He would blink at me and say, "I don't know." "Well stop it!" I'd say, I can't get any sleep! He would even laugh about it. So I am not worried by the moaning, but it does make it hard to sleep when you are less than ten feet away from him. None of this bothers Dad, of course. The moaning, the beeping, the nurses coming in. He doesn't care. He snoozes right on through all of it. I sleep fitfully and get a full hour and half between 1 and 2:30 am. At 4:30 am I give up and decide to wander around the hospital in search of a Diet Coke.

In the morning, the nurses and staff start coming in every few minutes. Finally, Dr. Azeem, the hospitalist, comes in. He manages to get Dad to open his eyes. He asks if Dad knows where he is. The hospital, Dad croaks. And who is this next to you? He looks at me. My daughter.

A bit later Dad asks me "where's Patty?" and I tell him she's gone home for now. He nods. Where is David? David is coming Friday Dad. Tomorrow. Another nod. Asleep again, I stand by his bed and smooth his hair back. I do this for hours. Respiratory therapy comes in and gives Dad a breathing treatment and then she sticks a small tube down his nose and into his throat to try and expel some of the secretions. Dad fights hard but he doesn't wake up. I have to hold his arms down as he tries to push the tube out of his nose. He scrunches his eyes up and groans and I tell him DAD, it's ok, it's ok, over and over. They go through this every couple of hours and I am beginning to wonder how in the heck I am going to do this for him when he goes home? Eventually I can't stand to be in the room when they do it. I walk the halls instead.

Thursday passes fairly uneventfully. I wait for the oncologist to come talk to me, and I never see him. Dad sleeps the whole day, only waking moderately when they suction his throat and lungs. I read, I write, I smooth his hair, I walk the halls some more. I go home and take a nap then return. Nothing has changed. I feel like someone is holding all the cards to this mystery and it definitely isn't me. I only have the two of clubs, someone must have the ace. Who knows what is happening here? Why isn't the nutrition making him stronger? Why isn't he awake more? I get no answers as the day goes on and morphs into Friday.

Friday morning sees the hospitalist checking on Dad and telling me "He is so weak." He tells me there isn't any way that Dad could withstand cancer treatment right now. He tells me that all we are waiting on is the oncologist to come talk to me, then Dad can go home. There is nothing more that the hospital can do for him. I don't read anything into what he is saying. I am still thinking we will take him home with home health and he will get better. I realize it might be a very slow, very long process but I don't for a minute think we are done here.

When respiratory therapy comes in she is alarmed by his low oxygen levels. Even though he is on full oxygen, his levels have dropped to a dangerous level. She gives him a breathing treatment, suctions his lungs, and frowns at the monitor. I am watching closely but I don't yet understand the impact of what she is seeing.

A couple of hours later I am sitting next to Dad's bed, typing away on my computer, when someone new walks in. I look up and see "palliative care" embroidered on her shirt. I close my laptop as my heart drops into my stomach. Somehow, I just know what she is going to say. She asks if she can sit down and I say yes of course. The look on her face is plain. She isn't bringing happy news. She tells me that they - the social worker, the hospitalist, herself - all think that Dad should be sent home on hospice care, not home health. "But the hospital bed has already been arranged by home health" I stutter. This is immediately where my brain went. Practical, as always. And then I ask the difficult question. You don't think he's going to get better? She looks at Dad, then looks at me and says no. I say, "but I have been waiting on the oncologist to come tell me what he thinks, and he is supposed to be here at noon." It's almost noon now, she says. Let's wait and see what he says, then we can talk again.

Noon comes and goes. One o'clock comes and with it the arrival of my brother. Thank goodness. I don't have to bear this burden alone. Not ten minutes later the oncologist walks briskly in. He introduces himself. He says Dad is not strong enough to withstand treatment. He says without treatment Dad only has at most a week to live. We are stunned. This is the answer. This is why Dad isn't waking up. We talk a bit more, he says he is so sorry, and he leaves. I ask my brother if it's ironic that the cancer doctor is bald. Then we both look at Dad and I lean into my brother's strong shoulder and ask him bitterly "when did it become just US?" We were always such a strong family unit of four. But that strength, passed on to us by our parents, is what will see us through this. We are still a team. We are still Bullworker's children and that is no feat for the weak. We talk quietly and make the hard choice. Dad will come home, on hospice care.

The rest of the day passes in a blur as we arrange to take Dad home. When we finally get him there and the EMT's are transferring him to the new hospice arranged bed Dad wakes up. His eyes are open. He is looking around intently. He stares for a while at the pictures on the wall. He sees me, he sees David. He is home and he knows it. I believe this gave him a great deal of peace. I do not know if he knew he was dying. His last twenty-four hours are just for me and my brother to remember. I won't write about them. But he knew he was home and that we were all with him. We didn't know it would only be twenty-four hours. He died on Saturday, August 21st at 6:21 pm. A date and time that will live forever in my heart. His last text to me was "love you" exactly one week before.

I am comforted now by the fact that I believe he is in Heaven, waiting for Mom. He'll have it all sussed out and be there to welcome her when it's her turn. He would have wanted it that way. I love you, Dad. I miss you like crazy. I'll take good care of Mom for you, don't worry.

CHAPTER TWENTY-TWO

The Eulogy

Late August 2021

As he had wished, Dad's service was held at the Central Texas Veteran's cemetery outside of Killeen, Texas. It was a beautiful August day, with lots of sunshine and lots of heat. It was a full military service and the flag was folded and handed to me, since Mom wasn't there. My brother and I had already decided we couldn't, wouldn't tell her. Her heart would somehow know. If she felt his absence, we would never know it. She never asked about him. She didn't mention his name. She seemed content and I let it stay that way, for better or worse.

My brother wrote the eulogy.

One of the things my father told me about his funeral was that he did NOT want us to play "Amazing Grace."

We were drinking beer in my garage. It was late. I thought about that for a bit.

Our conversations were never the hurried flurry of words you hear from most people. There were long pauses. Silence.

Reflection on what was said. Then searching for the right reply.

I gave up.

"OK, why no 'Amazing Grace'?"

"Because," he said. Another pause. "I've never been lost a damn day in my life!"

Did he mean spiritually, as the song intended? Or physically? Both?

He seldom explained his pronouncements.

He did have other ideas about what song to play at his funeral. We'll get to that.

We're going to talk about trees.

When my father retired from the Army, he moved just north of Tyler, Texas, about halfway between the Starrville Church of the Living God and Lambert's Liquor store, just across the county line in Gregg County.

(If you're thinking that's a metaphor, well, yeah. He was probably a little closer to the county line than the church.)

His place was in the country, essentially. He had neighbors, but he could ride a four-wheeler, fish in a pond, shoot a gun. And he had trees. A dozen or so huge, towering pine trees.

He loved trees and loved watching the animals that lived among them. He had been a hunter in his younger days but in his retirement years was essentially a bird watcher and animal lover. He took in several stray cats, including one that had been shot up by a neighbor's kid. He waged a peaceful battle against the raccoons that attacked his bird feeders. Shooting them was never an option for him. He had to outsmart them.

Still, he talked tough.

He texted me one day, while he was living out there.

"Shit! Bro! Mom saw a snake in the garage and it hid before I could get it!"

I texted him back, "Well, close the garage door and put a cat in there. If the cat gets the snake, you're good to go. If the snake eats the cat, you probably ought to move."

He texted me back: "Move! Hell! I'll throw the rest of the cats in there!"

He had tried a succession of jobs after the Army -- but he didn't fit in with the private sector. There wasn't a lot of room in the Northeast Texas good ol' boy network for a guy who was gonna tell the boss that he was wrong and this is how it should be done.

He worked for a car lot for a very brief time. Would you buy a used car from this man? No. Because if you asked enough questions, he couldn't help but tell you that the car was a piece of shit.

He loved those trees. Wouldn't cut one down unless it was dead. But he had no problem turning the remains of oak trees into family treasures. He didn't go out to Home Depot and pick out a few boards. Lumber was delivered to him on 18-wheelers.

So, Bullworker took the plunge and started his own business -- Solid Oak Wood Products. Did I say these were his retirement years? Hell, we were fifteen years away from that.

With a little bit of help, he could've made a good and comfortable living selling custom pieces to wealthy customers. But nobody in our family is a salesman and we had no way of connecting the craftsman to the customer.

Instead he sold display cases wholesale. Working himself stupid seven days a week out of his garage. Mom pitched in. Full time. Family members would come visit and find themselves cleaning the shop and sanding boards. If anyone thinks I picked up woodworking pretty quickly, keep in mind I spent hundreds of hours working and watching before I ever made a thing myself.

There was success -- he was proud to send cases to the George W. Bush White House. And to Super Bowl winning teams. He was proud his cases were the finest available -- "none of that plastic crap," he'd say.

He gave up the business when he got 100% disability from the Army. At this point he had money rolling in, and he didn't have to work -- couldn't work -- to get it.

Over those years the big pine trees started to die. Pine bark beetles killed most of them. Lightning struck the biggest one in the front yard. One by one, he'd have the dead trees cut down and hauled off.

If you think I'm going to make a Samson-esque reference to the dying of the pines and the loss of Bullworker's vitality, well, yes.

There were good times in the last years at Starrville. He was a fine grandfather -- he insisted on being called "grandpa." "None of that paw-paw shit," he'd tell me. Even though he was very fond of nicknames for everyone else.

He'd tirelessly drive the kids around on his John Deere riding mower. When my young boys identified him with his John Deere hat, he'd never fail to greet them in costume. We set up a zip-line. In true Bullworker fashion, we didn't do it half-ass. We're talking an 80-yard ride rigged up with professional rock climbing equipment.

And he and Mom would come to my house for birthday parties -- state visits, we called them -- and he'd come by himself to help me with some project or other, which usually involved us staying up past midnight drinking beer in the garage and pontificating -- his word -- on topics of all sorts.

But, the dying of the pines. I remember the time I came up to visit and found that he had actually left his tools out on the ground. A sin he had long warned against. There were projects left unfinished. There was a new silence at the house. He didn't talk about the future. He wouldn't answer questions. There was a depression. Perhaps a bitterness. Maybe even fear.

Of course he didn't take to old age. He was used to being vital. He was used to being in command. But it wasn't him. No, it was Mom. She had dementia. Alzheimer's. He couldn't leave her alone. He couldn't make the trips he loved.

He wanted, desperately, to protect her dignity, and wouldn't tell the family he needed help. He carried this burden even as his own health began to fail. "Bulletproof" he'd tell me. "I was damn near bulletproof."

When it came time to leave their home, only a single great pine remained. He needed to move to North Texas to be near my sister, Julie, so she could help take care of Mom. But he didn't want to go. I appealed to his pride: "You can still steer this boat," I told him. "Or you can wait a year and be a passenger."

He went, reluctantly.

Their new house overlooked the empty vista of a grass farm. They owned it for three years, but Mom only spent a year there before going to an assisted living facility. Dad spent most of the second year in a succession of hospitals and rehab facilities.

But in that first year, he planted a tree. Not a giant pine tree. Not a mighty oak. Just a tree. Any damn tree. Someplace to hang at least a single bird feeder.

In August. Just a month ago. When he was dying in that hospital bed in his living room, he was impossibly small. In a moment that morning between hospice nurses it was just me and him. "I love you," I told him. "But it's OK. I got this."

Looking out the window, that little tree he had planted was dying too.

That was the end.

But that's not where we're going to leave Bullworker.

We're going to build him up again. He deserves to live in our memories as the man he was.

When Larry McMurtry introduced Captain Woodrow Call in "Lonesome Dove," he wrote:

"The funny thing about Woodrow Call was how hard he was to keep in scale. He wasn't a big man -- in fact he was barely middle-sized -- but when you walked up and looked him in the eye, it didn't seem that way."

It was much the same way with Bullworker. Even in his 60s, when he had shrunk to my height and his shoulders had been worn to the point where he couldn't raise his hands in anger if he wanted, his hard stare and commanding voice would make a big man step aside.

Growing up, toughness was a hard-earned tradition for the Thomas family.

When my grandfather was a boy, his own brother accidentally shot him in the stomach during some foolishness with a rifle at the swimming hole. My great-uncle carried my gut-shot grandfather over his shoulder -- if you can imagine that pain -- and took him to the nearest road, where a passing horse-drawn wagon took them to the nearest hospital. The doctor took a quick look, decided my grandfather was going to die, and put him in an auxiliary room -- a shed really -- behind the hospital.

Grandpa lived. This was the blood in Bullworker's veins. This was the stock that he came from.

Toughness was the key to growing up on the farm. First in Magnet, Texas. Then in Wharton. He raised livestock -- became president of the local FFA chapter. He welded. He rebuilt cars and motorcycles. Raised hell on a motorcycle -- he talked about buzzing the local church on Sunday morning and passing a jug back and forth among his friends while speeding down the highway.

But most of all he worked. Because his dad did, and Bullworker was determined to be just as tough as his old man. He told me when he was under that farm truck trying to put that transmission back together, it didn't matter how heavy it was. It didn't matter how tired he was. If it was going to be done, he had to do it.

And it had to be done.

When it came time to go to college, Texas A&M wasn't his first choice. I would guess that the military was a sore spot in his immediate family. His uncles had served in World War II, but his father -- because of his childhood injury -- wasn't allowed to serve. It was a hard thing for my grandfather to live with.

Bullworker was going to be an agriculture teacher.

Dad told me he and a friend drove all day up from Wharton up to Texas Tech in Lubbock. Right as they entered town, a dust storm was blowing in. They turned around and drove home. Right then.

On the way back, they stopped at Texas A&M.

I'm not sure if dad had any intentions of a military career when he enrolled at Texas A&M, but he found his calling. He was traditional enough to love the farm life, smart enough to leave it behind and tough enough to handle whatever the Corps, and then the Army threw his way.

He was a senior at A&M when he met my mother. He called it a blind double-date. As much as an accidental meet-up as possible. But let's face it. The man had no problems with his dating life.

Look at this man. This looks like a still from a Hollywood movie. That is your good-looking leading man right there. The one who saves the day and gets the girl.

If you're here because you know me. And you've ever wondered why I was determined to be fearless, to work hard, to be stoic -- it was because that was all I could genetically muster to try to live up to Charlton Heston here.

This man didn't even break a sweat when he worked.

When he left Texas A&M, Bullworker and Mom were married in Austin and he was sent to Germany instead of Vietnam -- although he'd get there a few years later.

The old world was a romantic wonderland for the young couple. Here he was, half a decade away from driving a cotton picker from Wharton to the Rio Grande Valley at thirty miles per hour (you could see every rock on the side of the road, he told me) and now he's taking in Europe's wine and food and culture first-hand.

He didn't pass up an opportunity to point out that I was conceived during a trip to Italy, but I'm a bit more comfortable than Julie who recently made the mistake of reading some of their love letters -- and learning more than she wanted to know.

Once I was born, me and Mom came home to Austin, while he went to Vietnam. He only spoke about that year in the broadest of terms. He drove trucks. It was bad. He listened to Kris Kristofferson sing "Me and Bobby McGree" and wanted to come home.

If anything haunting happened there, he kept it to himself.

I've told you about the end and the beginning. Don't worry, we won't take another twenty minutes to run through the middle.

He was a good man. He worked too hard during the day. He drank too much in the evening. He smoked too much all the time.

He struggled hard to give me the raising that he had wanted. Most often I'd just work alongside him, but he took time out every now and then for a hunting trip. A fishing trip. A Dallas Cowboys game. Turns out, most of our adventures were misadventures. But you remember those better anyway.

He served in Desert Storm. And before that he spent a year in Lebanon as a military advisor. He told me a little bit after he got settled in at his apartment in Beirut (I'm guessing it was about fifteen minutes), he sent his driver out to find some whiskey. The guy was gone for hours. He finally returned with one small, dusty bottle of Four Roses whiskey. There basically was no whiskey to be had in Beirut. But Scotch? There was plenty of that. So Bullworker, practical as ever, switched.

We often talked about the "Thomas optimism."

I told him that the title of my autobiography was going to be "It Was Harder Than I Thought" -- because we both had a tendency to look at something and think "I can do that." He was right more often than I've been.

But over the last decade, I've realized he carried his disappointments a lot deeper than I ever thought. He retired a

Lt. Colonel in the Army, bitter that he didn't make full Colonel. The Army gave him 100% disability, but he was bitter when he could no longer work.

Old age brought with it fear. He wouldn't speak of cancer. He wouldn't talk about how he would do living alone. And when Mom got Alzheimer's, man he NEVER talked about his feelings about that -- at least not with me. He carried that heartbreak all by himself.

If he drank enough on a visit with me, he'd tell the same story he'd told me a dozen times. How, after he'd made it to captain or so in the Army, after he'd made himself a successful career, he went down to Wharton and took his old man camping down by the Colorado River.

It was the same spot they had camped when he was a kid. One of their few activities together that didn't mean working their ass off. But now Dad had all the gear. Top-notch tents. Army stuff. Coolers. Beer and whiskey and brand-new fishing poles. He wanted to show his dad he had made it.

And grandpa came and hung out for a while, but he didn't stay. After a few hours, he abruptly told Dad that he had to go. And he went home.

And Dad spent the night alone on the banks of the river. Wondering what he didn't do right.

Was grandpa really that ornery? Was grandpa already dying of lung cancer and too sick to stay? Or was he so proud that he was too choked up to stay? He never explained.

Fifty years later, Dad was still at a loss for words. Fifty years later, he still was looking for an answer. Confused enough to share that pain with his own son.

I told him it was probably a hard man struggling with his pride. But, hell, I didn't know.

My own father did particularly well in his life. But he wanted more than he got.

There's a Sam Peckinpah movie called "Junior Bonner." No, it wasn't one of his better-known ones. In it, a down-on-his-luck rodeo cowboy played by Steve McQueen finally returns to his hometown.

Of course, he wants to win the big rodeo, but one of the subplots is the backward-looking, wayward son reconnecting with his hard-drinking, idealistic old man, Ace Bonner.

Now you see what I'm getting at.

The day before the big rodeo the father signs the two up to compete in a wild cow milking contest. Not a serious competition, just a bit of entertainment for the locals before the big event.

But of course they give it all they got, and come up just short of winning.

The father is disappointed.

"We could have won," he tells his son..

The son sees the bigger picture. Junior puts his arm around his father's shoulder and says "We did, Ace. We did."

Well... we won Bullworker. I hope you know it now.

We won.

Here's that song you wanted.

(Plays "Whiskey River.")

CHAPTER TWENTY-THREE

Grief

September - December 2021

We tried to go on as normal. We really did. Skylar rode and horse showed. I taught lessons. Went to horse shows. Tony went to work and broke his stud colt in his free time. My brother and I went about the business of taking care of Dad's estate. His was all legal stuff, mine was dealing with the estate - the house and everything in it.

On September 18th we had a Celebration of Life for Dad. In Austin - Buda actually - so that most of the family could come. Aunt Patty was away on another cruise, but she was well represented by her kids. In fact, it was mostly cousins and old friends that showed up. None of his sisters could make it. It was a large hall, in the middle of nowhere, looking really rough on the outside and left you wondering where the entrance was. But the inside was lovely. Big and empty, we were able to hang the Texas and the American flags and decorate with centerpieces made out of Dad's favorite things - A Lone Star Beer bottle filled with an American flag to represent his patriotism, a stalk of cotton to represent his youth, a bluebonnet to represent Texas and a yellow rose for Mom. We set them on some old pieces of woodworking that Dad had done so the picture was complete.

My brother was mostly in charge of the event, considering it was on his home turf and not mine, and he did an outstanding job. Plenty of pictures and memorabilia filled the side tables and a portrait of Dad at Texas A&M greeted people at the door. I got choked up when Dad's old friend Dave Housman sat and talked to me a long while. It was like looking into Dad's past and even though I had never met him before, it felt like a message was being sent to me through him.

In spite of the fact that everything went well and it was a great time remembering Dad in all the ways he wanted us to, I was exhausted by the end of it and just wanted to get back home. Back to Pilot Point, back to Mom. I was worried about her, though I needn't be. I knew she was in excellent hands. But the fact that she wasn't at the celebration, that she couldn't perceive his death, that she would never see him again, really weighed on my mind. I felt a fierce desire to protect her from the knowledge that would wreck her temporarily and also felt sorry for myself that I couldn't cry on her shoulder.

Mom's hands have started curling up. From disuse I am told. Her fingers are clenched in a tight ball, and her right foot turns in at an angle. You can't un-angle it. I tried. These things bring home the reality, once again, that she's slowly getting worse. She can still move her hands and clutch things, but if she's not using them, there they sit, in a permanent clench she has no control over.

I take a lot of naps. It's the only way I can cope. I hold her hand a lot. I memorize the fingers, the knobs and the wrinkles. The sunspots and the softness. The skin is paper thin as I rub it. I want to whisper to her - don't let go Mom, don't ever let go. But that wouldn't be fair. So I don't. She's getting more frail and I am afraid she won't make it through another year. I try so hard not to be afraid. But I am terrified.

October rolls around and I go through all the things from my parents' house and find lots of old love letters. I read one. I learn my brother's nickname as a baby was "beetle" and that he had to wear two diapers because he peed so much. It makes me laugh but then I read another one from Dad to Mom - my eyes about pop out of my head and I vow not to read any more!

We take Skylar and her pony (and my clients) to a Halloween themed horse show in late October. She dresses up as a cheetah, and we turn the pony into a cheetah too. They win the best in show award! On Halloween night we go to our friend's neighborhood and the mom and I ride in the golf cart drinking wine while chasing the girls from house to house. We have a lot of fun, and I can put my grief aside for a small bit of time.

In November I finally get to buy my own golf cart, that I have always wanted. I name it Bullworker in Dad's honor. My brother has some stickers made up and I proudly display both that sticker (that says Bullworker) and one for Alzheimer's awareness on my new blue golf cart. I finally have the surgery I so desperately needed on my foot. The plantar fasciitis has gotten so bad I can't walk, plus there is a heel bone spur on my foot that grinds into the nerve every time I put my foot down. The surgery is a success, and while it takes time to fully recover, I can already tell that the pain is gone, and I am ecstatic about that.

On Veterans' Day I go to see Mom, and she is not her usual smiley self. She seems lethargic and down. I don't know what is causing it, but some days are just not as good as others, they tell me.

Well, Dad, it's been two and a half months. Ten weeks since you left. I suppose I am coping; I suppose things are going fine. I know you would want me to be strong, and brave, and holding it all together. But honestly, I'm a mess.

I've lost one of my main anchors. My stay, my rock. I'm out here drifting with one finger in the dam. I can't handle even the smallest things anymore. Skylar frustrates me every morning, every night. I'm not sure how she's coping with her Grandpa's death except to tell me every once in a while that she misses you. She has strong feelings, she has passion and grit. But she also is sensitive and can't handle anyone being upset with her. Yet, she continues to upset us by not listening, not doing as she's told, by giving me attitude and disrespecting me.

Dad, what would you do? You never told me how to handle her, your Fu-Fu. But you expected her to do exactly what you told her to do. And like the rest of us, she usually did. You never minded giving me a break, having her come to your house to play. You insisted the train table and toys stay in the living room, where you could watch her play. You had to know where she was if she wandered out of sight for a few minutes. She didn't know it, but you always had her back.

Just like you always had mine. You would never have let anything bad happen to me that you could help. You did anything and everything for me. Even as Mom became unable to communicate, you took over the everyday phone calls and nightly check-ins. I'm not sure if this was for my benefit, or yours. I know you were lonely, too.

I know the last three years were just damn miserable for you. Essentially losing the love of your life, your mobility, your independence, and your appetite. Losing your home in Tyler was a heartbreak you never got over. I still feel terrible that you had to make that choice, that what you (and all of us) felt was best for Mom turned out just to be a stopgap before the inevitable. We all wanted more time. With her. With you.

But I was grateful you were close. I am grateful that Fu-Fu had this time with you. The only light in your life these past three years, at least you had each other.

I miss you. Your belief that you were bulletproof, your confidence, your cussedness. Your willingness to do whatever it took to make us all happy. Family first. Pray to God. Be a good man and stand up for what you believe in. Determination, patience, persistence. Grit. But above all else, love. You loved us. You held on as long as you could out of love. I know you did.

Today is your favorite day of the year, Dad. You were always expecting a phone call on Veteran's Day. Once Fu-Fu and I made you an American flag cake. You were so pleased with it even though you only said "alright!" the way only you could. Conveying pleasure and appreciation with that one word. Today I am even more of a mess than usual. To not be able to call you and hear your voice is almost more than I can bear. I'm going to see Mom today instead. I'm going to go tell her how much we all love her and I'm going to think inside that I'm not really ready for her to join you, yet. I wonder if somehow she knows you aren't here anymore. I believe she does. I believe she knows because otherwise you would be there. You would never abandon her willingly.

But you knew we would take care of things. Mom, and Fu-Fu and ourselves. You knew you had done everything you could. You were more than ready to go.

In my mind you are still bulletproof.

I love you, Dad. Happy Veteran's Day.

A few days later my brother and his oldest son come to town, and we go to see Mom. We sit outside and Mom is covered up with a blanket. Mom was a little afraid of my brother at first, she didn't recognize him at all. This completely unnerved my brother, which is understandable. She eventually warmed up, and they ended up holding hands for a picture. Mom is happy to have all the attention, and she smiles big for the camera. My brother tells me later he was stunned at how she looked - she really had deteriorated a lot from the last time he saw her.

Over Thanksgiving Mom is really sick. Coughing and congestion. I go to see her and have to be content just sitting and holding her hand. She is well covered up with a blanket and has her favorite stuffed cat. In the silence I study her face. She looks so old. So much older than her seventy-five years. Her chin is sunken in, and you can tell she has very few teeth left. I don't like it at all. It makes me so sad. I know she would be horrified if she knew how she looked - outward appearances were very important to her. She has taken to pulling at hairs on her chin when she's awake. I would love to tweeze those suckers out, but it would hurt and she would not understand why I was hurting her. She might not even let me get that close to her face. So I don't try. I'm going to ask the hairdresser if she can at least trim all the stray hairs up. I watch her sleep and I wonder where the Mom I once knew went. Because this frail, tired, vacant person isn't her. Isn't the vital, tenacious, feisty Mom I had. I sigh in defeat and try to think of other things.

When I walked in to Just Like Home yesterday the first person I saw was Dad. Plaid shirt, patriotic hat, mustache, weathered face. Sitting there chatting with Nikki and Max (one of the residents). I did a double take and realized that it obviously wasn't him. But put a few more years on him and a cane in his hand and the likeness was startling. Turns out he is Max's son. I was momentarily thrown. I stole another glance just to pretend for a moment that it could be him, Dad. Just to have a little glimpse of how things used to be.

I breathed in slowly and then I asked Nikki to get Mom in her wheelchair so I could take her outside. As we entered her room and I said hi, she looked up at me with a smile in her eyes and reached her hand up to touch my face. I was, as always, relieved to see her still know me. I help her sit up while Nikki gets the chair ready and then helps her stand and rotates her into it. Mom's body is getting stiff. Her feet don't move well - they are curling up from lack of use. Her head permanently lists to the left. She has trouble bending her knees when we put the footrests on the wheelchair. In fact, she cannot bend them at all, and we have to help her. She doesn't seem to mind though. She is happy I am there and happy to be going outside on such a beautiful day.

As we walk around the perimeter of the building, she holds my hand to her face with her left hand, and I steer the wheelchair with my right. I tell her all about the last horse show, decorating the barn for Christmas and how we are going to a Festival of Lights in a few weeks. How I paid for the VIP tickets so I wouldn't have to walk too much. I tell her about everything and anything and she soaks it all up. We hear Crystal, one of the caregivers, out on the front porch animatedly telling stories about her lemon of a car and we go to investigate. Crystal is wound up, and Mom gets a big grin on her face just listening to her. Crystal and Nikki are laughing and so am I.

Nikki comes over to tell Mom she's leaving and she says, "I love you" and Mom responds, "I love you too." I quickly say, "but not as much as you love me, right?" Mom grins and says No! Nikki and I laugh. It is so good to see Mom like this. I ask her what she had for lunch and she pauses, then says "I have no idea." We laugh again. There is still so much life in her. I cherish these times I get to be with her because I know the darkness that is coming.

Roxie, her nurse, says she's aspirating some as she eats, which causes some coughing. Mom was very sick over Thanksgiving, and I was extremely worried about her. She's doing much better now, but I know our time together is winding down. Mom's body and brain are failing her. Slowly but surely the disease marches its advance and there's nothing left to fight.

I know Dad has gone ahead to "reconnaissance" the location. The problem is that he can't come back to tell us about it. "I'm on recon" he used to say as he headed out. He also used to say that you had to be "postured" correctly before you could expect to get something done right. And he definitely was postured before he died. He made it very easy

262

on my brother and I, he was a man that wasn't leaving this world unprepared if he could help it. He made sure that Mom was going to be well taken care of. That we all were. He's waiting for her there, so he can take her hand and show her the ropes of Heaven. He's waiting for his "Muff."

I, however, am so far from ready for it that I can't even wrap my head around what it will be like when she's gone. Right now, I can still hold her hand, still feel her love, watch her smile and laugh. I always ask her when I leave "will you be ok until I get back?" And she always answers "yes."

And I know she will be. The ladies here love her as their own. She is everyone's mom and a bright light in their lives as well as mine. And I know she'll be ok when she finally reaches out to Dad again - when she puts her hand to his cheek, instead of mine. When she sees the radiance of God and is free from the stranglehold life has on her. I know that Dad had to go first, so that none of us have failed her, so that she will never have been alone. She will have me until her last breath and then she'll have Dad again in Heaven. I understand that it had to be this way.

I understand it, and I am happy to be the one here with her, but Lord, what will I do when she's gone?

There is a Christmas Party at Just Like Home in early December. They dress Mom up in a Santa hat with twinkling lights. Skylar loves it and can't wait to put it on herself. Mom looks good and is in a good mood. She smiles a lot and touches my hand. Santa himself even comes for the party, and I get a picture of Mom with Santa. She smiles, but never at the camera. She no longer has the capacity to focus on someone taking her picture. We have a pretty good time, but I am always reminded of where we are versus where I would like us to be. It's pretty damn hard to have a good attitude about it all, all the time, when you just want to rant and scream and cry over the unfairness of it all.

On December 18th I drove out to the Central Texas State Veteran's Cemetery to visit Dad's grave for the first time. I picked up Val just this side of Ft. Worth and we were on our way.

We arrived at the cemetery at about 11:30 am in the morning. There was a lady sitting near a freshly installed headstone, just visiting her beloved. Val and I walk to find Dad's among the rest in his "unit" as we called the collection of graves in that area.

We looked at the inscription. The Christian cross at the top. David Lee Thomas. LTC US ARMY. Vietnam. (Why only Vietnam I wondered) Mar 5 1946 - Aug 21 2021. BSM & 3 OLC. DMSM MSM ARCOM. Bullworker. Loving Husband and Dad. Val texted her Army sister to find out what it all means. BSM - Bronze Star Medal. 3 OLC - Four Oak Leaf Clusters. Defense Meritorious Service Medal. Meritorious Service Medal. Army Commendation Medal. Your Dad was a Badass, Val says. Well obviously.

She keeps the atmosphere light, as I knew she would. We joke about pulling up some lawn chairs and cracking open a few beers with a tribunal whiskey at the headstone, while kicking back and watching an Aggie game on the laptop. I can hear Dad chuckling. Just the kind of humor he appreciated.

Val goes off to pick up all the fallen over Christmas wreaths in Dad's unit while I stay and talk softly to him. I tell him I miss him, that Fu-Fu misses him. That we're doing alright and that I'm taking good care of Mom. I don't talk a lot but just absorb where I am. I kneel behind the headstone with my arms draped over it. I feel closer to him that way, as if I'm giving him a hug. I stay that way awhile. It's very peaceful in this cemetery. I don't cry - I just try to remember. How we laughed, how he loved, how it was over much too quickly. I feel like he is at peace and in the presence of God. He can see us, and hear us, but he knows there isn't any need to "be" here. We've got this. We're alright.

I get up and wander around a bit. I notice coins on the tops of some of the headstones. Naturally I have to find out what they are for. I google it. A penny means someone visited. In military terms a nickel means they were in boot camp together, a dime means they served together, and a quarter means the person was with him when he was killed. Val and I decide we will leave pennies and start to walk back to the car to get them. I get close and stop dead in my tracks. Val - look! There is a bright red cardinal on my car. Peering and preening in the side mirror. He flies off to a tree as we approach but presently comes back again. Dad, I say, quit showing off. Val takes pictures while I appreciate the moment.

I decide to leave a quarter as well as my penny. The coins will be collected about once a year and used for cemetery upkeep. In civilian terms a quarter means you were with him when he died, and I was. So I go with it. We place the coins and tell Dad bye. It was good to see you Sir, Val says. I know he's answering "I'm glad you got to see me."

We stop to eat at Cheddar's and as we sit down at the bar I glance up and there is a bottle of Jameson straight ahead of my face. I smile. Dad, you are still larger than life. Still invincible. I feel something like the "let down" after Christmas - anticipation now satisfied and fulfilled. It was hard seeing that name in stone, but I am relieved to know it's perfect. The inscription, the place, the peace.

Bye Dad. I'll be back sometime. In the meantime I'm glad I got to see you.

I start planning for Christmas in September. I love the whole Christmas season. The lights, the music, the gifts, the wrapping, the magic and the joy. Making fudge. Making cookies. Making memories. But these last three Christmases have been anything but easy. I start planning in September because I know that come December, all hell has usually broken loose, and I had better be prepared.

Three years ago, my parents had first moved to Pilot Point and it was a month full of the flurry of unpacking and helping Mom to understand what was happening. Christmas Day with Mom was difficult. She was overwhelmed and couldn't even open, much less appreciate, her gifts. Though she tried mightily it was obvious to all of us that Christmas as we had always known it was gone.

Two years ago, Dad lay in a hospital bed in Ft. Worth, Texas, fighting for his life. It was me that bought, wrapped, gave, cooked and otherwise "made Christmas happen" for Skylar, my brother and his kids. Dad remembered none of it. He had no idea that we all trooped to Ft. Worth a few days before Christmas to visit. Mom cried when we visited her as well. Overwhelmed and emotional, it was hard on everyone, especially her and Dad, who didn't even get to see each other.

Then last Christmas Dad actually was here, in my home, celebrating with us. He spent the night and was present for the presents Santa brought. He helped Skylar un-do and un-box and set up new toys, and it was all just so bittersweet. He was here, but Mom wasn't. Mom wasn't forgotten, of course, but bringing her home for even just the day wasn't an option. Mom relies on security and being able to make sense of things. Routine is all important. For any of you that may wonder, "sun-downing" in Alzheimer's patients is a very real, and very scary thing. Tony made a brisket, and we ate that with a few other sides. Nothing crazy. Nothing that would make me break down and cry like I did on Thanksgiving when I couldn't figure out how to make Mom's famous gravy.

Fast forward to this year.

Dad - last night I cried. Huge grief filled balloon tears. I felt no Christmas joy, not an ounce of Christmas spirit. This month has gone so quickly. We did all the Christmas things - We made fudge. We made Christmas ornaments for teachers and friends. We went to a Christmas party. Skylar did a gingerbread house. We took a lot of pictures. But somehow, Dad, it all just seemed so.... quiet.

I just can't get used to the silence. To the emptiness that surrounds me. Last night it erupted within me. It was all I could think about, all I could focus on. You aren't here, you aren't here, you aren't here - like a broken record. I went to bed full of sorrow and tears.

I woke up this morning with a new purpose. I wrote my list out and started cleaning the house. I made banana bread. I vacuumed. I sorted and put away the laundry. I Windexed. I made corn casserole per Baby Girl's request. I did all the things. At 2 pm the in-laws showed up, and just before them was Sissy. Everyone was assembled and as we sat down to eat

I smiled to myself. Hello Dad, I said silently. I feel you. I know you would have been amazed at the concept of the frozen turkey. You would have eaten the store-bought gravy. And if you were here, I would have had cranberries from a jar. I smiled because I could hear you. I could feel you. You were here, even if I was the only one who knew it.

Amazingly, Dad, today I'm ok. Today I put it all together. For you. For the us that we used to be. And I think I did alright. Tonight, Skylar and I will make cookies for Santa and once she's asleep I'll sneak the gifts in and do the stockings. We have stockings for everyone in the house, Dad. All four of us, plus the three cats, two dolls and one stuffed cheetah. And trust me, they will all have been filled by Santa. The magic is still alive Dad, still here. Your Fu-Fu is having a wonderful Christmas and tomorrow will be even better. I won't cry when we visit Mom, I promise. I'll make sure that I hold it together. I'll make sure Mom feels you, too. By sharing with her my Christmas Spirit, the Spirit that you somehow gave to me last night while I slept.

Thank you, Dad. I love you. Merry Christmas in Heaven.

CHAPTER TWENTY-FOUR

Sunbirds

January - March 2022

My brother came with his kids for New Year's Eve. It was weird celebrating without Dad - especially when we brought the sparklers out. No one to tell us to "be careful" or to stop screwing around. We had to be the adults, my brother and I. I am not sure we liked it. Nobody stayed up until midnight, and my brother didn't go see Mom. I think for him, he realized that Mom didn't recognize him, and he didn't feel obligated or that it would do her any good, especially after Mom was a bit scared of him the last time he went. I understand how he feels.

She still holds my hand and reaches for me when I go. I'll hold onto that as long as I can. She doesn't talk much, but she'll say "I love you, too" if you say that you love her. Does she still know what it means? I don't know, but I do know that love is the last thing to go. And she still feels it. I don't know if language or speech goes away for everyone with Alzheimer's, but it did for her, and pretty early on, too. I remember her trying to talk to me on the phone and could not remember what she was going to say. Couldn't get the words out. It frustrated her badly. Some days she would laugh about it and carry on and other days she would get upset. I admire her courage. How can you laugh when you know what is coming? Once she told me, "Every day is a new day - a whole new ballgame, and I don't have to worry about whatever happened yesterday because I don't remember it!" She was in a good mood that day, standing in my kitchen and shrugging it off.

The caregivers have the great idea to get Mom one of those neck pillows you use when you're traveling. It will give her some support so she can hold her head up easier. She seems to really like it. Right now, she's stuck inside a lot as the weather has been brutal. We stay in the dining room, and I talk to her and hold her hand. Sometimes we sit in her room and I read to her. I get her a CD player and some audio books so that the caregivers can give her something to listen to. She doesn't hold the picture book of the family that I gave her anymore. She has forgotten about it. I take her outside on February 1st for a bit, to get some sunshine on a nice day. It's a good thing, too, because then it starts to snow.

Mom and I have always been sunbirds. We love to be outside, in the sun, enjoying nature. For her it was gardening, for me it's horses of course. With the weather coming about to be dreadful, today was a good day to go take Mom outside for a while. It's about 68° and Mom is in her high-back wheelchair. As I push her around and talk to her about everything from the weather to Skylar to horses, she

just soaks it all in, but without making a sound and without giving any indication at all that she is listening. But I know that she is.

Two weeks ago, Mom was very, very sick with Covid. I was very afraid that she wasn't going to make it. But with two IV infusions of vitamins, minerals, and whatever else they could throw in there she brightened up considerably. She made it through. She was smiling and talking again, and her eyes were bright. She was very aware of her surroundings.

Today Mom is not so bright. Her head lists to the left and they are using the neck pillow so that she won't strain her neck muscles. Her whole body kind of slumps to the left, and her legs stay straight even when they should bend. The two ladies that help her move from the recliner to the wheelchair do a great job, considering they get absolutely no muscle movement from Mom at all. I've bent down low so that she can see my face, and I take my mask off so that she'll know who I am. I say hi Mom and give her my best smile. She gives me a little half smile back and her eyes tell me she remembers me. But there's no more reaching up to my face and patting my cheeks with her hands.

I talk to Mom as we walk. We stop and fill up her bird feeder with the bird seed I bought. I fill up another feeder that's empty as well, because I've got some left in the bag. I don't know if Mom can even enjoy the birds anymore but that doesn't stop me from trying.

Mom's chest sounds awful. I've brought her a Coke from McDonald's, and she takes a sip with the straw. It takes her a few tries, but she can still do this. As she tastes the Coke her eyebrows raise up and I know she still likes the taste. Best thing ever, huh Mom? I say. But then she coughs and the gunk in the back of her throat sounds scary. It reminds me of Dad basically drowning in his own saliva and I am *concerned. I understand this is a constant now - she can't truly cough anything up and there's only so much the medication can do. COPD has been an important factor in her illness and not for the first time I wish she had never picked up a cigarette.*

We sit in the sun, and I take her hand in mine. I rub her fingers while she dozes. I can't stay long - there's always somewhere else I have to be or something else I have to do. Time is not my friend. Nor hers. I rewind the tape in my head and put us both on the back porch of their house in Tyler. Chilling out. Chatting while Mom smokes. Me in the swing drinking wine. Watching the birds and the squirrels. Talking about what to cook for dinner and where we want to go shopping tomorrow. Me telling her all about my life and her listening and trying to solve all my problems.

I would give anything to go back. Watching Skylar play in the little pool, or on the playscape Grandpa bought. Hearing Dad pontificate on some topic or tell a story I've heard a hundred times. Laughing and enjoying life, de-stressing and knowing that Mom and Dad still have my back. Not aware yet that there will be a time when they don't. When they can't. When I'm on my own and have to be the Strong One At All Times.

The past is gone, evaporated like smoke. So, right now Mom, I'll hold your hand and dream with you in this beautiful sunshine.

Mom's hospice nurse, Roxie, has gotten Mom a high-backed wheelchair so that she can sit up easier. We take it on a test run once all the snow has gone, just around the building a few times but Mom enjoys the walks. We wander up and down the hallways inside, too. Anything to beat the boredom and create some interesting thoughts. She gets a new haircut, and the girls curl her hair and put her in nice clothes. These ladies are so thoughtful, so nice, and so loving to Mom. I am so grateful for them. Mom is smiling big when she sees herself in the mirror.

March 5th was a hard day. Dad's seventy-sixth birthday. A day full of too many silences. Too many wishes. Too many empty spaces. In truth he's not seventy-six at all. He's forever seventy-five. I'm sure in heaven he's young again, young and carefree and full of piss and vinegar.

Today Skylar and I went to his house. The house he lived in for the final three years of his life. Three years that he was miserable, I know. Three years that I'm sure he wished he could've just skipped altogether. He was happy in East Texas; he didn't want to leave. He had to leave, for Mom, but he wasn't happy about it. So, I never really feel his presence here, in Pilot Point. I think I'd have to go to their old home for that. But still, I felt it important to have some sort of closure, some Goodbye, for Skylar. The closest I can get to his presence is sitting on the back porch, watching her play. He loved to watch her play. But if I look to the left, he's not there. It's just an empty space, where he should be.

We played some on the playscape and then collected rocks to take home for the roses. We went through the house room by room and imagined how it was, and I thought about how it will never be again.

After that we went to see Mom, and we brought her outside to enjoy the weather. Mom watched Skylar - her eyes followed her around - but other than that she was very unresponsive. I held her hand and played Willie Nelson songs for her, in honor of Dad. I told her it was Saturday, March 5th. No response. We listened to Seven Spanish Angels, A Good Hearted Woman and Whiskey River with no response. I kept hoping for a spark, but there was nothing today. Pancho and Lefty and the Highwaymen fared no better. She said she was happy I was there but other than that I got no words from her today. She often looks at me now like she's wondering who I am. It doesn't sadden me, I know she would know me if she could.

On the way home we stopped at Brookshires - I wanted to buy a piece of chocolate cake to put a candle in. Skylar argued for the bright blue frosted cupcakes and finally I gave in and let her make the call. Call me sentimental, I guess. I think I was hoping to feel something more akin to peace than to sadness. But it didn't work. It just made his absence even more painful to bear.

Saying Goodbye isn't something you can just do. You can call it goodbye, you can call it closure, you can call it whatever the hell you want but in the end it's just another way to remember the reason you're sad. Maybe in the long run I'll be glad I did it this way. It's hard to lose his house. The last place I saw him alive. The place where he died. The place where he tried so hard to be everything we all needed him to be. Until he just couldn't anymore. Even though Dad isn't there in any way, I will miss that house. Not as much as I miss the one back in East Texas, but I'll miss knowing he was there. Knowing your Dad was there is the hardest thing to lose.

I might've said goodbye to your house today, Dad, but you'll never be gone from me. It's my mission in life to make sure that your Fu-Fu remembers you and Mom. That she treasures who you were and how much you loved her. As long as she has me, she'll also have you.

Sometimes I wish I smoked. A terrible habit, to be sure, but it just looks so peaceful, relaxing. God knows I could use some of that. Seems like it's just the thing to take a bit of pressure off. A physical time-out. I often imagine that I could do it. A big inhale and a looonnnggg exhale, letting out all the worries of my mind. I wonder what the nicotine rush would feel like. It must be pretty good.

I'll never do it of course. You don't grow up with two parents who smoked - in the house, in the car, everywhere, and think smoking is cool. At least I didn't. I hated it. I would wave my hands dramatically in front of my face and act like I was dying of secondhand smoke inhalation. Every time one of my parents lit up, I would move a bit further away. I couldn't stand the smoke, the smell - the way it lingered on clothes and breath. My eyes watered, my throat closed up.

No matter how I tried I could never convince them to give it up. Mom tried - she tried a lot. But it never took long for her to pick up one, then two, then multiple cigarettes a day. Alzheimer's is the only thing that worked, ironic as that is - she forgot she was addicted. She forgot the pleasure, the sensation of holding something in her hand, the nicotine rush. She forgot the relief it gave her.

Almost fifteen years ago they finally decided they would no longer smoke in the house. Due to the birth of their first grandchild, they vowed to make the house smoke free. They kept their word and only smoked out on the porch or in the garage. They painted the entire house, ceilings as well, and the hazy, yellowed ceilings and walls came to life again. The garage was always fuggy with smoke, and I could never understand how they stood it. My brother would go out there to ruminate with Dad, but I never could. I'd open the door a half inch just for them to be able to hear me, then wait for them to come in.

Anytime I am stressed - which is the majority of each day - I think about how they smoked. I think about Dad's last years. The last of which he did not smoke again. He was forced to give it up due to his failing health. But he never stopped hankering for one. He never got over the mentality of it. I donated his last box of cigarettes to the homeless shelter at the Episcopal church in Denton. I still wonder what they thought when they saw that box of ciggies in with all the clothes. I wonder if they actually handed them out. I wouldn't normally be the person to perpetuate a terrible habit, but I couldn't help but think how grateful they'd be.

Mom's condition worsens with each passing week. These days it's a toss-up whether she'll know me or not. In the afternoons, after lunch, they lay her down to take pressure off her behind - they've had to adapt their care to her changing needs. She cannot move her body anymore, can't voluntarily move her legs or her feet - though they tend to twitch a lot.

I arrive today after lunch and she's resting, her eyes closed. I lean over and say Hi Mom, how are you? She opens her eyes but there is no recognition there. She is always now looking to the left, as if she sees something no one else can see. She meets my eyes briefly then looks off. Nothing in her face changes, no crinkling of her eyes, not a glimmer of her mouth turning up in a smile. I know that she doesn't know who I am. But I say, "I'm so glad to see you" and I smile and reach for her hand. I ask her if she wants to go outside for a while and she manages a yes. The ladies come in to dress her and put her in the wheelchair while I wait outside in the hall. I can't bear to see her inaction in action - I can't bear to see her so terribly helpless that she has no say in what anyone does to her now.

Once she's ready we head outside for the sunshine and the wind of an eighty-degree North Texas spring afternoon. We walk and I talk to her, of things she may or may not understand. I have no way of knowing if she comprehends what I say. We go around the building, and I remark on the snowy white buds on the trees and how beautiful they are. They're gorgeous, aren't they Mom? I say. She doesn't respond. We stop by my new car and I say, "look Mom, look at my car - isn't it beautiful?" She makes a sound I can't comprehend but I'll pretend she's saying yes, yes it is beautiful. I kneel down next to her and stroke her hair and say, "are you glad to see me?" She says yes, I think. I say do you know me? Am I Julie, your daughter? She looks at me but there isn't anything there. I wish I knew what she is thinking, does she think at all? How would anyone know?

I choose to believe she understands me at least. I choose to believe she's there somewhere, but I do wonder if she knows when I am NOT there. Like last Friday, when she recognized me and smiled hugely and listened to me talk - when I said I'd be back soon - did she know that I meant it? And now, when I come back and she doesn't remember me - will she know later that I was there? Will she wish I was there? Will she miss me? Or does she truly live only in the moment?

I stay about an hour, first trying Willie Nelson songs, then switching to Jimmy Buffett. Today nothing captures her memory, nothing makes her react. I sing anyway and hope she's not completely put off by my voice. Max is out there with us, and I worry about him. I see Dad in him - old and weak, but mentally still sound. I hope he has plenty of visitors. We chat for a minute, but then I let him enjoy the sunshine while I sing, badly, first Good Hearted Woman, then Highwaymen, then moving on to Cheeseburger in Paradise and Boat Drinks. I ask Mom if she remembers us going to New Orleans. There is a tiny spark there and I notice. I hope it means she does.

I can't stay too long - it hurts my neck and back to lean forward so I'm close enough for her to see me and hold my hand. Even if I only stay an hour at a time, I'm going to keep coming as often as I can. I don't want to regret anything when the time comes. I want to know that I did everything I could, everything I could do so she knew I loved her more than anything. Even if the time I'm there I could absolutely be getting a million other things done - there's time for that later. There's going to be time for me that she won't have. So, I sit and I stay as long as I can stand it. She can't talk to me, and today she isn't even looking at me, but I stay nonetheless.

Maybe next time she'll know me. Maybe she won't. But I'll be there anyway.

Mom and I used to adore Jimmy Buffett. I might be terrible, but I'll keep singing and remembering her there with me. *Changes in latitudes, changes in attitudes, nothing remains quite the same. With all of our running and all of our cunning, if we couldn't laugh we'd all go insane.*

CHAPTER TWENTY-FIVE

Praying For Rainbows

April - June 2022

I put one of the caregivers' huge sunglasses on Mom's face as we head outside today. She is sitting a bit more upright, has a bit more spark to her. She seems to love the sunglasses. She poses for pictures with me, and we have quite a good time. We do some selfies, and I take a few of just Mom in those glasses, which are quite stylish. I tell her she's looking good, and the ladies laugh and admire her. They are so kind, I just could not have found a better place for Mom to be. I thank God for it. I pray to God that someday, if I am afflicted with this terrible disease, that I will also have such wonderful surroundings.

Tony and Skylar and I take a break for Spring Break and head to Dinosaur State Park in Glen Rose, Texas. We have quite the time in the creek there, although it is cold as ice. Skylar is crazy, wearing her swimsuit and daring to get in the water. Tony and I politely decline. We see huge dinosaur footprints fossilized and protected by ropes. We hike through the park and then we go to dinner and get large slices of cheesecake for our efforts.

The next day is Fossil Rim Wildlife Center which is a drive through exotic animal park. A giraffe makes the line from car to car and sticks his head in for food. I have my sunroof open, and he obligingly stuffs his snout into it. The zebras are adorable and come right up to the car but Skylar's favorite animal, the cheetah, is thankfully contained behind chain link fences. We actually have a really great time and I'm glad we got to do this.

Horse show season has started up again, and Skylar has moved up to trot cross rails, instead of just poles on the ground. She is going to be eight soon and we plan for her birthday. We also upgraded her bedroom. She wants baby blue walls and unicorn curtains that match her unicorn bedspread. The chandelier that Mom picked out and bought for the nursery stays. I am not ready to let that go and honestly, it looks cute in the room. I think it could last her whole childhood, really. It's quite enchanting.

Easter comes and is really hard. This is a holiday that both my parents adored. It's a bit rough but Skylar still has a good time. She loves egg hunting and is delighted with her haul.

I find a field of bluebonnets to take pictures in. It's a beautiful day and the pictures turn out adorable. I am trying so hard to keep things normal for Skylar. To do all the things that a regular family does. But without them, without them it just sucks. I know eventually I'll get used to it, but I will never not wish they were here to celebrate and do these things with us. All I can think is that Dad must be glad we are trying to get on with our lives. Skylar doesn't talk about Grandpa. I don't know if she is traumatized or not. She won't talk about him at all. I am patient though. I know she is terribly sad.

Do you ever think about Heaven? What it is really like? I think most of us do, from time to time. The concept of Heaven has been on my mind most days lately, as I struggle to make sense of where Dad is, where Mom will be. What does Heaven look like in your mind's eye? I'm curious. Do we all have the same thoughts of beautiful clouds, angels with wings, golden roads and supreme peace? But here are some more thoughts...

When Dad died, I expected to feel something. Something serene and holy. I did not. I saw no light surround him, saw absolutely nothing out of the ordinary. I'm not even sure we were truly there when he passed. I think he might have already gone while we were all looking the other direction. It was only when the nurse said something that we gathered around and held his hand and talked to him. But I honestly think he was already gone.

Did he look back? Did he see us with his body? Did he have any regrets? Any time for regret? Did he see a light? Was there an angel there? Did he meet God right away? Or Jesus? When he's in Heaven does he still have a body? What does he look like? Young? Or is it just a presence that changes depending on what other souls he encounters? When Mom joins him, will they be young together again?

After he died a friend of mine sent me a book entitled "Many Lives, Many Masters" by Brian Weiss. She hoped that it would bring me some peace. In this book the author insists that, through hypnotherapy, he brought a woman back into other lives she had had throughout history. Reincarnation. Many, many times. The woman found peace through hypnotherapy and by visiting these other lives she was able to ease all her anxieties. Each time she was "between lives" she was just basically floating in peace. Not in Heaven as we know it. But just floating. The "Masters" came to talk through her and explained to Dr. Weiss that there are many things we must learn on earth and until we do, we will not be in the presence of God. We will just keep repeating lives on earth until we learn all our lessons.

This book brought me many more questions than answers. My friend meant well but honestly the book unnerved me. I had never thought about reincarnation before. Never considered it as a possibility. However, now that I have read about it, I must consider it. Just recently I read a story about a little boy that ran into a man's arms in a restaurant, and the man held him and rocked him until the little boy fell asleep. A complete stranger. But the little boy seemed to "know" him. When Mom met Tina, there was a definite kinetic energy there. It was almost as if Tina was Mom's mom in another life. Like she recognized her and had been waiting for her all her life. I've never seen her respond to anyone like that before. And maybe it's just the Alzheimer's, but whatever it is I'll take it. It almost hurt my heart; the love was so strong.

Is reincarnation real? Do you really just float in space between lives? Part of me does not want that to be true at all. I want to think of Dad in an actual Heaven, rejoicing at the feet of God. I want him there waiting for me, and for Mom. I want to know he is at peace. I don't want him, or Mom, to suffer through any more lives. Because life IS suffering, even if you have a fabulous life, it is never going to be like living in the Glory of God.

The other day I was out mowing the big paddocks, and I thought to myself, can Dad smell freshly cut grass in Heaven? A completely random thought, but not unusual for me these days. So, can you? Can you smell and think and feel? I don't mean feel emotionally but feel tactically. Maybe not on that one. *Eternity and Heaven are very difficult concepts to grasp. I don't think any of us are actually capable of it. Even with these stories you read, like "Heaven is For Real" and all these other tales of people coming back from Heaven to tell us about it ... I'm skeptical. Not of Heaven existing, but in what form? Maybe it is different for each of us. But the most important thing there is, is to be reunited with the souls you connect with. And if that doesn't happen – because you have been reincarnated – well when will I get to see Dad again? What if he's not there waiting for Mom? What if he's already "gone on" to another life?*

I did not want to think about all these things. I love my friend, but sometimes, you just want to think about things the way you think about them and leave it all well enough alone. The book was enlightening. And frightening. However, I still can see Mom's face when she sees Tina's face and I wonder.

Just Like Home has a lot of events that they do and host. One day they have some therapeutic mini horses come and all the residents just love this. The ponies wear little slippers to keep them from slipping on the hard floor or scratching it. I assume they are trained (somehow) to not poop inside the building. I try hard to engage Mom with the ponies but it doesn't really work. She is not with us today. They're also having a cookout and we go outside to chill with everyone for a while. Mom can't eat what they're making, but they mash some stuff up for her. I do not want to get to the point someday where I have to eat mashed up food. That is the worst! I feel so bad for her every time they (or me) spoon something into her mouth. Can she even tell what it is supposed to be? She certainly can't feed herself anymore and hasn't for a long time. She doesn't even really chew, thus the need to mash things up. She will move it around in her mouth for a while and then swallow. It's terrible to watch. Does she still get any pleasure from food? I can't tell. But I am a very picky eater, and I imagine the point where I can no longer tell people if I like something or not. I sure hope that by that time I can't taste anymore because I can think of very few things that are worse than being forced (even if by accident) to eat stuff you don't like.

Mom holds the Sonic Coke I got her with both hands. She sure isn't letting go of that! She reluctantly lets me take one hand off so I can hold it. Her hands get so bruised now. They are always black and blue, just from light touches on things like the table in the dining room. I rub the skin on her hand and as always, notice how paper thin it is. I will remember her hands, if nothing else, for the rest of my life. Years later I will be able to feel her hand in mine, I just know it.

One day I take a little video of her while I ask her questions. Can you say hi? "No" she says. Do you love me? "No." Did you miss me? "No." Are you tired? "Yes." All I can do is chuckle at her responses. They are, most likely, true. She knows me less and less these days.

As the months go on since Dad's death, my grief gets deeper and more insistent. Grief for Mom has overwhelmed me for years, and with Dad's death I feel like I have no one left to talk to. There's something about the way you can talk to your parents that just doesn't transfer over to anyone else. It's a selfish type of talking - knowing that your parents will listen and support you in whatever you say, knowing that they will have your back and will be there for you no matter what. At least, that is what I had with my parents, and when it was ripped away so suddenly with Dad, and so slowly with Mom, I found myself floundering and drowning in anger and sadness. I was in no way ready to lose them, at their age it just seems cruel. They are both only seventy-five, though Dad would have been seventy-six now. I prayed for years that they would be around a long, long time. I know that my plan is not always God's plan but still I find myself angry all the time.

I did not plan to raise this child, my Baby Girl, without them. I did not anticipate that I would have to. I assumed they would be there, rejoicing with me, and groaning with me, and celebrating each milestone and achievement. I imagined stories told of when I was young, comparing her attitudes and personality to mine. I imagined Mom just laughing and saying, "let me have her for a while, you need a break." I imagined Dad with his Fu-Fu wrapped around his little finger, letting her get away with murder and yet demanding his respect at the same time. I imagined her growing up with them so close, so much a part of her life. I can still see all that, in my mind's eye. I am wild with anger that it won't be so.

Even before today, I have thought that I am not worthy of the pain I feel. I try to hide it. I talk to people every day with a smile on my face, with my feelings deeply buried. I am tired, I'll admit that. I take naps - I try to hide from the grief. In sleep I can escape the pain. In my dreams I see Mom, sometimes without dementia but 99% of the time she is somewhere along the path of Alzheimer's. I never dream of Dad. Not once. I wish I would.

The other night I was sitting in Skylar's room while she was trying to fall asleep. I was sitting and singing to her, after she had had a hard day. I have to resort to the only songs I know all the words to - Twinkle Twinkle Little Star, Rock A Bye Baby, Rudolph the Red Nose Reindeer, Jingle Bells, and finally, Amazing Grace. As I sing, I think about her pain, and I wonder how I can ever help her if I can't even help myself. But then I think, maybe this is what she'll remember. Maybe she'll remember how hard I tried. That I was willing to sit with her in the dark until she softly whispers, "I'm ok now." Maybe she will remember how much I love her, so much so that I kill myself trying not to show her how sad I am. I know sometimes I fail. She sees me cry. She wrote me a note once that said "You are the best Mom I ever know. When you cry my heart breaks." And I want to tell her ditto, Baby Girl, ditto. She exudes love and empathy and caring and self-resilience. I think she'll be ok in spite of me.

With God's help maybe I'll be ok in spite of me, too. In time maybe there will be true happiness again. With wine, good friends, good clients, a loving husband and a child that needs me and loves me unconditionally, maybe one day I'll look back on this time and think "Wow, I am sure grateful I made it through." I pray for this. I pray for peace in my heart. I pray for joy. I pray for a life that I think is worth living. I am not worried about Heaven, I am worried about here, now, my earthly time. For all of you who are struggling with something - with grief and pain and unbearable sadness - I pray for you, too. I pray for rainbows.

CHAPTER TWENTY-SIX

Your Story

July - September 2022

This past year has been extremely challenging as I watched Dad's health deteriorate and then watched him pass away, handling all of his affairs along with my grief, and not being able to draw comfort from Mom, who has no idea he has passed, and probably doesn't remember him at this point anyway. When I go see Mom I keep a happy face, a smile and encouraging words. I wonder if she knows how fake I'm being. How anxiety grips me before and after each visit, how guilt and sadness can bring me down for the rest of the day. She searches my face sometimes as if she's looking for the me she used to know. As if this person in front of her, while very welcome, is a stranger she can't quite get used to.

And yet I *do* draw some comfort from her. Just to be able to still touch her face, hold her hands, and breathe her in. She's still *here* and that is everything. I know the day is coming when even this will be gone from me. I realize what an important role she has always played in my life - my parent, my cheerleader, my coach, my counselor, my rock and my friend. She always had my back, no matter what. Deep conversations and deep emotions never put her off. We laughed and we cried and we loved and I already miss that part of my life more than I can communicate.

However, in reading self-help books and doing a lot of soul searching, I have come to realize that now I must be all of this to my Baby Girl. It's her turn. Mine and her's turn. Of course, there are still a good dozen years before we can naturally morph into "friends", but my job right now is to set the stage for that eventuality. I need to set aside my fear, my grief and my anger and focus on what she needs from me. I'm afraid I haven't done a very good job of it as all these huge emotions took their toll on my mental and physical health.

I'm ready now. Ready to teach her that I love her no matter what, that she's important, not just to me and her daddy, but to God. I'm ready to show her that God created her through love and that He intended for her to be my daughter. I believe that He sent my Baby Girl to comfort me through these times and to let me know that it *doesn't end with my parents' deaths*. They set the stage and it's my time to act. Everything that they taught me, everything that they were - it's time to pass all of it along to her.

I have to start with my own health. Just last night I caught myself saying "I just feel fat." And Skylar not only heard me but commented "you always say you feel fat but you're perfect just the way you are." She loves me as I am, and so does Tony and so does God. That's pretty powerful. Instead of feeling fat and discouraged I will feel grateful and blessed. God put these people in my life, along with some great women friends, to continuously remind me that I am loved, and in turn, I will love as well. BUT I will also treat my body better - like the temple that it is, and I hope that I will be able to teach Skylar to love herself exactly as she is.

She's eight years old now, and I also realize that I will, in fact, *miss these days*. If I don't get out of my head and into her life, I will miss it entirely. And I will regret it. She's an amazing person, full of love and laughter and sensitivity and emotion and imagination. She's a lot like Mom. And a lot like me. Last night I sat and watched the complete rapture and joy on her face as we watched the fireworks at Lone Star Park. She has never seen real fireworks before, and she was super excited and enthralled with it. The last song they played was "God Bless the USA" and I teared up as I watched, and my husband put his arm around me (this was the song Dad and I danced to at my wedding). I looked up into those fireworks and at the joy on my daughter's face and I knew that I had to let her live in a world of happiness and peace and total love. Not grief or sorrow or anger. Dad would want us to be happy. Everything he ever did was for Mom, my brother, me or his grandkids.

Today's the day. Independence Day. I will live for you, my Baby Girl, and for me, and for God. We will take this life by storm, and we will not back down. I'll be here for you, until God calls me home. I pray that you will be strong enough to face whatever life throws at you, including having to put me in a home if I succumb to dementia. I pray that I am strong enough for you. I promise I'll do my best. And I promise that my heart will never, ever forget you. I know Mom's hasn't.

I've been dreaming about Mom a lot lately. In one dream she was having trouble making a sandwich and instead of asking for help she just gave up. I discovered the bread and mustard and everything out and asked her if she had eaten and she replied "No! I couldn't remember how to make one." She was upset and I told her it was ok to ask for help. I sat with her and made it for her while she said, "but I should have been able to do it." And I said of course she should, but that we all need help sometimes.

There was a lot more to the dream that I don't remember - this was the part directly before I woke up. I remember how flustered she was in the dream and how she said she guessed she needed a "big sister" to do it for her. I am not a dream analyst, and I have no idea what any of it means. But it's the fact that I can talk to her in these dreams that make them so incredible. Obviously, in this most recent dream she was at the forefront of Alzheimer's. But she could still talk to me. In reality, and oh there's a lot of stories I could tell, I remember the day she put the eggshells into a cupboard because she couldn't remember what she was supposed to do with them. The utter confusion as she held the eggshells. My heart wrenching because I knew I could not tell her to put them in the trash can. Waiting until I could move the eggshells when she wasn't looking.

If you want to know what Alzheimer's looks like, look closely at Mom's face. She is the face of Alzheimer's. This is the toll it takes. The vacant expression, the staring off into space - the listlessness and the leaning. Look at her eyes. She no longer sees the world around her; she can only rarely focus on anything. If she manages to look directly at me sometimes,

I'll still get a smile. Mostly not. Maybe she'll say a word or two to me, maybe she won't. Today I showed her a picture of Dad, all dressed up in his Army uniform standing in front of a flag. Who is this I ask, putting it carefully in her line of vision. Who is this? She glances at it before her eyes slide away. I don't know, she says clearly. You don't know who this is? I ask again. She mutters uh-uh. Usually, I don't do this to her. I don't ask the hard questions, and I don't try to make her remember.

But today I was curious. I set the picture down without another word and then I looked at her and said, "Do you know me?" I asked it twice and she just looked away. No response. Nothing in her eyes. So, I sat down and read to her, the storybooks she used to love. Where The Wild Things Are, Tikki Tikki Tembo, and Strega Nona. I did all the voices, and she was interested... I think. She didn't try to look at the pictures. She didn't watch me as I read. But she didn't fall asleep either, so I'll take that as a win. One of the care ladies stopped by and I think was sorry to have interrupted but I kind of wished she would have stayed and listened too. It made me have the idea to do a story time like Mom used to do. So, I messaged Lori, the Director, and asked her if I could do this for the residents sometime.

The time before when I visited, Skylar was with me. We sat outside for a bit and decided that it was too hot, so we took Mom inside, to her room. Skylar and I decided to "organize" Mom's room. It's always tidy but Skylar went through the postcards that Mom's best friend Panchita sends weekly without fail and decided which to hang on the wall and the door. I went through Mom's closet and found a ton of stuff to weed out. We thoroughly enjoyed ourselves and Mom sat and took it all in. She never said a word, but her eyes were open the whole time and she did look around a lot. We talked and *laughed anyway. Mom enjoys the commotion - she likes to listen to people chatter around her.*

Thursday July 22 is Mom's seventy-sixth birthday. The day before I am throwing a party for her. It's going to have live music thanks to Lori, and grilled salmon and lovely potatoes thanks to some of the ladies that work there. I'll bring the decorations and the cake and all of us, Tony included, are wearing purple to honor Mom. All the residents and caregivers are invited. It'll be a great day and I'm really looking forward to it. You might wonder why we would make all this effort for someone who will not know what is going on - but I tell you if I can make her feel the love that surrounds her then that is what I'm going to do. I'm going to celebrate the heck outta Mom! She deserves a party. We all do. Alzheimer's is an ass kicker for the entire family, so Alzheimer's awareness is the theme - purple and butterflies - because it needs a cure badly. Even some of her oldest friends are coming. Friends who I hope will understand that what they see is not the lady they knew, but that somewhere deep inside she still recognizes them.

I pray that I never have to be the face of Alzheimer's like Mom is. I pray that what she is suffering is not in vain - that if I can somehow make a difference that I will. I pray that my Baby Girl doesn't have to go through this twice. That she'll be around to see the cure. So please give us hope on this day, this day of Alzheimer's awareness. Thursday July 21st wear purple for Mom and thank your lucky stars or your merciful God that your brain is healthy and strong.

Memories matter. And in this family, no one fights alone.

On Mom's birthday this year I go all out. I am completely aware that Mom won't have a clue what's going on, that she won't smile or respond in any way. She probably won't even look at the cake or balloons or decorations. I am going to do it anyway. I am determined that if this is the last birthday she ever has (and I am pretty sure it will be), then it's going to be a great one. I decide on a theme of Alzheimer's awareness and purple butterflies. I buy shirts for me and Skylar. I even buy a purple plaid western style shirt for Tony. Normally I would not insist on him being there, but I want all the love and support I can muster for Mom. I invite friends from far away. Panchita comes. Mom's old friend Jeannie comes. Tina is there and Nikki and Kirsten and Lori and Crystal and Roxie and Angel - all the caregivers that love Mom so much. I've got the entire dining room of Just Like Home decked out in purple with purple butterflies hanging from the ceiling. The care ladies put on Mom's purple shirt and purple socks. I give Mom a tiny stuffed bird that chirps. I was hoping to get a reaction but there is none. We've got a gorgeous purple butterfly cake that I had made and some delicious sugar cookies. I put out pictures of Mom when she was younger. I've got a guy to play guitar (thanks to Lori!) and sing Happy Birthday, and we bring the cake out and sing to her. Skylar blows out the candles. Everyone cheers and we divvy up the cake among all the residents and guests. It's a great day, even if very poignant and bittersweet. I don't know if Mom even recognizes any of her friends, or the fact that this fuss was made for her. But it makes me happy to do it, and everyone is with me. I appreciate so much the love and support my family gets from Just Like Home.

At the end of July Skylar and I go to visit Aunt Patty in Georgetown where she lives. My brother meets us there to drop off Amy, Skylar's cousin. We have a great couple of days with her, swimming and riding the golf cart and getting in the hot tub. We color and play games. We watch the deer off the back porch and get lots of mosquito bites because we forget to put any bug spray on.

Aunt Patty has made me a quilt of Dad's clothes - his jeans, white tee shirts, his red sweatshirt and all his other plaid and striped shirts he used to wear. Even the gray flannel shirt he was wearing the day I took him to the hospital with the staph infection is there. I am overwhelmed. Aunt Patty admits it took her a while to even get started because she was so upset over her brother's death that she couldn't even look at the bag of clothes I sent. But thankfully she was eventually able to put together this quilt for me, and I will be forever grateful. He is fully represented in this quilt, and it means so much to me. She even made a tiny one for Skylar. Skylar cherishes that blanket to this day and still sleeps with it on her bed.

My nephew Matthew has taken to wearing Dad's "uniform". White Adidas tennis shoes, white tee shirt and jeans. He is driving Dad's truck. He even wears Dad's old John Deere cap and aviator sunglasses. It is unnerving when I see him, but I definitely understand. Everyone grieves in their own way.

Hey Mom, I need to talk to you. The other day I ran into a friend of mine and she made a point to tell me that the words I

write, in these blog posts, really mean something to people. That they touch the right people. She is suffering, too, Mom - her own mom also has Alzheimer's. She teared up when she told me that and I was humbled that my words could so affect someone else. I didn't know how to respond - I'm not great at expressing my feelings out loud.

But it moved me, all the same. I've written these blog posts for myself really, to let out my emotions and grief. But, Mom, maybe I could do more. Maybe I could tell the WHOLE story. The story of you. Your story, your fight, your memories. I could put it all down on paper and maybe someone would read it. I've long thought about this and have said to close friends and family that I intend to do it. Yet something has always stopped me. At first, I thought it was my own grief. I find it hard to write when I'm mired down in depression. But I know it is something more. It is your dignity that stops me. This is your story after all, not mine.

You would hate it, Mom, what I want to write. You would be embarrassed and upset, and angry. You did not want this to happen to you. You made us all keep it a secret for a very long time. When you could no longer tell me how you felt I took it upon myself to start telling the story in these posts. I did it for me. I did it so that others would understand. So that maybe someone else wouldn't feel so alone and discouraged. So, you see, I have already betrayed you.

I want to tell the gritty, dirty, terrible details. I want to start at the beginning and tell the truth of how this disease slowly steals your mind, your memories, your abilities and your life. I want to tell how it affects your family, how Dad couldn't stand your pain and how I wanted so bad to advocate for you every step of the way. How I wanted to be sure I never let you down, and how I both succeeded and failed. I want to tell about your feelings, and my feelings, your grief and my own, your fear and mine. I want to tell your history and all the skeletons in the closet.

What I need, Mom, is your blessing. I need to feel that you are ok with it. That maybe you would understand, and want to help others, too. When you were first diagnosed, I could find no books, no articles, or anything that really helped me understand not only what was happening at the time, but what would happen in the future. A few personal stories in books, yes, but nothing that went in depth, nothing that shared the deep, agonizing loss of both of us. Nothing that shared the mortification of losing your abilities such as going to the bathroom, knowing where the toilet was, or the trash can, or your bedroom. The effects of sundowning, and the terrible, terrible guilt over leaving you that first day in the memory care facility.

Through it all we have never lost each other, although I myself feel horribly lost from time to time. When I go to see you and lay my head on your shoulder I can feel you with me, truly with me. That physical connection has never been lost, that emotional connection still runs strong. You might have forgotten who exactly I am, but I know you will not forget that I am important to you. I don't know exactly who I'll be when you pass, the pain that will be etched on my heart when I can no longer feel you will be very hard to bear. I guess my point, Mom, is that I want to tell your story so that you and our story will never be forgotten. So that it might help others not feel so discouraged in their journey with Alzheimer's. And because your story matters.

I suppose I will have to go on without your blessing and hope that you will forgive me. Someone has to tell this story. I guess that someone must be me.

I am a strong woman because a strong woman raised me.

At the beginning of August when I visit Mom - I tend to go every few days - she is talking to me some. I told her I brought her a peanut butter shake, and she said "cool" which made me chuckle. I told her Tony had locked himself out of the house so I couldn't stay too long but I would come back on Monday and bring Skylar. Would that be ok? "Yes." Will you miss me? "Yes." Now we are outside, and I asked if she could hear the cicadas. She says yes again. Her eyes are closed - it's very hot - and she's just relaxing. I took her hands and said, "What if I write a book? About Alzheimer's and your story? Would that be ok?" She just closed her eyes again and didn't respond. Sometimes she frowns when I say I have to leave. It's like an oven out here. I ask if it's too hot and she says no.

August 21st is the one-year anniversary of Dad's death. It is a Sunday and so we all go to Cowboy Church. We each wear Dad's uniform - blue jeans and white shirt, except Tony and Skylar wear their boots. I wear the white tennis shoes Dad was so fond of. I get someone to take a picture of the three of us. I miss Dad terribly and at 6:21 pm I am sitting on the front porch thinking of that moment a year ago. I text my brother - it's 6:21 pm. And he texts back "I know'. We are both really broken still. A tear runs down my face as I watch the American flag blow in the wind.

The smell of the hot iron brings her to me. She stands at my shoulder when I am in my kitchen, chopping celery, making chicken pot pies the way she used to. She watches the timer when I make fudge. I'm baking banana bread and she's there - in her Julia Child's kitchen way while I clean up every little thing as I go. We're laughing until the song "More Hearts Than Mine" by Ingrid Andress comes on and all of a sudden, I'm alone again, standing at the sink bawling my eyes out and missing her so hard I can't breathe.

I'm in the bedroom with Tony while he changes out an electric plug but he's swearing because it's not going easy. "You gotta get postured" I tell him. He rocks back on his heels and looks at me. "You gotta get postured," I say again. "You can't do anything if you aren't postured." Dad always said that, I tell him. He stares at me, his face clearly saying, "what on earth?" "Well," I say, "you got to get positioned in a way that makes it easy for you to complete the task." I get another look. I decide to leave him alone.

Another song - "You should be here" by Cole Swindell - has me breathing deeply in the car trying to hold it together. He's missing out. His Fu-Fu misses him and so do I. We just aren't the same without him around. I can't even drive down his street. I never want to see the house where he was so miserable and our whole world fell apart again.

Almost four years ago Mom is with me in my house, and we are decorating for Christmas. A little figure breaks - one that I love - it is a pony with a little rider on the end of a lunge line, and there's a trainer holding onto the other end. It is me, of course, and Skylar on the pony. It comes off the table when Skylar (four at the time) accidentally pulls on the tablecloth and it shatters. I am shattered, too. I start to cry and Mom comes to me and hugs me and tells me she's so sorry. I know she is. I know also that it's probably the last Christmas I'll have her with me, the last time she'll be able to tell me she's sorry. The grief comes in knowing. The figure breaking wasn't the only reason she was sorry, nor the only reason I was crying.

Yesterday I ordered that little figure off eBay. I paid a pretty penny for it, but I can't wait for it to arrive. I need that figure. I need to hold it, to close my eyes, to remember clearly that moment. Those last moments, those last everythings. She'll still smile at me, but the words are gone. Her eyes no longer focus on me, except briefly. You can't leave me, Mom. Please don't leave me.

Everywhere I go Dad goes too. We have a blow out on the trailer on the way home from a horse show and I can hear him in my head because we don't have the small air compressor he bought me. Luckily Tony is there and can change out the tire that blew. We make it home, but Dad is sitting in the cab with us the whole way.

Every day, every moment, all the time and everywhere, they are with me.

And I miss them.

For the longest time Mom hasn't said more than a word. But lately she's really been trying to talk again. I can't help but wonder why, and what is happening inside her brain. This is one of those things that I think about daily. What IS happening inside her brain? Of course we'll never know exactly, other than what the Alzheimer's experts tell us, which is essentially that her brain is slowly dying. Fading memories and garbled words, the inability to take care of herself and the pain it brings to all her loved ones who simply want her to remember. That's what Alzheimer's is.

Be that as it may, she still recognizes me. The corners of her mouth will turn up slightly, and her eyes will soften and crinkle. That's how I know she's smiling. Yesterday she found my arm with her hand and started patting and rubbing it. That's how I know she's still there, still Mom. Yesterday she was leaning hard to the left and she was very tired, but she opened her eyes quite often, as if she was determined not to miss anything. I talked to her as I usually do, and we sat outside for a long time. Her breathing is slightly labored, and she has a very wet cough. I'm told she's better today but still I am worried. I bring my hand to her chest and ask her if it hurts there. But she doesn't respond.

When I'm there I simply chat to her and hold her hand. I ask her questions but rarely get an answer. Sometimes there will be a yes or a no. Sometimes I let her doze while I lean back in the rocking chair and contemplate life. I'll watch her face and wish things were different. I will think about the end and what that will be like. For me, and for her. I'll rub her hand and stroke her leg and make sure she knows that I'm there. I ask her what she wants for Christmas, and she smiles and kind of laughs. As if she knows there's nothing I can give her that will make up for all of this.

Her body twitches a lot, and her left foot drags while her right foot is permanently bent at a right angle. When we were walking yesterday I had to keep telling her to keep her feet up - and she was able to bring that left foot up some. I noticed that she could still do that, but she can't keep it up. It'll immediately start dragging again. So we walk very slowly and I show her the roses. There are two large pots there, one with yellow roses and one with pink roses. Mom can't focus on things - she won't look where you tell her to look. I snip a pink rose off and bring it up to her face. She focuses on it for a second and I bring it up to her nose. Smell it, Mom, I say, smell the beautiful rose. And she closes her eyes and sniffs. But her mouth also slightly opens as if she thinks it's something to eat. Isn't it gorgeous? I ask. I think she says "beautiful rose" but it's garbled and I can't be sure.

I give her the rose but she can't hold it. She's already lost interest in it. I tuck it into her sleeve, and we keep walking. But I keep looking at that rose. How full in bloom it is and how soon it will wither and fade away. A new rose will grow in its place, a new life in a new dawn. I decide to take that rose home and dry it. Turn it into something I can keep. So that I can remember that everything withers and dies, but something beautiful always will follow.

"

I may not be able to see it now,
but something beautiful will follow.

"

It might be just a small thing, it might be huge. I won't know until it happens. But I know that when it does, she'll be smiling down on me and holding tight onto that pink rose.

Mom is very unresponsive. I sit with her outside as she sleeps. She is tilted forward with her head to the left side. I want her to talk to me, but she can't. The only thing she has said is "I love you too" which should be enough but this time it isn't. I am just so tired of seeing her this way when in my mind's eye I see her as she was. In the kitchen, cooking, reading, shopping, smoking, and all the other things. I tell her that Dad couldn't have stood this. He couldn't have handled this. And I am glad he doesn't have to. That he didn't have to be there for this. Next time he sees her she'll be dancing to "Good Hearted Woman" with him in Heaven.

I ask God how much longer? When will this end? I'd rather her heart just stop beating in her sleep than to watch her starve to death slowly.

CHAPTER TWENTY-SEVEN

Waiting

October - December 2022

When does something you dreamed about become something that happened? And when does something that happened turn into a dream? What if you don't know anymore which is which, and what is what, but you can't stop thinking about it.

Years ago, I was maybe in college, Mom and I were driving somewhere. Mom really had to go to the bathroom but we were on a very long bridge and the traffic was backed up. She started to panic because she was sure she couldn't hold it. I was very concerned about her panic – and I tried to tell her it was ok – if she had to wet her pants then she did and we would just deal with it. I could run in somewhere and buy new stuff I told her, even a towel. But by this time she was crying and in full on panic mode, gripping the steering wheel with anger and fear. I remember the desperation in that car. I remember the traffic, and I remember how desperately I wanted to help her and that there was nothing I could do. I do not remember if she lost the battle of holding it in. I don't remember how the story ended. I just remember the reality of that situation and the panic and tears. I do know that she always carried toilet paper and a change of clothes in the car from then on. Always – up until the day I cleaned her car out they were in there in a Ziploc baggie.

Did this really happen? Was the scene on the bridge real? I can't tell you. I feel like it was. The Ziploc baggie forever taking space in her car is evidence that it happened. But I could have dreamed this particular situation. I no longer know what is real and what isn't. If I could have spared Mom this terrible day I would have – did I dream it based on her terror? It feels so real, even today.

Mom always had a bathroom obsession. Any store we went to, the first thing to do was to find the bathroom. Not just to know where it was, but to go in and use it. Anytime we left the house she had to go to the bathroom a dozen times before we could leave. She'd clutch her stomach and say, "I just don't know ... my stomach is so upset." I would try and be patient but eventually I would get annoyed. I think she knew this because she would snap "I'll be ready in a minute." Or she'd huff and puff and say, "I think we can leave now." And I would say nothing. I wouldn't point out that we could always stop at a store, or that she knew where every bathroom was in the thirty-mile radius of the house. (I wasn't that dumb – she would have killed me.)

But she knew anyway. She knew that I was annoyed. She knew that her fear wasn't justified – other than the time on the bridge (real or imagined) – she never had an accident in the car. Still, she was very afraid of leaving the house. She loved going out and going shopping with me, but until we left the house it was an ordeal every time. Once we were in the car she would usually relax.

Mom had a "witching hour." If we didn't leave town by 4 pm she would start getting twitchy. She would lose focus and get snappy. We used to joke about it. If I was trying to make a decision (or a joke) and she "clicked" her tongue and shifted from one foot to the other I knew my time was up. We'd better get going I'd say, witching hour is here! And then to make dinner after that was just too much. She was never a late afternoon/evening person. In the evenings she just wanted to sit and drink beer and read, later this turned into watching TV when reading was no longer easy for her.

But I digress, back to the bathroom thing. In later years getting Mom to leave the house was near impossible. She would never go to any doctor appointments – you couldn't get her to follow through on anything. She would get so distressed about leaving the house that Dad would just cancel the appointment. I know now that she was comfortable in her house, and that she couldn't compensate outside of it.

How long has she had dementia? She was always so smart and sharp. But somewhere along the way, and I don't think she was as old as I originally thought she was when it started, somewhere along the way she started to falter. The witching hour? Early on sundowning maybe? Witching hour used to be about 6 pm or 7 pm but as she got older that time moved up to 5 pm, then 4 pm. It even applied to me – if I was at a show and we didn't leave until 5 pm or 6 pm she would always say in dismay "it's SOO late!" Like she really felt for me. I remember leaving a show once about this time and her saying this to me as I called her on the way out – I answered by saying how I didn't mind, this was my job and some days it was just like this. She just couldn't fathom it. Even though she used to work at a bookstore until 11 pm and drive home at midnight. Those days were long behind us.

Leaving the house? Like I said, she couldn't compensate outside of her comfort zone. She needed to know where everything was to feel safe. The bathroom thing got worse as she got older, too. She had to be sure she knew where it was at all times. Even if I was with her, she was still uncomfortable. Going out by herself, which she used to love to do, slowly dwindled to never as well.

When should I have picked up on all the signs? When should I have known? It really doesn't matter because I could never convince her to do anything she didn't want to do. Dad couldn't either, though he was more successful than I was, just by virtue of always being in the house with her. But as the years went on she was less and less likely to leave the house, and less and less likely to let anyone in her house either. Even if I had known, even if I had an early diagnosis, there was precious little I would have been able to do about it. She wasn't a woman to let others make decisions for her. I convinced her to take the Prevagen, which is a supplement made from jellyfish and supposed to be really good for memory loss, but as soon as her memory really started to go, so did the Prevagen. She resented Dad telling her to take her pills. She resented him even more when he did the pill tray for her and put them in front of her every day.

But losing the ability to go to the bathroom on her own has to have been the most excruciating detail for Mom. I think about the dream I had, or the scene on the bridge and I wonder… was it real?

Does it matter?

I can't shake this feeling lately. Of a huge let down, a monstrous feeling of gloom. It is sneaking its way into everything I do, everything I feel and everything I eat. It could be that I'm missing Dad more than usual. It could be that I'm hyper aware that Mom doesn't have much time left.

It could be exhaustion, stress about finances, it could be just about anything.

But I think, I really think, it's just that I'm realizing how very alone I am.

Yes, yes, I know God is always with me, and believe me without Him I would've drowned a long time ago. And yes, I have a great husband who adores me most of the time and doesn't let on when he doesn't. He's a smart man. I have a daughter that has true joy in her heart and has the strongest will around. She has a precious heart, as her counselor says. I have friends, GREAT friends. Friends who listen, who walk with me, who care deeply and who will send me crazy memes when I need a laugh.

I have the ability to write about my feelings. An outlet that saves me constantly. An outlet that gives me the space to explore how I feel and what I need.

Because I have these terrible feelings right now, all I can do is wait it out. There is no magic cure. The ever-present awareness of Mom's disease is a scourge to me. I am powerless and helpless; no amount of my love can save her. No amount of her love for me can remove it. She would have done anything to avoid this, I know. Is it a sin to say I wish she was free? I wish she was dancing in heaven with Dad, free of pain and free of mental anguish. **My** mental anguish – she literally knows nothing anymore. I hate this for her. So much that I often feel nauseous just thinking about it.

And so I wait.

I'm waiting for Christmas. A time of cheer and goodwill. Fairy lights and brightly wrapped gifts. Giving and love and high spirits. I need a good Christmas party to go to. To bake cookies and shit. To spend time, without feelings of guilt, with my daughter. To know that it's ok to relax and enjoy the season. To make fudge, to make presents. To listen to

Christmas music that makes my stepdaughter cringe, but which Skylar loves. To sing Jingle Bells at her request until I want to throw up. To laugh, but NOT to cry.

I don't know what this season will bring. I am afraid of it, but also very much looking forward to it. I don't know the future. I don't know the answers to stress about finances, or if I will ever conquer the desire to eat my feelings.

I am waiting. Waiting for joy again. It will come. And peace will come with it.

Mom is deteriorating. When I go to see her now, she is mostly asleep, whether she's in her wheelchair, her recliner, or her bed. She stares off to the left and I have to get down on eye level to have any hope of her looking at me, even briefly.

When I get there, I touch her shoulder and get down to see her face and I say Hi, Mom, quietly. She doesn't look at me. But her eyes flutter and I wonder if she knows it's me. I am doubting more and more every time that I go that she knows me at all. She no longer reaches for my face or holds my hand - except for the grip with her fingers - like a baby will do when something gets close to its hand. She'll hold on then, until you let go, but I think it's just a reaction - not something she is consciously doing. Hi, Mom, I say again. Will you look at me today? Her eyes flutter but still she doesn't move her head, or her eyes.

Mom, I say, I've had such a crazy week. And I tell her all about it. She never responds, or moves, but I keep searching her face, keep talking, keep trying. She'll cough every once in a while, and it is guttural - she is definitely aspirating when she eats and drinks because her cough always sounds very wet. Her chest is a mass of bruises and her caregiver Nikki and I wonder why. Maybe she's scratching herself? Maybe it's the coughing? Something is causing her chest to have these deep red bruises and we can't figure it out. Mom's skin is tissue paper thin, so pretty much any contact with anything will make her bruise.

I am feeding Mom her breakfast today and I can tell its oatmeal with peanut butter in it. Trying to get those calories in. I bring her a chocolate donut, which used to be her favorite, but she makes a funny face when I give it to her, and I can tell she doesn't want it. She opens her mouth anytime the spoon gets close to her lips - just like a very young baby. She can still eat, but the swallowing seems to be taking longer. She can still drink through a straw. The entire time I am feeding her she just sits, staring straight ahead. I sigh and I lean in close to give her a hug. She smells like lavender. She's just had a shower and she's clean and fresh. Her hair is still damp. Every few weeks I buy her special shampoo, body wash, and lotion. It's about all I can still do for her. She doesn't need anything else. She's got a high necked sweater on today because it's so cold and she looks cozy and comfortable. I know that they'll settle her into her recliner as soon as she's done eating and Mom will doze for the rest of the morning.

I haven't been going to see Mom as much. It's heartbreaking for me to see her sleeping all the time. I know she's clean and comfortable. I know she's being well taken care of. I know she doesn't miss me when I'm not there. I have absolutely no concerns about her standard of care. And because of that, I have started to feel less guilty about how often I make it out there. Because, as much as I hate it, life does go on, and I am slowly adjusting to life without her. There is always so much to do every day, and guilt just doesn't fit into my life anymore. She's on my mind every day, and I am absolutely certain that some part of her knows that. What is the point of me sitting there while she sleeps? She doesn't know I'm there, only I know. So, I sit for about thirty minutes, I organize things in her room, and I check my phone. But other than that, there's not much to do, and the guilt now has transferred to all the *other* stuff that is waiting for me. I get up to leave. I'll be back soon, I whisper. You'll be ok? I always ask but she has stopped answering.

Y'all, Mom is in good hands. I could not ask for more. If you ever have to deal with a loved one that has Alzheimer's, the very best thing you can do for them is to find a place for them where they are **loved.** Where they are cherished. Where you can let that guilt go and live your life to the fullest in between visits. I can do this, and I am grateful.

Things happen fast. Especially bad things. In the blink of an eye it's gone, never to return.

The other day Tony was saying how fast his parents have deteriorated. I said to him "Babe, they are in their eighties! It's to be expected." And he said "just a month ago she was driving. Now I'm taking them to Walmart and the post office." I answered "I could say that a week ago Dad was having a conversation with me. Then he died. Four years ago Mom was standing in this very living room, helping me hang ornaments on the tree. Four years ago doesn't seem to be a very long time. Especially when it feels like yesterday." He acknowledged this with a heavy sigh. He knew it was coming - to be helping his parents to this extent. But he didn't get to ease into it. One bad infection later and here we are.

I am finally at peace with what happened to Dad. I know he is at peace, and that is all I need. I think that, even though it seemed to happen so quickly, it really was a long time coming in his opinion. I remember him remarking that he thought he only had a short time left, and he wanted to hire his caregiver back to make his life easier. So of course we did it. I never wanted to hear him talk that way, though, so I didn't pay any attention. I should have. I was in complete denial the entire last couple years of his life. I wanted him to live. I needed him to live.

But I needed him to be at peace more. Now he is.

It's not quite the same thing with Mom, but the end result will be. I need her to be at peace. I want her to be at peace. And happy again. Smiling, dancing with Dad, seeing her own parents, waiting for me. Knowing that I will finally be ok without her.

"

Slowly, steadily, Mom as I knew her has been erased.

"

It started with no longer being able to write a check or follow a recipe. Maybe it was when she stopped reading at night. Could have been when she no longer played games on her phone. Then the ability to know the time and weather.

Gone. The ability to dress herself appropriately. Vanished. Knowing where the trash can was. Her bedroom, her bathroom, the toilet. Silently disappeared.

Hoping I was doing everything I could for her and feeling like a failure. Her ability to cope, her ability to use the bathroom, walk in a straight line without help, communicate appropriately. All slowly, slowly slipping away. Just slipping away.

And then all of a sudden here we are four years later. Mom no longer communicates at all. She sits. Or lies in her recliner or her bed. Still and silent. No more tears. No more pain. No more unhappiness. No more awareness. She doesn't recognize me. She sleeps continuously. I go to see her, and I hold her hand but that is all I can do now. As far as I can tell she doesn't know if I am there or not. The silence kills me. Talk to me Mom. I miss you.

CHAPTER TWENTY-EIGHT

The End

January - February, 2023

January - Mom sleeps a lot. In fact, she is asleep most of the time. Alzheimer's has stolen everything from her and has stolen *her* from me and Skylar. When I go to see her now, she doesn't even open her eyes. She is lost in a world that I cannot find a door into. Mom, I say, hey Mom, can you hear me? She opens her eyes slightly with the squeak of the bed as I sit down. But she doesn't look at me. Hi Mom, hi - can you see me? Her eyes don't focus and almost immediately they start to close again. I sit for a while and watch a show on her TV. I put the Christmas decorations away.

Is there something wrong I wonder? I ask one of the lovely ladies when they think I should be coming to see her. Is there a time of day that she is more awake? They ponder but can't really come up with an answer for me. She is asleep most of the time they tell me, but she'll still eat. Even with her eyes closed, she'll open her mouth for food. I wonder at this - the human body is designed to keep us alive. Why has her brain capitulated in every other regard? I think to myself that I don't believe Mom will pass away due to anything other than her heart stopping. I don't think she's going to stop eating and starve to death, or that she'll choke on her food and end up with pneumonia. I pray that it doesn't come to that. My best scenario is that her brain will simply tell her heart to stop beating, and that it will be a peaceful transition. I also realize that this of course means that the chances of me being with her at that time are slim. But I would rather have her go peacefully than suffer due to hunger or pain. Even if I have to sacrifice being there in her final moment. Even though I know that they would not let her suffer. Pain will not come for her if the nurses can help it. I would still rather just have her slip away in her sleep - wouldn't we all?

I read today about a new drug that is coming. It has shown a 27% reduction in the advancement of Alzheimer's over an eighteen-month study. It is meant for those who have been diagnosed early. It is based on the amyloid plaque hypothesis of Alzheimer's - that amyloid plaques build up in the brain killing brain cells which leads to Alzheimer's and death. Many studies have shown little to no effect of such type drugs, and many companies have switched their research to gene therapy. I don't care who gets it right, but I would rather *not* know if I'm going to wind up in Mom's position. However, that being said, I do think I will know quickly if I am starting to show symptoms and will be first in line for any drug that will slow down the process.

If such a drug had existed at the time would Mom have taken it? Would she have jumped on board? If we had caught on early enough - if she had let us find out what was wrong sooner - would a drug like this have slowed down the process? *Would she have wanted this?* I wonder. She absolutely hated knowing she had Alzheimer's. She *hated* knowing what was going to happen and that she would be rendered helpless and dependent in the end. She called herself "stupid" and cried when she couldn't make words come out of her mouth. She could not understand that it was the disease causing her distress, or at least she refused to believe it. I still don't understand why she couldn't/wouldn't be more gentle with herself. Let herself have grace. Let herself accept what was happening so that we could have tried harder to do something.

The best she let me do was to put her on Prevagen, and to have her eat hardened coconut oil every morning. Eventually as memory failed the pills and oil became ignored... forgotten and discarded in the fridge. She was very suspicious, and it took a lot of convincing to get her to take her pills. I still believe that if someone had put her on an antidepressant early enough, she would have been a happier person those two years. However, considering how difficult it was to get her to a doctor at all, getting her to take an antidepressant was, while not the *least* of our concerns, was simply not a priority.

I won't share a picture of Mom now. She wouldn't have wanted anyone to see her this way, I know. At least I know she is comfortable. She is peaceful. She is unaware of my pain and heartbreak. Skylar still loves her Granny Susan and still remembers her as she was. May this be forever true for her. I do not want her to forget.

Please don't forget.

February - Mom's light is fading. I think I've really known this for a while now, but it became clear last night when I talked to her hospice nurse, Roxie. Roxie has always cut straight to the truth, and I appreciate that about her. She has told me every little thing that I need to know about Mom's health, and she is literally an angel on earth, along with her partners that see Mom when she's not available. I have felt completely supported this whole season of Mom's life and that goes a long way. It has made my life so much easier, and Mom's so much more comfortable. I highly recommend hospice care to anyone facing a life-ending diagnosis, and the earlier the better.

For a few weeks now Mom has been mostly asleep. She's been eating but also aspirating her food. This means that she has trouble swallowing, and that a lot of her food is going into her lungs instead of her stomach. The signs of aspiration include a wet cough while eating, and afterwards, taking a long time to swallow, and runny eyes and nose while eating.

Her food has been modified to be like baby food - mashed up and mixed to a consistency that's easier for her to swallow, but she is beginning to show a lack of interest in eating at all.

The body changes slowly with this disease. Mom doesn't need a lot of calories. She's completely immobile. But she does need protein to stay alive, and without eating it in her food, she isn't getting enough. She has a sore on her bottom that isn't healing and won't heal because she doesn't have enough protein in her body to heal anything.

She is retaining fluid. Her body can't absorb fluids or expel it like it should. Which leads to random swelling. If she lays on her left side, then the left side of her body will be swollen, and same if she lays on her right side.

Her hand has been swollen for a while now and we don't know why, along with this hard swollen mass she has in her chest. X-rays were done and show nothing. Her body just can't cope anymore.

My brother will be here today. Perfect timing Roxie told me. Alarm bells ring and I know what that means. I talk to Tony, and I tell Skylar. She pulls a long face and says she wants to go see Granny Susan with me today, but then she is quickly back to watching YouTube videos and rejecting her bedtime. I believe she let go long ago, and while it will still be hard for her to say a final goodbye, it won't cause trauma like it did with Grandpa. As brave and strong as she is, she still won't really talk about Grandpa. She says that's her memories, and they're special, and she doesn't want to talk about him with anyone else. Especially not with her counselor, which is a shame, but I can't force her to do so. And while she loves Granny Susan dearly, she was forced to confront her mortality many months back.

I text my brother to let him know what we'll be facing when he gets here. "I'll be ready" he says. I know I won't be.

February 18, 2023 - Sometimes the end is just a different beginning. For Mom, the end of her earthly existence is the beginning of her heavenly life with Dad and all her other loved ones that have passed before her, especially her daddy. If you asked her what the best part of her childhood was, she would tell you "Playing in the yard with Daddy." This is a girl that had a pet raccoon, a pet monkey and a pet rat (appropriately named rat-rat), who lived in Hyde Park of Austin, went on numerous vacations and had wonderful friends that played dress up and had doll tea parties with her.

Seems idyllic. But things aren't always as they seem, and life became harsh when her dad died (and probably before due to his manic-depressive disorder). She never got along particularly well with her own mother and Dad provided a much-needed escape and the security to live her own life.

Early love letters are filled with "darlings" and "dears." They were two halves of a whole and couldn't live without each other. Dad understood Mom in the way that most men understand women. She needed love, patience, a strong shoulder to cry on and security and he gave that to her and so much more. Early pictures of married life show a very happy couple and a gorgeous woman that I can't even believe is Mom - she just glowed - but always with a tinge of sadness in her eyes and way of being. Just a tinge. She was very private and wasn't going to share her emotions with everyone.

In a way, they never did have to learn to live without each other. As Mom's condition worsened, she forgot who people were, and while she recognized me the longest, after Dad died she never asked for him. In her fragile state it seemed too much to tell her he had died. I kept telling her that Dad was waiting for her, that he was there before her and needed her with him now. I didn't want her to somehow be "waiting" for him, needing to hear his voice one last time. I didn't know how much she understood, if anything, but I felt it was important to let her know he was there, waiting to dance with her again.

Dad couldn't handle living without Mom, either. I remember asking him once if he would be able to try and go on without her after she passed, and he wouldn't even contemplate it. He just said, "I'll try." He didn't want her to go into a care home, because even though she was angry and bitter (and scared) due to the disease at least she was *there*, with him. And not having her in the house with him was incredibly difficult for Dad. In a way, the cancer was a blessing for him, because they literally were only truly apart for eighteen months before being reunited in heaven.

"

He didn't want to live on without her, and he didn't have to.

"

If Mom hadn't had Alzheimer's (and I'm not saying it was a blessing) - she would have had to try to live without him. She was a very strong woman, but she couldn't make it without her man. God must have done what he felt best. That's the way I have to look at everything that has happened in the past four years.

It's the end of suffering for my parents' sake. It is the end of worry and stress and advocating on their behalf. These past four years have been the hardest of my life. I am all cried out. My eyes are as dry as a desert. As people filed in and said goodbye to Mom, there were plenty of red eyes, sniffles and tears. And I was jealous. I wanted to cry, to rant, to rage, to weep and to bawl. But I can't. I am numb. My grief has been spent over four long years and while maybe I should feel some relief at last, relief that Mom's suffering is at an end, and for Dad - that they are together again, I don't. I don't feel a thing. I must get all the last bits done for them. There's a visitation to be held, a service and a burial. There's banks to call, and the Army to inform. There's my house to clean and food to cook for after the visitation. There's her room to clean out. There's so much to do. I am not done yet.

I listened to songs this morning in my car. Songs that have made me cry in the past. Songs I can really relate to. Nothing. No tears. No lump in the throat. I am not without feelings. But what I feel most right now is just…. empty.

A new beginning is waiting for me. When it will start, I am not sure. When my heart fills back up again, maybe. When Mom is in her final resting place with Dad, maybe. When I see the headstone for the first time, maybe. I do not know what the future holds for me now. It's time to reinvent myself, in their honor, and with their undying love for me and each other, to step up once again and become me again.

This end is just a different beginning.

EPILOGUE

1/1/2025

In my head I see a rowboat. I'm sitting in it with no oars, no paddle. When I look down there's the deep, wide ocean under me. I'm not about to jump into that abyss. So, I sit. Day after day. Quietly going about my business. Quietly still living.

A bird comes. I see a dove. He sits on the bow of the boat and stares at me. I stare back. What are you doing here, I silently ask. Where did you come from? Where are you going?

The bird stays with me. Many days and many nights. I get used to him. I talk to him a lot. But I don't cry.

Then one day the bird flies away. Keening, I call "wait! Where are you going? I still need you! I'm not ready for you to go."

I watch it fly into the distance and disappear.

I look down. The rowboat I'm sitting in is now on a shallow lake. I can see the clear bottom. Surprised, I reach my hand down and touch the water. I pull my hand back, study it, and watch the drops from my fingers. But still, I don't dive in. I'm not ready to swim.

Then there's a fish. Swimming alongside my boat, he looks up at me and his fins sparkle like rainbows on water. We drift. The fish hangs out for a while. I sleep.

When I awake the fish has gone but now my boat is in just a small pool of water. I am touching the bottom. I contemplate. I finally stand up. I step out of the boat. I wade through the water to dry land.

And I cry.

ACKNOWLEDGEMENTS

This book was a work of love and catharsis for me. It would not have been possible without the help of my publisher, Adriel Publishing, and specifically Liz Lawless who guided me through every step with grace and humor. Along with that, I would like to thank Merrie Spaeth who has always been a top supporter of me for many years, and who gave me Liz's name so that this project could become a reality! I am grateful as I would not have known where to start without them both.

I must thank the care facility, Just Like Home, in Whitesboro, Texas and the caretakers there for taking such loving and excellent care of Mom and allowing me to become a family member there. What a relief for my heart to know how well taken care of she was in her last eighteen months.

My brother, who has always been by my side and exactly what a big brother should be, especially during my pre-teen years when he teased me mercilessly. Thank you for graciously giving me the eulogy you wrote for Dad, and for the earlier research you had done on Mom and Dad's histories. You are one of the best men I know.

I am extra grateful for my husband's quiet and complete back up support throughout these terrible years and always, and for the care he took of Dad whenever he was needed without complaint.

I have so many friends I haven't personally mentioned in the book that were such an integral part of this story, whether looking at care homes and rehabs with me, or taking my daughter trick-or-treating and providing nonstop love and laughter and shoulders to cry on. Kathy, Val – I can't thank you enough.

And finally, I wish to acknowledge my Baby Girl who may not always have been patient but always showered Granny and Grandpa with undying love and attention. I wrote this book partly so that she would never forget how much she was and is still loved by them and me.

FAMILY PHOTO DESCRIPTIONS

Susan Wade Thomas

1. *Age 2, circa 1948*
2. *High School*
3. *A little humor in the kitchen, circa 1985*
4. *Julie and Mom, circa 1977*
5. *Kitchen aprons – Ali (Sissy) and Mom Christmas 2014*
6. *Julie and Mom – October 2016*
7. *Susan and Baby Girl (Skylar)*
8. *Visiting during COVID, 2020*
9. *Planting flowers at Just Like Home, 2021*

David Lee Thomas

10. *On the farm, circa 1957*
11. *Texas A&M University Cadet*
12. *Stationed in St. Louis, late 1970's*
13. *Dad with David Dalton and Julie, in Germany, 1980*
14. *Writing letters during Desert Storm, 1990/1991*
15. *Mom and Dad with Baby Girl and Julie, 2014*

16. *Dad and my brother – June 2018*

17. *Tractor ride with Skylar – Easter 2018*

18. *Julie and Dad – 2016*

19. *Tea party with Skylar – May 2021*

David Lee and Susan Thomas

20. *Married 1/25/1969*

21. *David Lee and Susan at a formal Army affair – late 1970's*

22. *In Army training, circa 1970*

23. *In Europe, looking fashionable, early 1980's*

24. *Susan and David Lee early 1980's*

25. *David Dalton's wedding April 2003*

26. *Sitting on the porch at the house in Pilot Point, 2018*

Thomas and Tullos Families

27. *The Tullos Family December 2014 – Tony, Julie, Skylar and Ali*

28. *The Thomas Family in Germany, circa 1979, Mom, Dad, David and Julie*

29. *Skylar & Bruno Blue Ribbon Winners July 2022*

30. *Brother David and Boys (Matthew and David William) – August 2014*
31. *Julie, Dad, Mom and David selfie – early 2018*
32. *Mom and Dad with all their grandchildren – August 2014*

JULIE THOMAS TULLOS

Julie was an Army Brat growing up with her Dad a Lieutenant Colonel in the Army. Having grown up moving around a lot, she now has a great passion for staying grounded in Texas.

Julie is the owner and operator of Abingdon Park & Pony Farm, where she teaches English riding and goes to many hunter jumper and Welsh pony shows each year. She is the proud President of the North Texas Hunter Jumper Club and was also very involved in the United States Pony Club earlier in life.

Julie and her family live on 9 acres with several horses and ponies, a barn cat and a miniature dachshund named Luna. She loves to read, especially true stories, historical fiction and biographies. When she can be persuaded to leave the farm, her favorite vacation destination is a Cruise ship going just about anywhere she hasn't already been.

She was influenced to write by her Mom, a lifelong reader and librarian, and her brother, Dave Thomas, also an author.

Julie Thomas Tullos is married to her best friend, Tony Tullos, who is in Law Enforcement, and they have one daughter together. They reside in Pilot Point, Texas with the desire to move to the Piney Woods of East Texas someday when they both retire.